Published by Little, Brown and Company
by arrangement with D. C. Heath and Company

AUTHORS
GERTRUDE HARTMAN
AND
LUCY S. SAUNDERS

ILLUSTRATED BY
Marjorie Quennell
Assisted by Harold Cue

Maps by B. Magnuson Derwinski

PRINTED IN THE UNITED STATES OF AMERICA

BUILDERS OF THE OLD WORLD

BUILDERS OF THE
OLD
WORLD

SECOND EDITION

LITTLE, BROWN AND COMPANY · BOSTO

FOREWORD

Builders of the Old World, as it tells of the early nations, must often speak of war. Even today, in the midst of the hatreds and destruction of world quarrels, it is hard to believe that peaceful development is the really important part of man's history. Yet that is the truth which this book attempts to show. Throughout the ages, wars have occurred; but wars are best understood as interruptions of the continuing efforts of human beings, in ever larger groups, to work together in building a better world.

Man's history has been an adventure—a common adventure of billions of people since that dim time when primitive man first appeared in Europe.

The basic element in this adventure has always been the business of making a living: first by hunting and fishing, then by taming a few animals, then by tilling grain fields, then by simple trade in bronze and gold, skins and cloth, and finally by all the occupations of our own day.

Another important part of the adventure has been the development of means of communication between human beings. First a spoken language had to be built up, and then ways of expressing speech in writing. Pictures and syllables gave way to alphabets; and with each advance in the symbols, the range of the ideas that could be expressed increased.

Equally important has been the development of philosophy and religion from early myths and legends, and the first ideas of magic, to the teachings of wise men and prophets. Side by side with that

[v]

story runs the tale of how man gained skill in poetry, drama, music, and art.

Meanwhile, villages grew into cities, and distinct nations arose. With the empire-builders, the civilizations of different nations were brought into contact, and the lives of both the conquerors and the conquered were changed.

White, yellow, and black peoples, nations old and young, people of every religion, and people living under every form of government contributed to these developments. They are achievements in which human beings everywhere have shared. The rise of democracy has emphasized the historic truth that, over any long stretch of years, the people count for far more than the great men.

Builders of the Old World is a history that begins, as it should, with man when he shared the world with the cave bear and the saber-toothed tiger. It stresses the common experience of mankind and treats history as a continuous onward movement, showing how the world of Caesar grew from the world of the Sumerians, and that of Charles Martel and St. Francis from the world of Caesar.

All along the way, it traces the influence of the geography, the climate, and the natural resources of each country upon the people and upon their history. Each country and each great civilization had problems which the people of that period attempted to solve; and in doing so, they enriched human life.

The upward struggle this book records did not end with the discovery of the New World. The effort of men to achieve fuller liberty gives each rising generation new tasks to perform. It is the hope of the authors of *Builders of the Old World* that it will equip its readers with a sense of their place in the long caravan of humanity, and inspire them to assume the responsibilities that will fall to them in a world that is growing more and more unified.

ALLAN NEVINS

CONTENTS

UNIT I. Days before History   I

How the First People Lived   3
Sticks and Stones   6
The Fire Makers   8
Buried Treasures   12
The Cave Dwellers   16
Cave Artists   18
Man Begins to Worship   20
Animal Helpers   22
Wheels and Sails   24
The Beginning of Settled Life   29
Learning to Live Together   34
Trading and Counting   35
The First Nations   37
The Foundations of Civilization   38

UNIT II. The Land of the Pharaohs   43

Ancient Dwellers on the Nile   45
Tillers of the Soil   46
Watering the Land   49
Craftsmen   51
Boatbuilders   53
Picture Writing   54
Scribes   56
Telling Time   57
The Calendar Makers   58

Gods and Men   59
In the Hall of Truth   63
A Great Queen   66
Rich Man, Poor Man   68
The Pyramid Builders   71
Great Temples   75

UNIT III. *Early Nations in Southwest Asia*   81

The Fertile Crescent   83
Life in Babylonia   84
Tower-Temples   87
The Laws of Hammurabi   90
Books of Clay   91
School Days in Babylon   93
The Warrior Nation   94
King Nebuchadnezzar   97
The Shepherd People   99
Moses the Lawgiver   101
Life in the Land of Canaan   103
What the Hebrews Taught the World   105
The Sea Beckons   106
A Nation of Traders   108
Carriers of Civilization   110
Empire Builders   111

UNIT IV. *Greek Cities of Long Ago*   119

The City-States of Hellas   121
Greek Homes and Farms   125
Growing Up in Sparta and Athens   127
The Gods of the Greeks   130
The Olympic Games   133
The Tale of Troy   137

First Steps in Democracy 141
The Greeks Defend Their Freedom 142
The Athenians at Marathon 144
The Spartans at Thermopylae 145
The Wooden Walls Save Athens 147
The Golden Age of Pericles 150
Lovers of Wisdom 153
Greece Loses Her Freedom 156
The Gifts of Greece to Civilization 159

UNIT V. *Rome Wins and Loses an Empire* 163

The City of the Seven Hills 165
Early Roman Heroes 168
Rome Becomes a Republic 171
How the Early Romans Lived 174
Going to School in Rome 177
Rome Conquers All Italy 178
Rome and Carthage 180
How the Later Romans Lived 183
Cornelia's Jewels 186
Rome Extends Her Rule in Europe 189
Caesar Makes a New Calendar 190
The Death of Caesar 192
Rome, Mistress of the Ancient World 193
"All Roads Lead to Rome" 195
Christianity Comes to the World 196
The Christians Are Persecuted 199
The Last Days of the Empire 200

UNIT VI. *Wandering Tribes Become Nations* 205

The German Tribes Seek New Homes 207
The Moors in Spain 211
Gaul Becomes France 216

[ix]

Charlemagne, King of the Franks 217
Britain Becomes England 221
King Alfred the Great 224
The Vikings Sail the Northern Seas 227
William the Conqueror 231
Lords and Vassals 234
Pagan Gods 236
Christianity Spreads over Europe 238

UNIT VII. New Ways of Living 245
In a Medieval Castle 247
Learning to Be a Knight 249
Feasting and Revelry 252
Hunting and Hawking 254
A Tournament 255
Serfs and Nobles 258
How the Land Was Divided 259
How the Peasants Lived 260
Holy Men Help the People 262
Making Books in a Monastery 265
The Good Saint Francis 267
Men Follow the Sign of the Cross 270
In a Medieval Town 274
The Cathedral Builders 275
Butcher, Baker, and Candlestick Maker 278
Markets and Fairs 281
The Towns Win Their Liberty 283
Traders East 285
Kings and Towns Unite against the Nobles 288

UNIT VIII. Foundations of Freedom 293
Guilty or Not Guilty? 295
The Beginning of Trial by Jury 297

The King Must Obey the Law   298
The Great Charter of English Freedom   302
The Beginning of Parliament   304
A Champion of Freedom   306
Government by the People   308
Parliament Makes the Laws   310
Parliament Is Divided into Two Houses   311
The Serfs Seek Their Freedom   312
The Black Death   314
All Men Are Created Equal   316
Wat Tyler Leads a Revolt of the Peasants   318
The Rebellion Is Put Down   322
The Power of the People   324

UNIT IX. *The Great Awakening*   329

The New Spirit   331
Religion Takes New Forms   332
A Monk Brings Changes in Religion   334
Reforms within the Catholic Church   337
The Struggle for Freedom of Worship   338
Men Create New Forms of Beauty   340
Block Books   346
The Printing Press   350
The Making of Many Books   354
How Printing Helped Men to Be Free   355
Education Spreads among the People   357
Great Poets and Playwrights   361
From Superstition to Science   363
The Man Who Knew Too Much   365
The Father of Modern Astronomy   367
Magic Glasses   368
The Struggle to Advance Knowledge   372

UNIT X. *Europe Looks East*   377

    The World Grows Larger   379
    Ancient India   381
    In Far Cathay   386
    Marco Polo Visits the Great Khan   393
    The Polos Give a Banquet   397
    Tales of a Traveler   401
    Ships in Unknown Seas   403
    Prince Henry's Dream   407
    The Cape of Good Hope   411

UNIT XI. *Finding a New World*   417

    Is the Earth Round?   419
    Westward to the Indies   422
    Crossing the Atlantic   426
    The Indies at Last   428
    Prince Henry's Dream Comes **True**   434
    The Last Days of Columbus   438
    Discoveries in the West   439
    America Gets Its Name   442
    A New World   445

List of Dates   450
List of Maps   452
Index   454

I

DAYS BEFORE
HISTORY

WESTERN EUROPE. *Scientists have found remains showing the ways early people lived in different regions of Europe.*

Most of the land in those days was covered with dense forests, with open meadows here and there. Fierce animals wandered through the forests searching for food. There were huge elephants, called mammoths, with long, curving tusks. There were savage wolves and cave bears. There were terrible saber-toothed tigers with long fangs curving down from their upper jaws. Wild horses and cattle roamed the plains. The first people lived in the forests very much as the animals did.

It might seem as if the animals were better equipped for the struggle for existence than man was, for some of the animals had tusks and horns to protect them when they were attacked; some had hoofs with which to trample their enemies; others had wings with which to fly away from danger. Man had none of these things. Compared with many of the animals he was small and weak. But man had some gifts which no animal had. For one thing he could walk upright on two legs. This walking on two legs was very important, for it left man's arms and hands free to be used in other ways.

Two other important gifts man had. He had a wonderfully made hand with a thumb that could meet the tip of each of his fingers. Because of this he was able to take hold of things and could use his hand in a great variety of ways. Man also had a better mind than any animal. He could learn and think and plan and invent. By the use of his good mind and his skillful hands, early man discovered ways of making nature help him.

At first, people lived in constant fear of being attacked by some of the larger animals. The safest place was up in the trees, for few big animals can climb trees. Because the earliest people spent much of their time high up in the branches of trees out of harm's way, they are sometimes called tree dwellers. Of course they had to come down to the ground to get food. They wandered about hunting

anything they could find. They gathered nuts, wild fruits and berries, and the tender roots of certain plants. They ate the eggs of wild birds, which they found in nests, and honey made by the bees. Sometimes they were able to catch small animals or small fish with their hands.

When darkness came, they climbed up into the trees for the night. Vines grew around the trunks of the trees and twisted themselves about the branches. Sometimes the vines were so thick that they made a kind of hammock in which people could sleep. Mothers made cradles of vines for their babies. There, in the branches of big trees, the first people were safe during the night.

STICKS AND STONES

For thousands of years, scientists believe, people spent most of their time searching for food and trying to protect themselves against the animals. Gradually they found in the forest things that helped them in their hard struggle to keep alive. In streams they found pebbles that had been worn by the water until they were round and smooth. These were helpful in cracking nuts and other hard objects; they were the first hammers. Other stones were sharp-edged and could be used for cutting and scraping the skins of animals; they were the first knives. Sharp splinters of bone or the tusks and horns of animals were good for boring holes. A sharp-pointed branch of a tree was useful for digging in the earth for roots. A stout branch made a strong club with which to beat off an animal.

DAYS BEFORE HISTORY

HOW THE FIRST PEOPLE LIVED

History tells how people lived in the past. The writing of history began when men learned to keep records of what they did and what happened in their time. These first records may still be seen on the stone walls of temples and tombs. But the oldest history in the world does not go back more than six or seven thousand years, and men had been living on the earth for many thousands of years before that time.

Although the earliest people left no written records, learned men called archaeologists and other scientists have discovered in many places remains of early times. Digging down in the earth they have come upon shells, bones, fragments of pottery, stone tools and weapons, and other objects used by prehistoric people. They have found many common things in ancient rubbish heaps called kitchen middens. In some places the scientists have found caves in which people lived long ago, and under the beds of some lakes they have discovered the remains of villages. Patiently and carefully working over their findings, year after year, these men of science have been able to tell us much about the way people lived in the far-off days before the beginning of written history.

Thus the sticks and stones which people found in the forests became man's first tools and weapons.

People soon learned ways of trapping the larger animals. They dug pits in the ground and laid over them a thin covering of branches and leaves. These pits were usually made in the paths which the animals took when they went to streams to get water. When an animal walked over the thin covering, it gave way, and the animal fell into the hole and was caught by the hunters.

At first, people used things just as they found them in nature and did not change them in any way. Very likely they often had to search for a long time before they found the right kind of stone for their purpose. By and by it was discovered that if one stone was struck sharply with another, small pieces could be chipped off. Thus a stone of the size and shape needed could be made. One kind of stone, flint, was particularly good for making tools, as it was hard and yet brittle, and could be easily shaped. People chipped pieces of flint to make them more useful and thus took the first steps in toolmaking. They no longer

[7]

had to depend on nature to supply them with ready-made tools and weapons; they could fashion their own.

As most of the tools and weapons of this early part of the prehistoric period which have been found are made of stone, scientists call this time the Old Stone Age. How long people lived in the Old Stone Age no one knows, but this period probably lasted for thousands of years.

As time passed, people gradually gained greater skill in toolmaking. They invented new tools and improved their ways of making old ones. Instead of merely chipping stones, they learned to grind and polish them. By fastening a wooden handle to a sharp-edged stone, someone made an ax. With this useful tool trees could be chopped down and wood cut into shapes and sizes needed. By fastening a sharp-pointed stone to a long stick, someone made a spear. A clever hunter invented a bow by stringing a sinew of an animal to the two ends of a springy sapling. With this bow a stone-tipped arrow could be sent with great force and swiftness for a long distance. This time of improved toolmaking is called the New Stone Age.

THE FIRE MAKERS

In that early time man learned to use fire. The early people must often have seen fires in the forests. Perhaps some hunter saw lightning set fire to trees during a thunderstorm. As the fire spread from tree to tree, roaring and crackling, no doubt he fled in terror from what seemed like a frightful monster belching flames and black smoke.

[8]

In time the fire died down and the hunter crept back. As he came near the place where the fire had been, the smoldering remains warmed his body and felt good. Perhaps the hunter picked up the branch of a tree that was still burning, and carried it to show to other people. He gathered some dry leaves and twigs and threw them on the burning branch and the fire blazed up. The people enjoyed its pleasant warmth. When the fire died down they quickly gathered armfuls of twigs and branches and threw them on it to make it blaze up again. A fire in front of the cave frightened away wild animals.

For a long, long time people did not know how to make fire. They could have one only when they happened to find a tree on fire in a forest and could get a burning branch to start a blaze of their own. They therefore tended their fires very carefully. Usually one person had this duty. But even with great care the fire sometimes did go out. Then might follow a long, hard time before people could find more embers from a forest fire.

[9]

No one knows exactly how men first learned to make fire for themselves. Very likely early people began making fire after they noticed that sticks became hot when rubbed together. This may have given some early thinker an idea. He took two pieces of wood and tried rubbing them together. Faster and faster and harder and harder he rubbed them. After a long time he was rewarded by seeing a little curl of smoke. He blew on this and a tiny flame flared up. Quickly the fire maker threw the sticks on some dry leaves and grass. Soon he had a good fire blazing.

Early workers boring holes in wood when they were making tools and weapons may have noticed that the wood dust around the hole grew hot. This may have suggested to some man another way of making fire. He may have used a sharpened stick to bore a hole in a piece of soft wood. Holding the stick between the palms of his hands he turned it very fast, first in one direction, then in the other. As he twirled the boring stick,

he pressed the point down on the other piece of wood as hard as he could. As the hole grew deeper, a little circle of wood dust collected around it. The point of the boring stick grew hotter and hotter and began to smoke and glow. The edges of the hole grew hotter, too. Finally the wood dust caught fire.

These ways of making fire were slow and hard. Someone discovered a better way. He wound a string around the boring stick. When he pulled the string, the stick twirled rapidly.

After men learned to use fire, they could cook their food. Before they had fire they ate pieces of raw flesh and sucked the marrow out of bones. Perhaps a piece of meat fell into the fire and was quickly snatched out by someone. When he ate it he discovered that the heat of the fire had

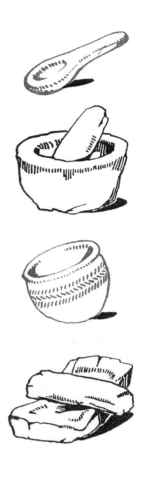

improved its flavor. After that, people fastened pieces of meat to the ends of long sticks and held them over the flames. They buried the roots and other parts of plants in the hot ashes of the fire to bake them.

One of the things early people learned with the help of fire was how to make pottery. They had found that a certain kind of earth, called clay, could be rolled and smoothed and fashioned into various shapes. They formed it into little bowls, which they set in the sun. When these were dry they could be used for holding nuts and fruits, but the clay soon became soft and lost its shape. It was discovered that hollow gourds could be used for holding food to be cooked if the outside of the gourd was smeared with clay to protect it from the fire. The heat of the fire made the clay very hard. It was not long before the gourd was discarded and the clay was molded into the shape of a gourd and hardened in the fire. Thus the making of pottery began. Jars, bowls, pitchers, cups, and other things made of clay were useful as dishes and for cooking and storing food, for carrying water, and for many other purposes.

BURIED TREASURES

Tools and weapons were made out of stone for untold ages. The use of fire gave people a better material out of which to make them. In the early geologic ages, when the earth was being formed, molten metals collected in many places beneath the earth's surface. As the earth cooled, these formed wonderful deposits of copper, tin, iron, and other metals, which were discovered and became useful to man in his work. The earliest people knew nothing of these hidden treasures; they knew only about things they found on the surface of the earth.

Although most metals are buried deep in the earth, some rocks containing metals were thrown up to the surface by the great upheavals in the earth's crust which took place in early times. When these rocks were broken up by the action of the weather, bits of these metal deposits were often exposed.

It is thought that some early hunter, building a fire, happened to gather for a fireplace loose rocks in which there were bits of copper. The fire heated the metal and it oozed out of the rocks in bright reddish streams. These hardened into glittering lumps. They attracted the attention of the hunter. He wondered whether this new kind of material was good for anything. He laid a piece of copper on a stone and beat it with his stone hammer to see whether it would break. The trouble with stone tools was that work with them was very hard and tiring and that they often broke. Copper did not break. It flattened out when it was beaten and could be hammered into various shapes to make tools and weapons.

Without knowing it, the early hunter who found copper made one of the most important discoveries in the world. When people learned that they could make better tools and weapons with copper than with stone, the Stone Age came to an end, and the Age of Metals began.

Copper is a soft metal. Because tools and weapons made of copper soon lost their sharp edges, early people were always on the lookout for some other metal which would make stronger weapons.

In the course of time they came upon a new, silver-white metal, called tin. Some early metalworker thought of smelting this with copper. By mixing the two metals he made another metal, called bronze, which was harder and stronger than either copper or tin. This new metal was found to be so useful that for ages all tools and weapons were made of it.

The long period during which the new metal was used is called the Bronze Age.

Centuries later, men discovered iron, which is the most useful of all metals. As there is plenty of iron all over the world, it took the place of bronze for making all sorts of things, and the Age of Bronze gradually gave way to the Age of Iron.

Iron is much harder to melt from the rocks than copper or tin. On some high place in the hills, where there was plenty of wind to make a fire burn well, early ironworkers heaped up big piles of wood. They broke up rocks containing iron ore and piled the pieces on top of the wood. They covered the pile of wood and rock with a layer of dirt to keep in the heat. Next they made a hole at the top to let out the smoke, and several holes at the bottom to let in the air so that the fire would burn better. Then they started a fire in the wood. After a while the intense heat melted the iron out of the rocks and it trickled out of the bottom of the pile.

These hillside furnaces worked well enough when there was a good wind, but sometimes the wind did not blow hard enough to make a sufficiently hot fire. Then the ironworkers forced air into their fires by blowing into the holes at the bottom of the furnace through long tubes. This method of blowing to make a hotter fire was very exhausting to the workmen. In time the ironworkers discovered a better way of forcing air into their fires by means of bellows made from the skins of animals.

During the Iron Age men were able to make many new tools and weapons, for iron was the hardest metal that they had yet found.

THE CAVE DWELLERS

In the beginning the climate of the earth was warm. Later there were several times when huge glaciers, moving southward, made it very cold. This change in climate brought about many changes in man's way of living. The bitter cold caused much suffering and made it necessary for people to find some kind of shelter from the weather. In some places there were caves which were inhabited by fierce cave bears and other animals. The people drove out the animals and took possession of the caves.

In their cave homes people were safer and more comfortable than they had ever been before. A fire built at the entrance of the cave kept the animals away. A fire within the cave became the center of the life of the people. It shed its warmth and light as they gathered around it, making their tools and weapons and scraping the skins of animals. The women made needles of bone and thread of sinews to sew the skins together, and fashioned the first clothes.

During long winter evenings the cave people told one another about their hunting experiences. Perhaps one story-teller would entertain the others by telling of the great feats and mighty deeds of some especially brave leader.

Sometimes the stories were turned into plays. After an exciting hunt those who had engaged in it would tell about their adventures to those who had not been with them. In trying to make the others see just what had happened they would act out a particularly thrilling part.

In those days the first musical instruments were made. A good string on a well-bent bow gives a humming sound as the arrow flies. Hunters noticed this, and they also noticed that long bowstrings twanged with a deeper tone than shorter strings. They liked the sound of the long strings and short strings humming together. Perhaps, as the cave people sat around the fire at night, several hunters twanged their bowstrings together. Someone stretched strings across the hollow shell of a turtle and picked at the strings, making music as he sang. Someone stretched a skin across a hollow tree trunk and beat on it. Thus the first drum was made.

Often the cave people had feasts. Afterward the young men danced in a circle around the fire. Others kept time for the dancers by clapping their hands and stamping their feet. Some of them beat together pieces of wood, like clappers. Some shook rattles which they had made by putting pebbles in hollow gourds. The sounds which these things made pleased people and helped them to express their feelings.

[17]

CAVE ARTISTS

Not so many years ago an archaeologist discovered other wonderful things done by the cave people. This man was a Spanish nobleman. He was taking his little girl through a big cave on his estate, exploring it to see whether prehistoric people might have lived there. His little girl had wandered off by herself into the cave. Suddenly the father was startled by hearing her cry, "Father, come quick! Bulls! Bulls!"

Quickly the father ran to the child. He did not see any bulls; instead, he found his little girl pointing up to the roof of the cave. He looked up and there, to his great astonishment, he saw a big painting of a bull in a soft red tint. He looked further and found more bulls, as well as galloping horses, reindeer grazing, and bison charging. The whole roof was covered with the paintings of animals. Some were black; some were yellow; others were red. Here was the work of cave artists who had lived in the cave thousands of years ago.

Other men of science visited the cave and admired the lifelike figures. They searched in other caves and found many other paintings on walls and roofs. These are some of the oldest pictures in the world.

In the early forests were all sorts of things which the cave artists found useful in making their pictures. Along the banks of streams they found bright red and yellow clay. They ground the clay by pounding it in stone bowls, and they poured the powdered clay into the hollow bones or horns of animals for safekeeping. Bits of charred wood made good black marks, and the juices of certain berries made pretty colors. The shoulder blades of big animals served as palettes.

The artists of those early days carved as well as painted. With their axes and chisels of flint they sculptured horses and other animals out of the solid rock. When they made handles for their tools, they engraved the outlines of animals on them, and cut away the wood or bone or ivory to make the outlines stand out better. With sharp horns or bones they scratched pictures on their clay bowls or made pleasing designs on them with colored clays. They ornamented shells or cut the teeth of animals into different shapes, then strung them and wore them as necklaces. They carved drinking cups from the horns of animals.

When the cave people saw that fire gave them warmth, cooked their food, gave them light, and kept the wild animals away, they were grateful to it for making their lives easier. Fire seemed to them a sacred thing and they thought of it as a sort of god. They showed their thanks by bringing offerings to the fire which had given them security and comfort.

Early men saw the sun rise in one part of the heavens in the morning, travel overhead during the day, and set in another part of the sky at night. They knew that the heat and light which they needed for their lives came from the sun, for they saw that when the sun did not shine for a long time everything suffered. In the night sky they saw the moon and the millions of stars gleaming like diamonds in their deep blue setting. They saw day turn into night, and the seasons—spring, summer, autumn, and winter—follow one another over and over again. They did not know what caused these changes. They wondered about the strange world in which they found themselves—how it came to be, how they came to be in it, and what would happen to them after they died.

Some things in nature were terrifying. Sometimes gathering storm clouds made the day as black as night. There were deafening roars of thunder and the heavens seemed to be split wide open with blinding flashes of lightning. At such times early men saw at work a tremendous power which they did not understand. They crouched in terror under a friendly protecting rock until the angry god passed by. Other terrible things happened—floods and earthquakes and fires.

People knew that man had no power over any of these things. It seemed to them that other beings greater than themselves ruled the world and that the things which happened were caused by these spirits. In this way they came to worship many things in nature. They thought that their actions sometimes made the spirits angry. Then there were unhappy times for men. They prayed to the spirits to keep away any harm that might come to them. They were thankful for the things that helped them in their hard struggle to live. People made gifts to the spirits, hoping that they would be kind.

Offerings were burned on stone altars. In one place in England a wide circle of great upright stones has been found with an altar of rocks in the middle, where, it is thought, early people placed their offerings.

There came to be certain men, called priests, who were believed to know more than the ordinary people about how to please the gods. The priests had great power over the other people, for men who could advise others how to live so that they would gain the good will of the gods were held in great reverence.

ANIMAL HELPERS

In the beginning man had no friends among the animals. As time passed, people learned that some animals could be tamed and made useful to man. It is thought that the first animal to be tamed was the wolf. Perhaps a hunter came upon a mother wolf and carried home her puppies. His children probably enjoyed petting the young wolves and feeding them. When these puppies were fully grown they were no longer wild and fierce. They liked to live where they had plenty of food. In time many wolves became friendly to the people who fed them. These tamed wolves were the first dogs.

The dog was a wonderful help to man. This four-footed friend served his master well. He guarded the cave and kept other animals away. With his keen scent he tracked animals and guided his master when hunting.

Other animals that man tamed were cattle, hogs, sheep, and goats. With these animals about him he was sure of having plenty of food, for they supplied him with meat and milk. He no longer had to spend so much of his time hunting. He became a shepherd, caring for his flocks and herds, and they made his life easier.

When sheep were tamed, people found that these animals could give them better clothing than they had ever been able to have before. They discovered that by twisting the wool of the sheep between the thumb and the first finger they could make a long thread. In the spring the men clipped the thick fleece from the sheep, the women washed it in the clear running water of streams, and combed the tangles out of the wool. A bunch of wool was attached to one end of a long stick and the other end was held under the arm. Pulling out a small piece of wool, the woman fastened the end of it to a small round stone with a hole in the middle. With a quick, turning motion of her hand she set the stone whirling and let it dangle at her side. When the motion died down she gave the stone another whirl. This process is known as spinning the thread.

As a great length of thread was spun, it was wound around the twig of a tree to prevent it from tangling. A notch was made in one end of the twig to keep the thread from unraveling. This notched twig was the first spindle.

To make cloth the thread was woven on what is called a loom. The weaver set up two forked limbs of trees a little way apart and fastened two sticks across

them, one at some distance below the other. Between these she stretched many woolen threads. In and out, between these up-and-down threads, she wove other threads. Forward and back the threads were interlaced over and over again, in time making a long piece of cloth. Clothing which was made from wool in this way was softer and much more comfortable than clothing made from skins.

WHEELS AND SAILS

When a cave man went hunting he often had to go long distances, and he had to carry back to the cave the animals he had killed for food. The easiest way to carry a large animal was to sling it over the shoulders and carry it on the back, but when the animal was too heavy the hunter had to drag it along the ground. Sometimes two hunters carried an animal hung from the branch of a tree, the ends of which rested on the shoulders of the hunters.

When the cave people needed to seek a place where food was more plentiful, they had to walk and carry their belongings with them. They carried things in their hands and on their backs. Sometimes they carried burdens on their heads or shoulders. Perhaps they fastened two saplings together, making a sledge. On this simple framework a number of things that had to be moved could be dragged along the ground.

Through endless centuries man was his own beast of burden. Backs and arms and legs were always weary from the effort of carrying things from place to place.

After people learned to tame animals, they found that some animals were capable of carrying heavy loads over long distances. Then burdens were shifted from the backs and shoulders of men to the sturdy backs of beasts. Harnesses were made of leather thongs, with which certain animals were trained to draw sledges over the ground. For this work the horse was tamed and the ox. In warm countries the camel was used, and in cold places the reindeer and the musk ox.

It was discovered that logs placed under a heavy object would roll and make the object move more easily. Some

man thought of fastening rollers to the bottom of a sledge. He cut two round slabs from the trunk of a tree, cut a hole in the middle of each, and attached one to each end of a pole called an axle. When the axle was fastened across the bottom of the sledge in such a way that it could turn, man had a cart with two wheels.

The solid wheels were heavy and clumsy. They made the cart very hard to pull. After a while it was discovered that the wheels need not be solid. Someone thought of cutting three-cornered pieces out of them to make them lighter. This made them look as if they had heavy spokes and a rim. Finally a wheel with spokes and rim was made. As time went on, men put four wheels on their carts instead of two.

Thus began the use of wheeled vehicles. With them men could travel and haul heavy loads much farther than before. The use of carts made roads necessary and men began widening and straightening the forest trails to make the first roads.

Water is as necessary to man as food. Therefore many people in early times lived near bodies of water. These people probably made the first attempts to travel on water. The first boats may have been merely floating tree trunks. Often loose branches or trunks of trees float downstream. It may be that a weary swimmer, in danger of drowning, saw a tree trunk floating near him. He clutched at it and found, to his delight, that it helped to hold him up. He wondered whether it would float with him on it, and he scrambled up on it to see. It did not sink.

In some such way as this early men discovered that floating logs would hold them up in the water. They found that by paddling with their hands and feet, or by shoving the log along with the stout branch of a tree, they could make it go wherever they wished. After fire was discovered, men learned that they could hollow out logs with fire. A hollowed-out tree trunk made a comfortable and serviceable boat in which man could sit and put his belongings.

Probably an early boatman noticed that sometimes the wind blew his boat about and it occurred to him to try to use the force of the wind to move his boat for him. Perhaps he held up the skin of an animal in his outstretched arms. When the wind was blowing from behind, it blew against the skin and drove the boat along. This was the first sailboat. Someone thought of tying the sail to a branch of a tree which he stuck up in the middle of his boat. With such rude wind-catchers small boats could be blown over the water. The boatman sat and steered, while the wind did the work of moving his boat.

When a man needed a larger boat to move his family and his possessions, he fastened a few logs together with strong vines or strips of hide, and thus made a raft. He moved it along by pushing on a long pole which he stuck into the bank of the stream. In the course of time men learned to improve the raft by fitting the logs together and building a wall of rough planks around the outside to keep the water from sweeping over the raft. This was the first step toward making a flat-bottomed boat with square ends.

Thus, little by little, people learned to build bigger and better boats, with which they were able to travel farther and farther over the water.

THE BEGINNING OF SETTLED LIFE

People had long known that the seeds growing in the tops of certain wild grasses were good to eat. These grasses were wild wheat or other grains. Perhaps a woman noticed that at certain times of the year the seeds fell to the ground and in time new plants appeared there. This gave her the idea of gathering seeds and planting them where she wanted grains to grow. With her digging stick she scratched the ground and loosened it to make it soft so that the rain could reach the seeds and the roots could spread out. She dropped the seeds into the places she prepared and covered them with earth. Planting seeds in this way was slow, difficult work. Then someone discovered that dragging the branch of a tree over the ground made a little trough into which seeds could be dropped. This branch was the first plow.

The seeds lay in the ground until the warm air, the sun-
shine, and the showers of spring started them growing.
As summer passed, the grain changed from green to golden
yellow and the top of each stalk grew heavy with many
little seeds. Then the stalks were cut in wide swaths with
a stone blade fastened to a handle. The stalks were beaten
together to shake out the seeds.

The women put the grains in hollow stones and ground
them by crushing them with heavy rocks. This made a kind
of coarse flour. Adding a little water to it, they mixed a sort
of paste which they formed into little cakes and set in the
sun to dry. In this way they made the first bread. Later on
they found that bread would dry more quickly if it was
placed on stones and heated in the fire.

This planting of seeds was to change man's whole way of living. When people had to depend on hunting and the raising of herds and flocks for food, they had to move from one hunting ground or pasture land to another. They could settle down in one place only temporarily. This meant that they must have homes which could be easily carried by a pack animal when they needed to move again. Simple shelters, like tents, were made by sticking three or four poles in the ground and covering the top of them with the skins of animals. Sometimes round huts were made from the branches of trees woven together and smeared with clay. These did not take long to construct and were left behind when the people went on to make new homes in another place.

When people learned to plant seeds they no longer had
to wander about in search of food. They could stay in one
place and raise the plant food they needed for themselves
and their animals. They learned to build permanent homes.

In places where there was plenty of stone the builders
gathered together flat rocks and arranged them in a small
square or circle. On these rocks they piled up more rocks
until they had a wall higher than their heads. At one place
in the wall they left a hole for a door. To keep the wall
above the hole from falling down they used two long flat
stones which they placed upright with another flat rock
joining them at the top. For a long, long time people did not
know how to make any better form of building than this.

Groups of houses were built close together for greater
safety. Thus the first villages grew up.

Where there were lakes people sometimes built their houses well out over the water. They sharpened the trunks of trees at one end and drove them into the soft mud at the bottom of the lake far from the shore. On the tops of the tree trunks they laid wooden platforms and built houses of wood on them.

The lake dwellers made nets which they let down into the water to catch fish. Narrow bridges built to the shore made it possible for them to reach the land. There they pastured their flocks and raised their crops.

Such lake villages provided secure places in which to live. They were protected from the attacks of wild animals and hostile people, for in times of danger the bridges which connected the villages with the land could be easily defended or could even be destroyed.

[33]

During the thousands of years that people were learning how to make life easier for themselves, they were also learning how much better life is for everyone when people help one another. In the beginning each family lived alone, but people early discovered that they were safer and better off if groups of people lived together. Constant danger made it necessary for men to rely upon one another for help. One man by himself might be helpless when he was attacked by a powerful animal, but many men, combining their powers, could overcome the most dangerous beasts. Thus a group of people, using their strength together, made the life of each one safer.

When men began living in groups they also learned to work in ways that were best for all of them. At first each person made for himself everything that he needed. If he did not know how to make a certain thing, he did not have it. In the course of time it was discovered that some men could do one kind of work better than others could do it. So, instead of one person trying to do everything for himself, each one did the thing he could do best. In this way various occupations arose. When a person did the same kind of work over and over, he became very skillful at it. As a result, the things he made grew better and better.

This way of working is called division of labor, because the labor is divided among different people. Some men became boat builders, some were carpenters, many were herdsmen, others were farmers and fishermen.

People began to exchange things when they saw that by so doing they could get many things they wanted but could not find, or raise, or make for themselves. If a hunter had more skins than he needed, he would willingly give them to his neighbor for something else he needed but did not have—perhaps some cattle which his neighbor owned. If the neighbor had more cattle than he needed and wanted some skins, he was willing to make the exchange. It was in this way that trade began. This way of trading one sort of goods for another is called barter.

It is easy to see that this kind of trading was difficult. Suppose a farmer had a cow which was worth ten sheep and he wanted only five sheep, what would he do? Suppose a man had more grain than he needed and wanted to exchange some of it for a cow. He might have a good deal of trouble finding a person who had a cow and who also happened to need some grain.

[35]

These examples show how hard it was for people to carry on trade by barter. They tried to find some better way of exchanging things. They decided upon some one thing, like cattle or sheep, which expressed the value of other things. After a time they came to use little things for this purpose, like shells or beads, that could be easily carried around. This made trading much simpler. After metal was discovered, little chunks of it were used as money.

A knowledge of arithmetic grew up in those early days. When man came to have possessions he had to count to keep track of what he had. Suppose a shepherd had eight sheep. They were very valuable to him and he knew that he owned eight. Every evening, when he led them into an enclosure where they would be protected from the wild animals during the night, he counted them to make sure that they were all there. Suppose, one evening, when he counted his sheep, he found that there were only six. Then he knew that two of his sheep were lost and that he must go out and find them. That early shepherd had done a little example in arithmetic.

The easiest way to count is on the fingers. Because men had ten fingers, they began counting by tens. When they

were counting and reached ten, they put down a little mark and began counting over again on their fingers. When men exchanged things they often needed to weigh them; when they built structures, they needed some way of measuring lengths. Various parts of the body, such as the finger, the foot, and the distance from the elbow to the tip of the finger, were used in measuring. Thus counting, measures of weight and distance, and computing had their beginning in the early days.

THE FIRST NATIONS

Groups of families lived together for protection. These groups were called tribes. The strongest and bravest man in the tribe became the chief. The other members of the tribe obeyed his orders because they knew that their safety depended on their obedience. The chief decided how all matters of importance should be settled. The decisions of the chief became the laws of the tribe, which the people obeyed.

When a chief died, it was at first hard to decide who the next one should be. Often there were several strong men who wanted to be chief. This sometimes led to fighting, as people took sides with the different leaders. Gradually the custom grew up of having the oldest son follow his father as chief.

Some places are better to live in than others, for in certain places nature helps people, while in others life is a hard struggle. In the fertile valleys of rivers, where there is plenty of water and the climate is warm and sunny, crops grow easily. In such places people can have good homes and work out comfortable ways of living.

In the early days, when the wandering tribes came to such good places they settled down. As they were able to raise their food and get the other things they needed easily, they had time and strength to improve their life and they learned to do many wonderful things. That is why the first civilizations grew up in the fertile valleys of rivers.

When the people of a tribe settled down on a piece of land, they thought that it belonged to them. If another tribe came to the same valley and tried to settle there, the tribes fought until the stronger tribe drove out the weaker one or made slaves of its people. Perhaps a tribe whose harvest had failed would raid the land of another tribe to get food. In some such ways as these war began in the world. Fighting and warfare were going on most of the time.

When the land of one tribe joined the land of another tribe these tribes might unite. The head of the strongest tribe became the king. Thus the first nations grew up.

THE FOUNDATIONS OF CIVILIZATION

For untold ages the earliest ancestors of modern people lived and learned in primitive ways. The people of those times kindled the first fires, invented the first tools and weapons. They were the first workers in wood, clay, stone, leather, and metal. They made the first carts and boats to carry them and their goods over the land and the water. They were the first traders, the first artists, musicians, storytellers, and dramatists. They learned to live together in communities with a kind of government, and they began that worship of a power greater than themselves which is called religion.

In those early days people began seeking new ways of doing things to make their lives safer and more comfortable. At first they had to take whatever nature provided. To get food they simply hunted for it and gathered it wherever they could find it. Later they tamed animals and began raising plants. The first homes were merely the tangled boughs of trees, or caves, or other nature-made shelters. Gradually people learned to build homes. The first clothes were the skins of wild animals thrown about the body. In time came spinning and weaving and the making of garments. Those early people were taking the first hard steps along the road of progress. They were beginning the search for better ways of living which has continued since that time and will continue as long as man lives on the earth.

The world owes much to those unknown thinkers and workers who laid the foundations upon which the people of later times gradually built up civilization.

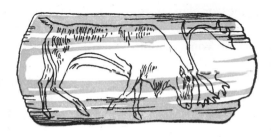

TALKING TOGETHER

1. Early man moved from one place to another in search of food. Do you know of any group of people today who move from one place to another to find work?

2. Discuss the different ways in which man has lighted his home from the days before history up to the present.

3. How many kinds of metals are used for things in your home?

4. What is the difference between iron and steel? Which makes better tools and weapons?

5. When were carts and rafts used in our country as important means of transportation?

6. Why is little weaving done in our homes today?

INTERESTING THINGS TO TRY

1. See if you can start fire by rubbing sticks together, or striking one stone against another.

2. Cut a forked stick and try to plow the ground with it. This helps you to realize how handicapped early farmers were by the lack of tools and implements.

3. Grind some grains of dried corn or wheat between stones. From this you will see that the primitive process of making meal or flour was very slow.

4. Talk to one another with signs and sounds such as early man might have used as a means of communication.

5. Make drawings or clay figures of prehistoric animals. Find the pictures in this unit showing wild and domestic animals.

6. In a corner of your schoolroom construct a floor scene to represent the homes and activities of man before the days of history.

7. Make models to show the types of tools, looms, boats, carts, and musical instruments used in early days.

8. Name some places in the United States where traces of early men and animals have been found.

9. Plan a pantomime to show how early tribal life was carried on.

Man and His Tools, by William A. Burns. This book tells of the beginnings of tools, transportation, and other contributions made by early man.

Graven with Flint, by Frederick L. Coe. Here is a story of a courageous boy in the Dawn Age.

Our Earth and Sky, by Gerald S. Craig and Sara E. Baldwin. You find many good illustrations in "Plants and Animals of Long Ago."

In the Beginning: A First History for Little Children, by Eva Erleigh. Be sure some of your group read "The First Man" and "Wandering Sailors."

How the World Grew Up, by Grace Kiner. Here you find stories of the first fisherman, the first builder, and other early workers.

Building Our World, by Clyde B. Moore, Helen M. Carpenter, Gertrude M. Lewis, and Fred B. Painter. Read "Early Man and How He Lived."

Looking at History, by R. J. Unstead. You will enjoy the descriptions of the Stone, the Bronze, and the Iron Ages. You will also like the illustrations of life among these people.

Introduce Yourself to Your Book

Look at the *table of contents* in the front of your book. How many units do you find? How many pages in the first unit? Glance over the titles of the units. Which do you think you will enjoy most?

In the contents of "Days before History," select a heading that interests you. Turn to the page shown by the number after the heading. Read what it says about the topic. You will save time by using the table of contents for reference.

The *index* in the back of your book is an alphabetical list of the important topics, persons, and places mentioned in the book, with the page number where each reference can be found. In the case of difficult words, the pronunciation is also given. Look up topics from this unit, such as Art, Food, Homes, in the index.

Quiz Yourself

Choose the Right Word

From the list below choose the word or group of words needed to make each of the following sentences complete and true. Write the numbers 1 to 10 on a separate sheet of paper. After each number place the correct word or words that will complete the sentence that has the same number. Then read the sentence with the right word in it. *Do not write in this book.*

1. The homes of early men were in ———.
2. The ——— was one of the first animals to be tamed.
3. The first hammers and knives were made of ———.
4. When men discovered ———, they were able to make better tools and weapons.
5. Early man hollowed out the trunk of a tree to make a crude ———.
6. The cave artists used colored clay and ——— in making their drawings.
7. The ——— ——— were early groups of village people.
8. Permanent ——— came about when people began to raise crops.
9. A stone blade fastened to a handle was used for cutting ———.
10. One of the most important advances in transportation was the invention of the ———.

homes	lake dwellers
grain	copper
boat	dog
wheel	berries
caves	stones

II

THE LAND OF
THE PHARAOHS

EGYPT AND THE NILE VALLEY. *The people of Egypt built a great civilization in early times as they developed this fertile valley where the Nile River flows between desert lands.*

THE LAND OF THE PHARAOHS

ANCIENT DWELLERS ON THE NILE

Egypt is a long, narrow strip of green, fertile land in the northeastern part of Africa, with endless wastes of desert sands on each side of it. Flowing through it is a long river, called the Nile. To this fertile Nile valley came, in early days, a roving people. It seemed to them a good place in which to live.

The climate was warm, water was at hand, and grains good for food were growing wild. With the desert on both sides of it, the valley formed a protected home. In the course of time the Egyptians built up in this fertile valley one of the great early nations.

For hundreds of years the Egyptians lived in little scattered villages along the banks of the Nile. Each village was ruled by a chief. The people of the villages often fought one another, and the stronger sometimes took the land of the weaker people. In time all the settled land along the river was organized into two kingdoms—Upper Egypt and Lower Egypt.

Upper Egypt lay to the south. The kingdom of Lower Egypt occupied the Delta of the Nile, where the river spreads out into many branches, like a fan, and flows into the Mediterranean Sea.

About 3400 B.C. a strong leader, Menes, gained control of both kingdoms. He built the city of Memphis near the mouth of the Nile, and this was the capital of Egypt for many years. Menes and the rulers who followed him developed Egypt into a prosperous and powerful nation.

The Egyptians thought of their ruler as akin to the gods. They held him in such reverence that they did not use his name, but called him Pharaoh, which means "great house" and referred to the palace in which he lived.

TILLERS OF THE SOIL

The months of April and May were times of terrible heat in ancient Egypt. Up from the south swept the burning desert winds. Everywhere the soil was dry and cracked with the heat. The air was filled with sand. There was no vegetation anywhere.

But in the mountains far to the south, where the Nile River has its source, something took place which brought about a change each year. In those mountains the snow melted in the early spring and there were heavy rains. The mountain streams swelled to overflowing and poured torrents of muddy water into the river.

With ever-increasing speed the water came rushing along. Higher and higher rose the Nile. By the middle of July it had overflowed its banks and was spreading its waters farther and farther over the low-lying lands on both sides. Each year a flood covered the valley through which the Nile flowed.

[46]

For six or eight weeks the whole valley was flooded. Then the waters gradually went down. When the river returned to its banks once more, it had left a layer of rich, black earth over all the valley to the base of the hills on each side.

As if by magic, Egypt was transformed. Seeds began to sprout; trees and shrubs came to life again and put forth leaves and blossoms. The Egyptians rejoiced at the rich earth which the life-renewing flood had left behind.

As soon as the Nile fell, the new farming season began. The low-lying lands which had been under water for a long time were so soft that plowing was not necessary. The farmer sprinkled seeds over the soil and dragged the branch of a tree along to scrape the moist earth over them.

The higher ground dried quickly and had to be plowed. The plow was very simple—just three rough pieces of wood fastened together so that the end of one piece dug up the soil as it was dragged along the ground, the second reached up to the yoke of the oxen, and the third formed the handle of the plow held by the plowman.

When the grain had grown to its full height and its long stalks bore their precious seeds, it was cut and bound into sheaves, which were carried to the threshing floor. There the grain was spread out, and oxen were led back and forth over it to tread out the seeds. As they did this, the farmer sang:

> Thresh, O ye oxen,
> Thresh for yourselves!
> Thresh straw for your fodder!
> Thresh grain for your master!
> Take ye no rest;
> Cool is the air this day.

The next step was getting rid of the little shells, or husks, of the grain. This is called winnowing. The Egyptians winnowed their wheat by tossing it high into the air with wooden scoops. As the grain fell, a man fanned the air so that the light husks would blow away.

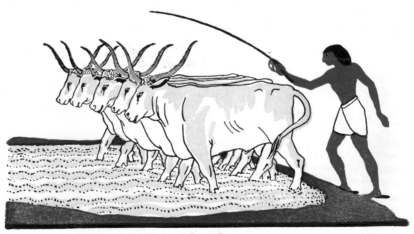

The flooding of the Nile year after year left thin layers of soil which gradually raised the land, so that the surrounding fields came to be higher than the land nearest the river. The river gave the Egyptians enough water for about six months. During the rest of the year the water was very low.

The farmers noticed that some water stayed in hollows in the low ground. There the land remained green and fertile after the higher ground was dry and cracked by the heat of the sun.

They began enlarging the hollow places into pools which would hold the water long after the flood season had passed. Then, when their land began to dry up, they let water from the pools run into ditches which they dug through the fields. As far as the water reached, the land remained green and fertile even in the dry season.

[49]

The farmers had to find a way to raise water up to the high fields. To do this they invented the shadoof. This was a long pole on which a skin bucket was hung by a rope. The other end of the pole was weighted with a ball of hardened mud. The worker pulled down the empty bucket and dipped it into the river. When it was full he raised it and swung it around so that it could be emptied into a ditch five or six feet above the river.

Still higher fields were watered by a series of canals or ditches, the water being raised by shadoofs from one level to another until the highest ground was reached.

This way of watering dry land and making it fertile was one of the earliest methods of irrigation.

When the water of the Nile overflowed its banks each year, it often washed away the boundaries between the field owned by one man and that owned by another. It was therefore necessary to find a way of measuring the land so that each person would know what belonged to him. The way of measuring land by using straight lines and angles is called surveying. The Egyptians were the first people to survey their lands.

With such abundant crops from the fields, the Egyptians needed containers in which to store grains and other foods. Egypt abounded in clay suitable for pottery. The potter kneaded the clay with his feet, then placed a lump on a wheel and skillfully shaped it with his hand as the wheel whirled round and round. When the soft clay vessels were finished they were baked in closed furnaces.

The Egyptians also discovered that the clay made excellent bricks. They mixed it with sand and a little chopped grass and straw and then left the bricks to dry and harden in the sun.

The art of making glass was probably first learned in Egypt. Glass is made by melting sand with other substances. At first the glass is like a thick sirup. The Egyptian glassmaker would put some of the hot, soft glass on the end

[51]

of a long tube. Then he would hold the other end of the tube in his mouth. As he blew through the tube the hot glass swelled up into a hollow sphere. While it was still soft he molded it into some beautiful or useful shape.

The flax growers learned that the inner part of the flax stalk could be divided into thin strands which could be made into thread. The stalk had to be soaked in water for several days, then dried in the sun and cracked open. From a bunch of flax stalks, hundreds of thin strands of flax, each eighteen or twenty inches long, were obtained. The strands were twisted into threads, and from these flax threads weavers made fine linen. This cloth was almost as soft as silk. Pieces of it have lasted for more than four thousand years.

There were many other skilled craftsmen in Egypt. Goldsmiths fashioned rings and necklaces and bracelets set with jewels or inlaid with brilliant enamels. Workers in wood decorated furniture with mother-of-pearl, ivory, gold, and silver. Leatherworkers made girdles and sandals. Metalworkers made shields and spears.

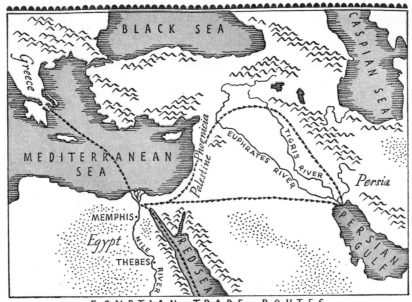

EGYPTIAN TRADE ROUTES

BOATBUILDERS

The Nile was a fine waterway through the country, and the Egyptians soon learned to make excellent river boats of reeds. The ends of the boats were shaped like the papyrus flower. Up and down the river the people of a village rowed or sailed, carrying their produce and trading with the people of another village. In the early days there was no money in Egypt. All trading was carried on by exchanging wares.

In later days larger boats were built, which made it possible to trade with faraway places. In exchange for the things he wanted, the Egyptian trader offered the beautiful and useful things made by Egyptian workmen.

[53]

On the big ships there was one large square sail which could be used only when the wind blew from behind the boat. The rest of the time the ship was moved by oars. The rowers were usually slaves. They were chained to their seats, and if they did not row hard enough they were sure to feel a blow from the slave-master's whip. There was no rudder. At the stern was a pilot who steered by means of a broad oar fastened to the ship's side.

PICTURE WRITING

For a long time the people of Egypt did not know how to write. They began writing by making little pictures. When they wanted to write about water, they made a picture of wavy lines. If they wanted to write about a boat, they made a picture of a boat. For the sun they drew a circle, for the moon they made a crescent, and so on. But this way of writing was very slow.

In time people got into the way of making fewer marks to show what they meant. For instance, instead of drawing a bird, they might make two little marks that looked like the wings when the bird was flying. Instead of drawing a man, they might make two marks to represent the legs of a man walking.

[54]

In the earliest days, pictures were sufficient to express what the Egyptians wanted to write about. As time went on, they wanted to write about things that were difficult to represent by pictures. So they made up little signs for these. It was possible to express even the most difficult ideas by means of signs. It took hundreds of different signs to tell a long story, however. The next step was to have signs stand for syllables instead of for whole words; and finally a mark stood for a simple sound.

Growing in the low marshes along the Nile was a reed-like plant, called papyrus, which proved to be good for making a kind of paper. First the stem of the reed was cut into long strips. These were laid lengthwise, side by side, with their edges overlapping. Other strips were placed crosswise over them. Then the strips were dampened and pressed with heavy weights and dried in the sun. Thus a sheet was formed which was much like a sheet of paper.

To write on this paper, the Egyptians used a sort of ink made by thickening water with vegetable gum and mixing in a little soot from pots that had been blackened over the fire. A pointed reed served as a pen.

The Egyptians made some of the first books in the world. Their books, however, were not bound in pages. The sheets of papyrus were joined together into long rolls. Sometimes these rolls were over a hundred feet long. Of course, such a long piece of papyrus would be difficult to manage in reading; so the Egyptians rolled it up on a stick. The reader unrolled the papyrus a little at a time, and then rolled it up on another stick as he read.

Few of the Egyptians could write. There were special people, called scribes, whose business it was to do writing for other people. The scribes were very important and were greatly respected. An ambitious boy was advised to "set to work and become a scribe, for then thou shalt become a leader of men. He who is industrious and does not neglect his books may become a prince."

The life of a scribe was far better than that of most workers. One father who wanted his son to become a scribe said:

Be a scribe who is freed from forced labor and protected from all evils. The coppersmith has to work in front of his blazing furnace, and his fingers are like the crocodile's legs. The mason is always overhauling blocks of stone, and in the evening his arms are heavy and the bones of his thighs and back feel as if they were coming asunder. The waterman is stung to death by the gnats and mosquitoes. The ditcher in the fields works among the cattle and pigs; his garments are stiff with mud. The caravan man goes in terror of lions and nomads whilst on his journey, and he returns to Egypt exhausted. When the baker layeth his bread in the fire, his head is inside the oven and his son holdeth fast to his feet. Cometh it to pass that he slippeth from his son's hand, he falleth into the blaze. But the scribe, he directeth every work that is in this land.

TELLING TIME

At first the Egyptians guessed the time during the day by looking at the sun to see how high in the heavens it was, but this was not an accurate way of telling time and they learned a better way. They divided the time between one sunrise and the next into twenty-four hours.

Someone noticed that a tree casts a shadow and that this shadow is shortest in the middle of the day. As the sun rises higher in the sky, the shadow of the tree grows shorter and shorter until noon. Then it grows longer and longer. The Egyptians could tell the time by measuring the shadows cast by rocks, trees, or sticks.

Later they made a shadow clock. This was a long piece of wood with a crosspiece at one end. In the early morning the crosspiece was set toward the east and its shadow fell along the whole of the long arm. As the sun rose higher, the shadow shortened. There was a scale on the long arm marked off for the hours. The place of the shadow on the scale showed the hours until noon, when the shadow disappeared. Then at noon the crosspiece was set toward the west, and the hours of the afternoon could be measured by the lengthening shadow on the long piece.

Egyptians liked to watch the stars on clear nights. Their wise men noticed that some stars rose each night a few minutes earlier than the night before. From the movements of the stars in the heavens, they learned many things. They came to know that the rising of a certain star was a sign that the Nile was rising. They used the stars to guide them when they traveled at night.

Egyptian shepherds, guarding their flocks by night, had a fine chance to observe the moon. They noticed that on certain nights it was like a silver sickle in the sky. Each night after that it grew larger and larger until it became a great ball of light. Then it grew smaller and smaller until it disappeared entirely. After a while a new moon appeared and grew into a full moon. These early watchers of the sky discovered that the moon reached its full size once in twenty-nine or thirty days and that there were twelve new moons between the risings of the Nile. The Egyptians called the time between two new moons a month.

When the dwellers on the Nile had watched the moon for a long, long time, they made a calendar to measure time. They decided that each month should be thirty days long. This made three hundred and sixty days for twelve months. At the end of the year they celebrated five feast days, a kind of holiday week. This gave them a year of three hundred and sixty-five days. Their year was made up of three seasons, called the Inundation, the Coming Forth, and the Harvest. Each season was four months long.

[58]

In everything about them the Egyptians saw the work of gods. They believed in a creator, the source of all things. But they could not understand how one being could have all the qualities needed to control the whole world. So they thought there must be many gods.

The sun, which shines so gloriously in the cloudless Egyptian sky, was the greatest god of the Egyptians. They called him Ra. He gave them light and heat, the source of all life. Every morning he appeared on the eastern horizon, victorious from his fight with the powers of darkness, and began his daily journey in a boat called "Millions of Years." On his way he looked down upon his people and saw their deeds, good and evil. In the evening he passed beyond the mountain of the west. When dawn came he issued forth again, to begin once more his journey across the heavens.

The Egyptians were very grateful for the river which was so good to them. They did not understand why it overflowed its banks. They knew only that when it did, the fertile soil came to make their crops grow. When it did not, there was famine, which caused much suffering among the people. They thought the rising of the waters was under the control of the Nile god. They believed that by praying to him they could persuade him to make the waters flow over the land and make it fertile.

Every year when the waters began to rise, a great festival was held in honor of the Nile god. From all parts of Egypt flocked crowds of people to worship and give thanks.

[59]

Led by their priests, the people went in a procession to the river bank, chanting a hymn of thanksgiving:

Praise to thee, O Nile, that issueth forth from the earth and cometh to nourish the dwellers in Egypt.
Thou waterest the fields which Ra hath created to nourish all cattle,
Thou givest drink to the desert places which are far from water,
Thou makest every workshop to flourish.

Lord of fish, that maketh the water fowl to go up stream,
That maketh barley and createth wheat.
If the Nile be sluggish, the nostrils are stopped up and all men are brought low;
When the Nile rises, earth rejoices and all men are glad; every jaw laughs and every tooth is uncovered.

Thou art the bringer of nourishment, creating all things good,
Creating herbage for the cattle,
Filling the barns and widening the granaries; giving to the poor.

[60]

Osiris was the god most widely worshiped by the people. He was the god who came down from heaven in the form of man to teach the people to live together in brotherly love. Another god held in great reverence was Thoth. He represented the divine intelligence, and so became the god of wisdom and learning. In the religion of the Egyptians there were many different kinds of gods.

Many animals were looked upon as sacred by the Egyptians, because they thought that the gods often took the forms of animals when they visited the earth to watch the doings of men. Some of the gods were represented with the body of a man and the head of an animal.

The Egyptians believed that the soul of a man lived on after his brief life on earth. They thought that it might sometime want to re-enter his body. When a man died, they treated his body in certain ways to preserve it. Then they wrapped it carefully in long strips of linen which had been soaked in resin and spices. A body so treated was called a mummy. The mummy was placed in a coffin shaped like the body and beautifully painted and decorated in color. The coffin was then placed in a tomb with food, furniture, and many other things which might be needed in the life after death.

The rich nobles, who had always had slaves to work for them, had hundreds of little statues placed in their tombs to do their work in the next world. The master was supposed to say to them: "O ye figures, be ye ever watchful to work, to plow and sow the fields, to fill with water the canals, and to carry sand from the east to the west."

Whenever the noble was called upon in the afterworld to do any work, he could summon one of these little statues, who would answer, "Here am I, ready when thou callest." So the statues were called Answerers.

After death the soul set out on its perilous journey to paradise. The dead man had to cross bleak deserts, climb high mountains, ford streams haunted by serpents, dragons, and demons. These dangers he was able to escape from or to overcome because he had with him a book, now called the *Book of the Dead*. This contained hymns, prayers, and magical phrases, which he could recite on his journey to the spirit world.

Before being admitted to paradise, the soul had to go to the Hall of Truth. At the far end of a mighty hall, on a splendid golden throne approached by nine broad steps, sat the dread judge, Osiris. Forty-two gods on thrones of ivory and gold were ranged around the hall. Each one had the power to punish some particular sin.

Near by was a pair of scales. Behind them yawned a deep pit, and behind this crouched a monster with the head of a crocodile, the body of a hippopotamus, and the hind legs of a lion.

The forty-two gods began questioning the soul.

"Hast thou been guilty of theft?" asked one.

"Hath thy tongue spoken falsely against thy neighbor?" asked another.

"Hast thou taken the life of thy brother?" questioned a third.

"Didst thou honor thy gods?"

"Didst thou love thy neighbor as thyself?"

Thus the examination went on and on.

[63]

Solemnly answering the questions of the gods, the spirit replied:

"O ye Lords of Truth, I have not done evil against mankind.

"I have not oppressed the poor.

"I have not caused the slave to be ill treated.

"I have not spoken ill of any man.

"I have not dealt deceitfully.

"I have not stirred up strife.

"I have not given false weight.

"I have not stolen.

"I have spoken no lies.

"I have given bread to the hungry, water unto them that thirst, and clothing to the naked. I have done that which is right and pure, and my God I have faithfully served in spirit and in truth."

Did the soul speak the truth? Horus, the falcon-headed son of Osiris, came forward and led the spirit-man to the scales of justice. The heart of the man was placed on one side of the scales, and on the other a feather, symbol of truth. If the scales did not balance it meant that the soul had lied, and it was doomed to terrible punishment. If the balance remained level and the heart was not outweighed by truth, the soul was allowed to enter paradise, which it was to enjoy forever. This was a pleasant land of fields and rivers, where a man would meet his ancestors and live as he had lived on earth but in glorified form.

It is clear that the Egyptians believed that a man's character was important, and that he would be rewarded or punished in the next world in accordance with the life he had lived in this world.

[65]

One of the greatest rulers of Egypt was a woman, Queen Hatshepsut. Her father had decided that she should rule after him. The people had never had a woman ruler and were afraid that Hatshepsut would be too weak to maintain the glory of their country. But the Pharaoh commanded that preparations should be made for the coronation of his daughter.

On the appointed day, the Pharaoh spoke to the people, saying: "Hatshepsut shall sit on my holy throne. She shall lead you and ye shall harken to her word. He who praises her shall live, and he who says aught evil of her shall die."

So after the death of her father, Hatshepsut became queen. Her reign was one of peace and prosperity.

One day the queen heard the voice of a god bidding her send an expedition to a distant country known as the land of Punt. Accordingly, she fitted out a fleet of five ships and filled them with Egyptian goods.

The fleet sailed down the Nile and through a canal which led from one of the mouths of the river to the Red Sea. The ships kept on down the African coast of the Red Sea till they finally arrived at the land of Punt.

The people of Punt were greatly excited by the arrival of the strangers. Headed by their chief, a great crowd came down to the shore to welcome them.

[66]

"Why have ye come hither unto this land which your people knew not?" they asked. "Did ye come down upon the ways of heaven, or did ye sail upon the water, upon the sea of God's land?"

The natives of Punt gave the Egyptians the rarest products of their land in exchange for "all good things of the land of Egypt," which the Egyptians had brought with them. Many strange and precious things were carried up the gangplanks to the ships. There were gold, precious stones, ebony and ivory, sweet-smelling myrrh and incense, even strange animals—baboons and apes—which the Egyptians had never seen before.

Heavily laden, the five ships sailed back home. Great was the welcome the sailors received when they stepped ashore. There was a triumphal procession, led by the sailors bearing the rich cargo. Such riches had never before been known in Egypt. This expedition to Punt was one of the great events of Queen Hatshepsut's reign.

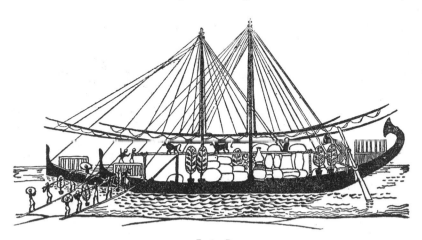

All the land of Egypt belonged to the Pharaoh. He gave parts of it to his great nobles. The nobles lived in spacious houses with shady balconies. There was usually one long room with low windows, facing north, where the master of the house and his family could sit in summer and make the most of any cool breeze. Around this were a number of smaller rooms.

The rooms were beautifully decorated. Sometimes the ceiling was painted to look like the sky, with stars shining out from a deep blue background. Sometimes the floor was painted green and represented pools of water with marsh grasses growing in them, with fish and waterfowl among the marshy reeds.

On the large estates of the nobles were stables and storehouses and servants' quarters. There were high-walled gardens where fountains flashed and sparkled in the sun. Beautiful white lotus blossoms and the round green leaves of the lotus floated on pools of clear water.

Wealthy people dressed in fine garments of linen, richly embroidered. As decorations they wore necklaces and earrings, bracelets and anklets. They were fond of feasting. Often they gave banquets, after which they and their guests reclined on couches, listening to the music of the harp or watching entertainers in stately dances. When nobles went out, they rode in chairs borne on the shoulders of slaves or in chariots drawn by beautiful horses.

Only a few people were rich. Most of the people were poor and many were slaves. The houses of the poor were mud huts with only one room. They contained little furniture and that was of the simplest kind. In their house a poor Egyptian family had only a rough wooden table, a few stone blocks that served as seats, and a bed of woven reeds and fibers.

The life of the poor people was very hard. They worked for the Pharaohs and nobles. Barefoot and bareheaded and dressed in a single cotton garment, they went to work at dawn. For food they carried with them two or three little cakes of barley bread which had been baked in the ashes, a skin filled with goat's milk, perhaps one or two onions, sometimes a bit of fish. They worked always under the watchful eyes of overseers who had whips.

THE PYRAMID BUILDERS

The early Pharaohs, who lived in Memphis, began about the year 3000 B.C. to build tombs called pyramids. There are many of these near the Nile River. The largest is that built by Khufu—or Cheops, as he is sometimes called. This great tomb is a solid mass of stones, each one weighing several tons. An ancient writer tells us that a hundred thousand workmen, most of them slaves, worked for twenty years building it.

No one is quite sure how the work was done—how the great blocks of stone were quarried from the rock; how they were moved to the place where the pyramid was to be built; and how they were lifted into place.

Most of the stone came from a place nearly six hundred miles away. To break the blocks from the solid rock, it is

thought that a groove was cut and that holes were bored along the groove at intervals. Into these holes wooden wedges were forced. Then the groove was filled with water, which caused the wood to swell, and this cracked the stone along the groove. Heavy rollers were probably used to move the blocks of stone to the banks of the Nile. Next they were floated down the river on rafts buoyed up by the inflated skins of animals, and unloaded onto sledges.

Where the stones were landed, workmen built a road leading up a long slope. Along this slope gangs of slaves must have pulled and pushed the blocks of stone. Hundreds of men tugged in front and hundreds pushed from behind. Slowly the heavy stone blocks moved higher and higher to their places in the huge mountain of stone. Each block was so perfectly fitted to the next that the joining could scarcely be seen. At length the last block was laid

in place, and slabs of smooth granite were fitted over the stones so that there was an unbroken slope from the base to the top of the pyramid.

The pyramids lost most of their smooth covering as winds and sand wore away the stone. Many of the blocks of stone have been removed, so that the sides of the pyramids look like rough, giant stone stairways.

Part way up one of the slanting sides of the pyramid was an opening to the tomb inside. It was cunningly concealed so that robbers would not be able to find the entrance. Through the solid rock a long, narrow passageway led deep down to a room in the center of the pyramid.

This room was the tomb in which the embalmed body of the Pharaoh was placed when he died. Many beautiful things were put in the tomb with him. Pictures and inscriptions on the walls told of his good deeds as ruler and of the life of the people during his reign. It is from these pictures and inscriptions that historians have found out much about how the Egyptians lived.

Rising out of the sand near the pyramids is the Sphinx, one of the strangest statues in the world. It has the huge body of a lion with the head of a man. It is carved from solid stone.

For centuries the sand blown by the desert winds piled up around this enormous statue, covering most of it. Then the sand was cleared away, showing the gigantic paws of the lion. Between the outstretched front paws was found a small temple. The doorway of the temple is often blocked by sand.

The features of the Sphinx have been greatly damaged, but it still has a mysterious dignity. There it stands, the riddle of the ages. No one knows when it was carved or what it represents. Perhaps it was made in honor of some Egyptian god.

The capital of the later Pharaohs was at Thebes, which was about four hundred miles up the Nile River. Thebes was the most magnificent city in the world. Every Pharaoh added to its splendor, building a temple or adding to one already built, or setting up a gateway or a statue. In front of a temple there was usually a tall tapering column of pink granite called an obelisk. It was tipped with gold and its sides were adorned with pictures and writings telling of the greatness of the Pharaoh who had it set up.

Of all the temples the most magnificent was the Great Temple of Karnak near Thebes, built in honor of the sun god. It took hundreds of years to build it and many Pharaohs helped in the building. It was approached by a broad avenue lined with sphinxes. At each entrance were two pylons of stone with slanting walls like a fortress. At the top was a winged sun disk, the symbol of the sun god, with a serpent on each side. The outspread wings of the sun disk were the symbol of divine protection. The serpents were the symbol of royalty. The Egyptians thought that this sign brought safety to all within the building. They often carved or painted it over doorways.

The largest part of the temple was the great hall. Its roof was supported by many enormous columns painted in brilliant colors. Their tops were carved to look like the bell-shaped lotus blossom, which the Egyptians loved more than any other flower. Enormous pictures were sculptured on the walls from floor to ceiling.

[75]

Across the river from Karnak, Queen Hatshepsut built
a beautiful temple on the sloping ground at the foot of
towering cliffs. It was built in three terraces, one above
another, and on each terrace incense trees from Punt were
planted. On the walls were carved scenes telling the story
of the expedition to Punt. There may be seen the sailors
loading the ships, the arrival of the ships in Thebes, and
the festival held in honor of the safe return of the fleet.
One inscription reads:

The loading of the ships very heavily with marvels of the country of Punt: all goodly fragrant woods of God's land, heaps of myrrh with fresh myrrh trees, and pure ivory with the green gold of Emu, with cinnamon wood, eye cosmetics, with apes, monkeys, dogs, and the skins of the southern panther. Never was brought the like of this for any king who has been since the beginning.

For many centuries the Egyptians lived in their well-watered Nile valley, building up a wonderful civilization. The later Pharaohs were strong military leaders who extended their rule over other nations. Egypt became a great empire and rose to the height of her power by 1500 B.C. But little by little, the greatness of Egypt passed. Neighboring people conquered the Egyptians, and the power of this mighty empire was broken. The things which the Egyptians had learned were not lost to the world, however, for their contributions were passed on to benefit the people who came after them.

Talking Together

1. Some of you know rivers which have spring floods. What is the effect of these on the surrounding country? Do the people rejoice in a flood as they did in Egypt?

2. In what sections of our country do people irrigate their crops? Compare modern methods with those used by the Egyptians.

3. In our present-day life, who does the kind of work done by the scribes in the early days in Egypt?

4. The Egyptian slaves did the heavy work in building, such as breaking stones, lifting, pulling, and rolling. How is this work done in our country?

Interesting Things to Try

1. Imagine that you are an Egyptian slave. How would it feel to do the heavy work in building or farming? Dramatize this to your classmates by your arm movements, your slow step, your stooped body, and your tired face. Some children like to do such things with the rhythm of music.

2. Begin to keep a "Story of Records." Make a scroll such as the Egyptians used for writing. On this draw some of the Egyptian pictorial signs. This "Story of Records" may be continued as you study other countries.

3. Construct a model of a shadoof, using the picture on page 50 as a guide. Carve a model of an Egyptian boat like the one in the picture on page 67.

4. One group may plan and construct a shadow clock on the school grounds.

5. Have your class select a committee to paint a colorful frieze illustrating the story of Egypt as "The Gift of the River."

6. If you have a movie projector in your school, ask your teacher to get from the school, city, or state film library the movie "The Kingdom of the Nile." After you have seen the picture, name the historical monuments in the film.

Communication: From Cave Writing to Television, by Julie Forsyth Batchelor. An interesting story of communication from stone tablets to paper books and block printing.

Rivers of the World: Stories of the Great Rivers of Each Continent, by F. Raymond Elms. Here is told the part the Nile has played in the history of Egypt.

Here Is Africa, by Ellen and Attilio Gatti. "Egypt, the Desert's Biggest Oasis," gives glimpses of the past and the present of this country, the home of early civilization.

Sokar and the Crocodile, by Alice Howard. This story makes old Egypt seem very real to you.

Never to Die, by Josephine Mayer and Tom Prideaux. You and your group are sure to be interested in the pictures of Egyptian life shown in this story.

The Gift of the River, by Enid L. Meadowcroft. "A Walk with Uni" tells what an Egyptian boy might have seen on a walk a thousand years ago.

Joseph. This story arranged by Elizabeth Yates tells how the Hebrew boy became a leader in Egypt.

Looking at Pictures and Maps

There are many illustrations, or pictures, in this book. They say in a different way or add something to what has been told by the author. This is the way the artist gives his message.

Look at the pictures in "The Land of the Pharaohs." Study each picture carefully. Does the picture tell you the same thing that is told in the text? What other thoughts or feelings does the picture give you?

Make a map of Egypt with near-by lands and waters. Use the maps on pages 44 and 53 for reference. Decorate your map with pictures to show important places and travel routes.

[79]

QUIZ YOURSELF

Put These Sentences Together

On a sheet of paper copy the first list, labeled "Beginnings." Then from the second list select the right ending for each beginning and write it so that you have a complete and true sentence. *Remember that you must not write in this book.*

BEGINNINGS	ENDINGS
1. The Egyptians invented the shadoof	linen that was nearly as soft as silk.
2. Waters receded from the river valley,	at the time of the year when the Nile began to rise.
3. Plowing was unnecessary in lands	leaving behind rich soil for the planting of crops.
4. Surveying was used to restore	the development of picture writing.
5. A festival was held by the people of Egypt	which had been under water a long time.
6. The Egyptians thought that Osiris taught	built by King Khufu, or Cheops.
7. Egyptian weavers showed skill in making	to help irrigate their fields in the dry season.
8. One of the first trading journeys was	boundaries of the land washed away by the Nile.
9. The largest of the Egyptian pyramids was that	Queen Hatshepsut's expedition to Punt.
10. An aid to the keeping of records was	that men should live together in brotherly love.

III

EARLY NATIONS IN
SOUTHWEST ASIA

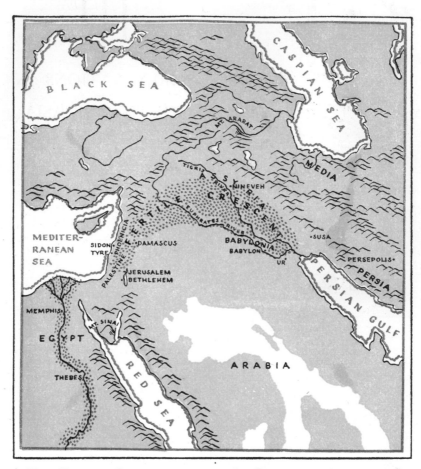

THE FERTILE CRESCENT. *People of different tribes formed early nations in southwest Asia and used the resources of land and sea in building their cultures.*

EARLY NATIONS IN SOUTHWEST ASIA

THE FERTILE CRESCENT

In the southwestern part of Asia near Africa and Europe, different peoples were settling down, and early nations were developing in the fertile lands of this region.

The Fertile Crescent is a broad belt of rich land. One end stretches along the shore of the Mediterranean Sea and then curves like a huge crescent with its other end at the head of the Persian Gulf.

In one way the people living in this region were less fortunate than the Egyptians. Egypt was protected on both sides by the desert, but the Fertile Crescent was an open plain which could be easily reached.

From the earliest times tribe after tribe crossed and recrossed it and sought to settle in it. One tribe would succeed in getting possession of some of the fertile land. Then another, stronger tribe would invade the region and try to take a piece of the rich land for themselves. This struggle went on constantly for many years.

In spite of these wars, the people who lived in the Fertile Crescent made many contributions to man's progress. Five nations—the Babylonians, the Assyrians, the Hebrews, the Phoenicians, and the Persians—at one time or another became important in the history of this region.

[83]

Two great rivers, the Tigris and the Euphrates, rise in the snow-capped mountains and flow southeast through a broad, level plain. The waters of these rivers join and empty into the Persian Gulf.

These rivers, like the Nile, overflow their banks each year and leave their gift of rich, fertile soil when their waters go down. The land between the Tigris and the Euphrates came to be known as Mesopotamia, which means the "Land Between the Rivers."

The earliest people who lived in the southern part of Mesopotamia were the Sumerians, who became highly civilized. The Sumerians were conquered by the Babylonians, who built up one of the great civilizations of the early world. Their most important city was Babylon, on the banks of the Euphrates River.

There was not much stone in Babylonia. There was plenty of good clay, however, and the Babylonians shaped this clay into bricks, which were dried in the hot sun until they were hard and could be used for building.

From these bricks, which were beautifully colored and sometimes enameled, the Babylonians built splendid palaces and temples.

The Babylonians learned to make many useful things. Their weavers made rugs of brilliant colors in beautiful designs. Many of the signs they used in weaving had special meanings. The palm tree was the sign of immortality, a zigzag line meant water, and a pine cone meant fire.

Their smiths made bronze tools and gold and silver jewelry. Their potters learned to use the wheel in molding bowls and jars into lovely shapes. There were also skillful cabinet workers and workers in leather.

Strange boats were used on the Euphrates River. Goatskins blown up with air were tied underneath rafts to make them float better. With these blown-up skins of animals the rafts could carry enormous weights. The great blocks of stone sometimes used in building a palace were carried hundreds of miles on these rafts. Other boats were made by weaving together reeds and grasses.

The Babylonians became merchants and traders. They were good businessmen and had banks to manage their money. In Babylon were busy markets where traders met to buy and sell the products of city and country. Merchants from foreign lands exchanged their wares for things made in Babylonia.

In carrying on their business, Babylonian merchants and traders had to use arithmetic. They worked out systems of counting by twelves as well as by tens. The idea of the dozen came from them.

The Babylonians needed to measure goods and to weigh the things they bought and sold. For use in their trading they worked out a system of weights and measures. The king made a law that the weights and measures were to be the same in all parts of the country.

Among the weights were the pound and the ounce. One of the measures they used was the foot. These weights and measures were found to be so useful that they were adopted by many of the countries with which the Babylonians traded.

To measure time the Babylonians invented the sundial. The shadow which the sun cast on the sundial indicated the hour of the day. Some of the sundials they made were small enough to be carried about easily.

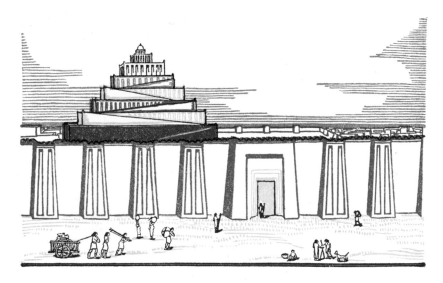

TOWER-TEMPLES

Like the Egyptians the Babylonians believed in many gods. Their supreme god was Marduk, the creator of all things. The Babylonian account of him says:

He formed mankind;
The beasts of the field and living things in the field he formed;
The Tigris and Euphrates he created and established in their place;
The grass, the rush of the marsh, the reed and the forest he created.
The lands, the marshes and the swamps, he made;
The wild cow and her young, the wild calf,
The ewe and her young, and the lamb of the fold.

The belief of the Babylonians in the life after death was quite different from that of the Egyptians. The Egyptians looked forward to a happy life after death; whereas the

[87]

Babylonians thought life in the future world was gloomy and desolate. The world of the dead, they believed, lay under the ground. There the spirits of the dead flitted about in the darkness like bats. They were hungry and they had nothing to eat but dust. They were cold and they were "clad in thin garments in which they fluttered to and fro uttering mournful cries." The future home of the soul was called the "Land of No Return," for the Babylonians believed that there was no escape from it.

The Babylonians built temples to their gods, but they were quite different from those of the Egyptians. They were built of sun-baked brick and were like square towers built one above the other, each one a little smaller than the one below it. Some of the tall skyscrapers in cities today, with each story set farther back than the one below it, are somewhat like the Babylonian tower-temples.

Each story of the tower was painted a different color. The lowest story was black, the next was orange-colored, the next red, the fourth gold, the fifth pale yellow, the next a deep blue, the next silver. At the top was a little temple which was thought to be the dwelling place of a god. The people believed that the god often rested on the couch in this temple and feasted from a golden table placed before it. Processions of priests climbed to the shrine to offer the gifts of the people to the god.

The seventh day of the week was kept as a holy day in Babylonia. No food could be cooked, no new clothes put on, no medicine taken. Even the king was forbidden to ride in his chariot or to issue any royal decrees.

From their high places in the temples the Babylonian priests studied the stars. They observed twelve groups of stars arranged in a broad belt which they called the zodiac. They believed that the sun and the stars were gods under their great god, Marduk. They thought that Marduk told the stars what was going to happen, and the priests believed that by studying the stars they could see into the future and predict events to come. Such a belief in the influence of the stars over the events of this world is called astrology. It is interesting to know that this belief comes down from the early days in Babylonia.

In some parts of Babylonia the people worshiped the moon-god. This worship of the moon led to the making of a calendar in which the twelve months corresponded to the twelve appearances of the moon. The worship and study of the sun, moon, and stars led to the beginning of the science of astronomy.

The most famous king in the early days of Babylonia was Hammurabi, who ruled about 2000 B.C. Before his time many laws had been made in different parts of the country. Sometimes the laws in one part allowed people to do things which were not allowed by the laws in another part. Hammurabi gathered together all the laws of the different parts of his kingdom and made them into one set of laws for all his people. He did this, he said, so that people might live together in peace.

In order that everyone might know what these laws were, he had them carved on a huge block of stone which he set up in a temple. At the top was carved a picture of the king receiving the laws from the sun god, and above the laws were inscribed these words: "Let the oppressed who has cause for complaint come and stand before my image as King of Righteousness. Let him read the inscription and understand my precious words. The writing shall explain to him his case, he shall see his right, and his heart shall become glad."

This is the oldest known system of laws. Some of these laws were good, but according to modern ideas many of them seem harsh and cruel. There were thirty-four things which were punished by death. Here are some of the laws:

> He who steals from a temple or palace shall be killed.
>
> If a builder build a house for someone and do not construct it properly and the house which he built fall and kill its owner, that builder shall be put to death.
>
> If in a man's house a fire be kindled and the man who comes to put out the fire steal from the owner of the house, that man shall be thrown into the fire.
>
> If a man put out the eye of another man, his eye shall be put out.
>
> If he break another man's bone, his bone shall be broken.
>
> If he knock out the teeth of his equal, his teeth shall be knocked out.

There were certain laws like this one: "If a man has stolen an ox, or a sheep, or a pig from the priests or the king, let him pay thirtyfold. But if he has stolen from a poor man, he shall repay tenfold." Thus a poor man was not so well protected by law as a rich man.

Sometimes today people make use of the expression, "an eye for an eye and a tooth for a tooth." That expression is first found in the old laws of Hammurabi.

BOOKS OF CLAY

When the Babylonians wanted to record their thoughts they used the clay which was so plentiful in their country. First the clay was made into flat tablets. On the smooth surface the Babylonians wrote with a sharp reed. It is not easy to make round marks in soft clay. So instead of making any circular letters, the Babylonians made their signs wedge-shaped. There were about three hundred of these queer wedge-shaped characters. The tablets were baked until they became as hard as stone. Each tablet was like the page of a book. Sometimes it took fifteen or twenty tablets to make a book.

In time the Babylonians built up large libraries of these clay tablets. In the books, they wrote the stories of their gods and heroes, what they knew about science, and many of their customs. By reading these ancient books men have learned a great deal about how the people of Babylonia lived long ago.

The Babylonians also wrote letters on clay tablets. Instead of signing his name to his letter as we do, the Babylonian pressed a seal against the soft clay. This seal was a little cylinder with a design carved on it. When the seal was rolled over the clay tablet, the design was stamped on the clay. Every Babylonian gentleman had his little cylinder, which he wore hanging on a chain around his neck or from his wrist.

When a letter was finished, it was sprinkled with dry clay and wrapped in a thin layer of moist clay which made an envelope. The address was put on the outside and the letter was baked in the sun.

SCHOOL DAYS IN BABYLON

There were schools in Babylon for boys and girls of well-to-do parents. These schools were attached to temples and conducted by priests. School must have begun very early in the morning, for one of the old Babylonian sayings was, "He who would excel in the school of the scribes must rise like the dawn."

Of course the children learned reading and writing. Both of these studies were very hard, for the children had to learn over three hundred wedge-shaped signs which were used in writing.

Men who are interested in Babylonia have found out how the children learned to write. In the school-room was a lump of wet clay out of which they made tablets on which they wrote with reeds from the river. On their tablets they practiced making rows and rows of signs. Then they copied wise sayings many times. Some tablets have been found which have on them the sayings which the children copied. One of these was, "He who shall excel in tablet-writing shall shine like the sun." When the tablet was full it could be smoothed over with a flat stick, or a new tablet could be made from another lump of clay.

THE WARRIOR NATION

In the northern part of the Land Between the Rivers another nation, Assyria, grew up. The Assyrians were a cruel, warlike people. They were ruled by ambitious kings who wanted to extend their dominions, and who were constantly making war on their neighbors. They had strong armies of spearmen and thousands of war chariots drawn by wild, strong horses. Wherever they went they destroyed everything in their path. The approach of the Assyrians struck terror among all peoples.

Nineveh, the capital of Assyria, became one of the most beautiful cities of the time. There the kings built splendid palaces and adorned them with the finest sculpture. At the doorways were immense stone figures with the bodies of bulls, the wings of eagles, and the heads of men. On the walls were carved pictures of the kings riding in their chariots against their enemies or going out to hunt the fierce lions.

The Assyrians decided to invade Babylonia, and the people there were unable to resist them. So Babylon fell into Assyrian hands.

The power of Assyria was not to last, however. It could endure only while its army was strong. In time the army was exhausted by the ceaseless wars. In the year 612 B.C. Assyrian tyranny came to an end. The once proud city of Nineveh was destroyed by the Chaldeans. These strong people swept into Babylonia, overcame the Assyrians, and they, in their turn, became the rulers of the Land Between the Rivers.

The news of the fall of Nineveh was carried all over the ancient world, and great was the rejoicing everywhere among the peoples who had suffered from Assyrian cruelty. No longer were subject people like the Hebrews forced to bring tribute to their Assyrian masters.

The joy and relief of the Hebrews was expressed by one of their prophets:

Woe to the city of blood!
Hark, the whip!
And the rumbling wheel!
And the horses galloping!
And the rattling dance of the chariot!
Cavalry charging—the flash of the sword, the gleam of the lance,
The slain in heaps!

Nineveh is laid waste! Who shall bewail her?
All who hear the news of thy fate shall clap their hands over thee!
For whom hath not thy wickedness afflicted continually?

After the destruction of Nineveh, Babylonia once more became the center of civilization. A strong king of the Chaldeans, Nebuchadnezzar, came into control of all the Land Between the Rivers.

Nebuchadnezzar rebuilt the city of Babylon. It was surrounded by strong walls to protect it. They were so thick that it was said that a chariot with four horses could turn around on top of them. They had a hundred gates of glittering brass plates, hammered in beautiful designs by the metal workers.

Nebuchadnezzar was proud of the new city of Babylon which he had built. He said, "Is this not great Babylon which I have built by the might of my power, for the house of my kingdom and the glory of my majesty?"

The wife of Nebuchadnezzar was a princess from one of the mountain tribes. She did not care for the low, flat country of Babylonia. She missed the mountains of her homeland and was unhappy. To please her and make her more contented, Nebuchadnezzar decided to build a mountain for her. He had his builders make a series of terraces, one on top of another, supported by strong arches. Each terrace was a little smaller than the one below it, somewhat like the stories of the tower temples. The terraces were covered with earth in which were planted beautiful flowers and vines and even trees. Water was pumped up from the Euphrates River and poured in cascades here and there in the gardens.

[97]

Seated in a bower on the topmost terrace of this artificial mountain, the queen could imagine that she was on one of her native hills. From a distance the gardens looked as if hanging in air. The Hanging Gardens of Babylon were considered one of the wonders of the ancient world.

Nebuchadnezzar was the last great king of Babylonia. After him the land was always a subject country.

The western end of the Fertile Crescent lay along the eastern shores of the Mediterranean Sea. This region was cooled and made fertile by the rain-bearing winds from the Mediterranean, and there were good pastures for sheep. At some early time wandering shepherds made their way there and decided to settle down. They called themselves the Children of Israel, which means "those whom God rules." By other people they were called Hebrews.

In later times the Hebrews wrote the story of their early settlement. The great ancestor of the Hebrews, they said, was Abraham, who had lived at Ur, near the mouth of the Euphrates River. Abraham and his family wandered westward with their flocks and herds, searching for a good place in which to live, and after many years they settled in the land of Canaan, later called Palestine.

Not long after Abraham's arrival in Canaan his son Isaac was born. Isaac married Rebekah and they had two sons, Jacob and Esau.

Jacob had twelve sons, one of whom was named Joseph. Joseph's brothers were jealous of him because he was his father's favorite, and one day they sold him as a slave to some merchants who happened to be going to Egypt.

Soon after his arrival in Egypt, Joseph was brought to the notice of the Pharaoh. The Pharaoh had been greatly troubled by a bad dream. He was told that Joseph could explain the meaning of dreams. The Pharaoh sent for the young slave. Joseph told the ruler that his dream meant that there would be seven years of plenty in Egypt, followed by seven years of famine. He advised the Pharaoh to store grain in the barns during the years of plenty so that there would be food for the people in the years of famine.

The Pharaoh was much pleased with Joseph and put him in charge of storing the grain. Later, when the famine came, Joseph was able to give out grain from the storehouses to the hungry people.

The famine spread to the land of Canaan. Hearing that there was grain in Egypt, Joseph's brothers went there to buy grain for their people.

They were led before Joseph. He knew them, but they did not recognize their long-lost brother whom they had sold into slavery. He forgave his brothers, however, and let them have grain from the great storehouse.

Later Joseph sent for his people. They were given land near the Red Sea, one of the fertile parts of Egypt. There they and their descendants lived for many years with their flocks and herds.

All went well with the Hebrews in Egypt until some years after the death of Joseph, when a new Pharaoh came to the throne who treated them very cruelly. By that time there were so many Hebrews that the Pharaoh was afraid they might become powerful enough to rise up against him. The Egyptians made slaves of them and forced them to do all sorts of hard work under overseers who beat them if they worked too slowly. In spite of their sufferings the Hebrews continued to grow in numbers. The Pharaoh then ordered that all boy babies born to Hebrew families should be killed at birth.

A certain Hebrew woman who had a little son was determined to save him. For three months she kept him hidden. Then she put him in a cradle which she made from bulrushes, and laid the cradle among the reeds which grew along the Nile River.

It happened that the Pharaoh's daughter came to the river with her handmaidens to bathe. When she saw the cradle among the reeds, she sent one of her maidens to bring it to her. Looking inside, she saw the baby. Though she knew that the baby was a Hebrew child, she took him to the palace and adopted him as her son. She named him Moses, which means "taken from the water."

When Moses was grown and came to realize the suffering of his people at the hands of the Egyptians, his heart was filled with pity. He wanted to set his people free. Again and again he begged the Pharaoh to let the Hebrews leave

Egypt, but the Pharaoh did not want to lose his Hebrew slaves and refused to let them leave. All sorts of trouble came to the Egyptians. The people were afflicted with the plague and many of them died. Then the Pharaoh sent for Moses and said, "Get ye forth from among my people, both ye and the children of Israel. Take your flocks and herds and go."

In the year 1230 B.C. about six thousand Hebrews started out in a great caravan over the desert toward the land of Canaan, which they called the Promised Land because they thought that God had promised it to Abraham.

The Hebrews journeyed toward Mount Sinai, where they made a camp and remained for almost a year. During that time Moses left his people and went alone to the top of the mountain to pray. When he came down after forty days, he

brought two tablets of stone on which were carved a set of laws which he believed had been given to him by God. Ten of these rules for right living are called the Ten Commandments.

For forty years the Hebrews wandered about in the desert. Moses had hoped to lead them to the Promised Land, the land "flowing with milk and honey," but he died while his people were still living in the desert.

LIFE IN THE LAND OF CANAAN

When the Hebrews reached the land of Canaan they found it occupied by other people, and it was only after years of fighting that they were able to get possession and settle down there.

For many years there were twelve tribes of Hebrews, each tribe ruled over by a religious leader called a judge. Gradually, however, the people realized that they should unite as a nation under one leader; so, in a great assembly of the people, Saul was chosen king.

The next king was David. David was not only a good king, he was also a great poet and musician. He had been a shepherd boy, and had learned to be a skillful harpist and to write beautiful songs called psalms. David made Jerusalem the capital of his kingdom When he died, his son Solomon became king. Solomon built a magnificent temple in Jerusalem. Thirty thousand men spent seven years building it. Under David and Solomon the Hebrew nation reached its height.

After the death of Solomon there was a revolt among the people, and the Hebrew kingdom was divided into two parts. The northern part, made up of ten tribes, formed the kingdom of Israel. This kingdom was prosperous for many years, but it was finally destroyed by the Assyrians in the year 722 B.C. and the people were taken to Nineveh. The ten tribes scattered and became mixed with other peoples. For this reason they have been called the Lost Tribes of Israel.

The two southern tribes of the Hebrew kingdom became the kingdom of Judah. Judah remained independent until 586 B.C., when it was attacked by the Babylonians under Nebuchadnezzar. He captured Jerusalem, destroyed it, and took the Hebrews captive.

The captivity of the Hebrews in Babylon was a sorrowful time. One of their psalms tells of their unhappiness:

> By the waters of Babylon,
> There we sat down, yea, we wept,
> When we remembered Zion.
> Upon the willows in the midst thereof
> We hanged up our harps,
> For there they that led us captive required of us songs,
> And our tormentors required of us mirth, saying,
> "Sing us one of the songs of Zion."
> How shall we sing the Lord's song
> In a strange land?

Babylon was later conquered by Cyrus, king of the Persians. One of the first things Cyrus did was to free the Hebrews and allow them to return to Palestine and rebuild

Jerusalem. After their return from captivity in Babylon, the Hebrews began to be called Jews. Later, Palestine was taken by the Greeks and then by the Romans. Under the Romans, Jerusalem was destroyed and the Jews were driven out to become wanderers without a country of their own. Today they live in many countries.

WHAT THE HEBREWS TAUGHT THE WORLD

The Hebrew people did not form a powerful nation as some of the neighboring countries did in early times. The great gift of the Hebrews to the world was their religion and their belief in one God. Their holy writings form the Old Testament of the Bible.

The religion of the Hebrews emphasized their duty to God and their duty to their fellow men. "Thou shalt love the Lord thy God with all thy heart, and with all thy soul,

and with all thy mind." "Thou shalt love thy neighbor as thyself."

The Hebrews sometimes forgot the worship of one God and fell into sinful ways. Then there arose among them teachers, called prophets, who brought them back to right ways of living. The greatest of the prophets was Isaiah. For forty years he lived in Jerusalem preaching and teaching. Isaiah looked forward to the day when fighting would cease and there would be peace all over the earth. He described the kingdom of the spirit which would one day be established. Then, said Isaiah, "the nations will beat their swords into plowshares and their spears into pruning hooks. Nation shall not lift up sword against nation, neither shall they learn war any more."

During all their years of misfortune the Hebrews looked forward to the time when a great leader would arise among them. At a later time there came among the Hebrews a great teacher, Jesus Christ. From his teachings sprang Christianity, or the Christian religion. These teachings are the holy writings found in the New Testament of the Bible.

THE SEA BECKONS

North of the land of the Hebrews lies a narrow plain along the eastern coast of the Mediterranean Sea. From the palm trees which grow luxuriantly along the coast this land gained its name, Phoenicia, which means the "Land of the Palm Trees." On the east of it were mountains which were called the Mountains of Lebanon.

Shut in by the rocky, towering mountains, the Phoenicians could not make a good living on the land, and so they turned to the sea and many of them became fishermen.

These early fishermen made a remarkable discovery. Near their shores they found great numbers of a small shellfish. Inside the shell, near the head of this tiny animal, was a little sac containing a few drops of a creamy liquid. The people of Phoenicia discovered that from this liquid they could make a beautiful dark, purplish-red dye.

It was necessary to use many shellfish to make even a small quantity of dye. When the supply in one place became exhausted the Phoenician fishermen ventured farther away, even to neighboring shores. One fishing village after another grew up along the coast, and in the course of time some of them became thriving towns. The most important of these towns were Tyre and Sidon. Because most of the dye was made in Tyre, the color was called Tyrian purple. Cloth of Tyrian purple became famous and was everywhere sought as a great luxury. It was considered so beautiful that the kings' robes were made of it.

As the Phoenicians traveled farther away from the waters near their homeland, they needed larger, stronger ships. Fortunately the slopes of the Mountains of Lebanon near by were covered with tall cedars and other trees good for shipbuilding. The Phoenician ships had large square sails gaily painted in bright red, purple, or blue. When the wind was not right for sailing, oars were used.

It took many oars to move those big boats. One man managed one oar, and there might be as many as a hundred rowers. The rowers sat on benches one above another, and the oars were stuck through openings in the sides of the ship. Sometimes there were two and sometimes three rows of oars on each side. In the middle of the boat sat a man who beat time to keep the rowers all pulling together. A boat with two rows of oars on each side was called a bireme, and one with three rows was called a trireme.

A NATION OF TRADERS

The Phoenicians became the first great traders of the world. Their ships coasted all along the Mediterranean Sea, gathering cargoes of gold, silver, bronze, precious stones, ebony and other rare woods, ivory, incense, and perfume. They made their way from island to island of this great inland sea, to Greece, Italy, Spain, and all along the northern shores of Africa. They stopped at all places which they thought might be good for trade.

A writer of the time describes the way the Phoenicians traded:

> They take the merchandise from their ships, they set it along the beach and embark again in their ships, and after that they raise a smoke. The natives of the country, seeing the smoke, come to the sea, and then they lay down gold for the merchandise and retire. The Phoenicians come to the shore and examine the gold, and if they think the natives have left enough, they take it and go away. But if they think there is not enough gold, they go to their ships again and wait there. The natives come to the shore and add more gold, and this keeps on until the Phoenicians think there is the right amount of gold for their merchandise.

Wherever they went, the Phoenicians established trading stations. In time the shores of the Mediterranean were dotted with them. Always searching for new opportunities for trade, these sea rovers made their way through the narrow passageway at the western end of the Mediterranean which is now called the Strait of Gibraltar. This outlet to the sea is guarded by two immense rocks, which the people of the ancient world called the Pillars of Hercules.

Between these Pillars and out on the great unknown ocean to the west of Europe sailed the Phoenician seamen in their big sail-and-oar boats. It is said that they went as far north as the island of Britain, where they exchanged their wares for tin, which was much needed for making articles of bronze. This was indeed a bold undertaking for those days, for seamen had nothing by which to guide their ships except the sun by day and the North Star by night.

PHOENICIAN TRADE ROUTES

CARRIERS OF CIVILIZATION

As the Phoenicians traveled about on their trading voyages, they carried with them more than the wares in their ships. From the various peoples they visited they picked up many new ideas and ways of doing things. This new knowledge they passed on to other people with whom they traded. Thus they spread the learning of Egypt and western Asia to countries along the Mediterranean Sea. They are sometimes called the "carriers of civilization."

The Phoenicians needed some convenient way of keeping records of their business transactions. At first they used the Egyptian signs. Later they learned from some of their neighbors to make simpler signs. Finally they found somewhere in western Asia a still simpler system by which they were able to write all the words they needed with an alphabet of only twenty-two letters.

[110]

A	B	C	D	E	F	Z	H	T-H	I	K
⟨symbol⟩	⟨symbol⟩	⟨symbol⟩	⟨symbol⟩	⟨symbol⟩	⟨symbol⟩	⟨symbol⟩	⟨symbol⟩	⟨symbol⟩	⟨symbol⟩	⟨symbol⟩

L	M	N	X	O	P	S	Q	R	S	T
⟨symbol⟩	⟨symbol⟩	⟨symbol⟩	⟨symbol⟩	⟨symbol⟩	⟨symbol⟩	⟨symbol⟩	⟨symbol⟩	⟨symbol⟩	⟨symbol⟩	⟨symbol⟩

When the Phoenician traders went to other lands, the people saw them handling bits of papyrus on which they made strange signs. These people had no such convenient way of making records. They learned to use the simple set of letters which they saw the Phoenicians using.

The Phoenician alphabet was thus carried to Greece. The Romans learned it from the Greeks. From Rome it made its way to the rest of Europe, and finally to America. This alphabet was greatly changed in the course of time, as the people of each nation altered it to suit their needs.

EMPIRE BUILDERS

When Babylon and Assyria were building flourishing empires in the valley of the Tigris and Euphrates rivers, the region to the east of the Persian Gulf was inhabited by hardy tribes known as the Medes and the Persians.

The Persians became a mighty people. One of their kings, Cyrus, started the Persians on their way to conquest. With his well-trained armies he overthrew the Medes. He made just laws for the peoples he conquered, but he never allowed the laws to be broken. Sometimes today people speak of the "law of the Medes and Persians," meaning a law that cannot be broken.

Cyrus decided to conquer Babylonia. Nebuchadnezzar, who had succeeded in making Babylonia strong and powerful, had been followed by a weak king by the name of Belshazzar. Belshazzar was betrayed by traitors in Babylon and the city was taken by Cyrus.

In one of the Hebrew writings an interesting story is told of how Cyrus succeeded in taking Babylon. One night Belshazzar was giving a feast to his nobles. In the huge banquet hall revelry was at its height. Suddenly a hush fell upon the merrymakers. All eyes were looking at something high up on the wall. There the fingers of an armless hand were tracing strange words: MENE, MENE, TEKEL, UPHARSIN.

What did this writing mean? No one could explain it.

Hastily Belshazzar sent for his wise men and said to them: "Whoever shall read this writing and show me the interpretation thereof shall be clothed with scarlet, and have a chain of gold about his neck, and shall be the third ruler in the kingdom."

But none of the wise men could tell what the words meant.

The king was greatly troubled. Then the queen remembered a young Hebrew called Daniel. "There is a man in thy kingdom," she said, "in whom is the spirit of the holy gods. Now let Daniel be called, and he will show the interpretation."

When Daniel was brought in, the king said to him: "I have heard of thee, that the spirit of the gods is in thee, and that the light of understanding and excellent wisdom is to be found in thee. If thou canst read the writing and make known to me the interpretation thereof, thou shalt be clothed with scarlet, and have a chain of gold about thy neck, and shalt be the third ruler in the kingdom."

Daniel answered: "O thou King, the most high God gave Nebuchadnezzar, thy father, a kingdom and majesty and glory and honor. All people and nations feared and trembled before him. Whom he would he slew and whom he would he kept alive; whom he would he set up and whom he would he let down.

"And thou, his son, O Belshazzar, hast not humbled thy heart, but hast set thyself up against the Lord in heaven. And this is the writing that was written and this is the interpretation: MENE—God hath numbered thy kingdom and finished it; TEKEL—Thou art weighed in the balances and found wanting; UPHARSIN—Thy kingdom is to be divided and given to the Medes and the Persians."

That night, while the revelers slept, the Persians secretly entered Babylon. You remember that Nebuchadnezzar had built strong walls around the city to protect it. Cyrus thought out a plan by which the city might be taken in spite of this. The Euphrates River ran under one part of the wall of the city. Cyrus had some of his men turn the water of the river to one side into a canal which they had dug. When the water of the river was shallow enough, his army was able to get into the city by going along the river bed under the wall.

So in the year 539 B.C. the Persians became masters of Babylonia.

[113]

Cyrus was followed on the throne of Persia by his son Cambyses, and after him came Darius. Darius set up his first capital at Persepolis, east of the Persian Gulf. After his conquests he had a new capital, Susa, at the mouth of the Euphrates River. He built a magnificent palace at Persepolis, and at Susa also he had a fine residence. These palaces were adorned with sculptures and gaily colored glazed bricks.

Darius built good roads to the different parts of his empire. He also had a postal system by which messages could be sent quickly to the farthest point in his dominions. Riders on horseback were stationed at intervals so that there would be no delay. "Neither snow, nor rain, nor heat, nor darkness of night prevents each of these from accomplishing the task proposed to him, with utmost speed," says an old account. "The first rides and delivers the message with which he is charged to the second, and the second to the third, and so it goes through, handed from one to another."

Royal officers went about to different parts of the empire to report anything wrong. These officers were called the King's Eyes and the King's Ears.

Darius made Persia the largest and most powerful empire the world had known up to that time. It included Egypt, Babylonia, Assyria, and stretched from the borders of India to the shores of Greece. The Persians boasted that their empire "extended so far to the south that man cannot live there because of the heat, and northward to where he cannot exist because of the cold."

TALKING TOGETHER

1. You have seen modern skyscrapers in cities or pictures of them. Do you recognize any points of similarity between some of these buildings and the "tower-temples" of Babylon?

2. The Hebrews in Palestine lived on the caravan routes between the rich countries of Babylonia and Egypt. What were the advantages and disadvantages of this fact to the shepherd people?

3. From the map on page 82 you notice that Phoenicia was a land by the sea. Discuss the conditions that helped the Phoenicians to become shipbuilders, and carriers of new customs.

4. The power of the Assyrians in the Fertile Crescent did not last long in spite of the fact that they were fierce warriors. What caused their downfall as a nation?

5. The Persian empire under Darius was far reaching and powerful. How was this king able to control such a large area and to develop his empire?

INTERESTING THINGS TO TRY

1. Have you ever thought what hard work was done by people long ago? Try the experiment of making bricks of mud dried in the sun. Why is this difficult?

2. Dramatize the banquet scene in the court of Belshazzar and the entrance of the Persians into the city.

3. Imagine you are living in Babylonian days. Make a clay tablet and write on it as the Babylonians did. Make a seal, such as the Babylonians used, and put your name on it.

4. Ask your teacher to secure for your class the film "Ancient World Inheritance." As you watch this picture, list the different things ancient peoples gave us.

5. Make two wall hangings, one showing the "tower-temples" of Babylon, and the other showing an Assyrian war chariot.

6. Your class is sure to enjoy singing or chanting the Twenty-third Psalm, which was written by David.

Let's Read

Man and His Records, by Franklin Barnes. Read "How the Alphabet Was Born" to learn about the letters you use every day.

In the Beginning, by Eva Erleigh. The chapters "Babylon and Egypt" and "Hebrews and Assyrians" are interesting.

A Boy of Babylon, by Frances K. Gere. This story shows that boys liked adventure in early days just as they do now.

Allah: The God of Islam, by Florence Mary Fitch. This book tells of Moslem life and culture. The photographic illustrations are good.

Bible Children, by Pelagie Doane. The stories of Isaac, Benjamin, Miriam, Samuel, David, and others make the children of the Bible seem very lifelike.

The Picture Story of the Middle East, by Susan R. Nevil. This story shows life today in the Middle East.

In Bible Days, by Gertrude Hartman. In "Tales of Early Hebrews" the author has told the dramatic story of Joseph and his brothers.

A First Bible, illustrated by Helen Sewell. In this beautiful book you find some of the Old Testament stories.

Mediterranean Spotlights, by Attilio Gatti. In this present-day story read "Palestine, the Promised Land of Jews and G.I.'s."

Can You Read Maps?

Each map in your text tells a story. Look at the map of the Fertile Crescent on page 82. What does the caption say? What do the colors tell you? What countries do you find? What rivers do you see? What other large body of water is near these countries? Did the fertile river valleys and the near-by sea affect the growth of these countries? How does this help you to see that the geography and history of a country are related?

Study the map of Phoenician trade routes on page 110. How does it show you that the Phoenicians were carriers of civilization?

Who Was It?

Here is an opportunity for you to show how well you remember the things you read about "Early Nations in Southwest Asia." Write the numbers 1 to 10 on a separate sheet of paper. After each number write the word from the list below that will answer the question that has the same number. *Remember that you must not write in this book.*

1. Who made a set of laws for all his people in Babylon?
2. Who made the Hanging Gardens for his queen?
3. Who was the great ancestor of the Hebrew people?
4. What people were famous for their cruelty and skill in warfare?
5. Who led his people out of captivity in Egypt?
6. What people have been called the "carriers of civilization"?
7. Who saw handwriting on the wall?
8. Who read the meaning of the message written on the wall?
9. Who captured Babylon by turning aside the waters of the Euphrates River?
10. Who developed a postal system that covered his entire empire?

Phoenicians	Hammurabi
Belshazzar	Abraham
Darius	Nebuchadnezzar
Cyrus	Assyrians
Daniel	Moses

IV

GREEK CITIES OF
LONG AGO

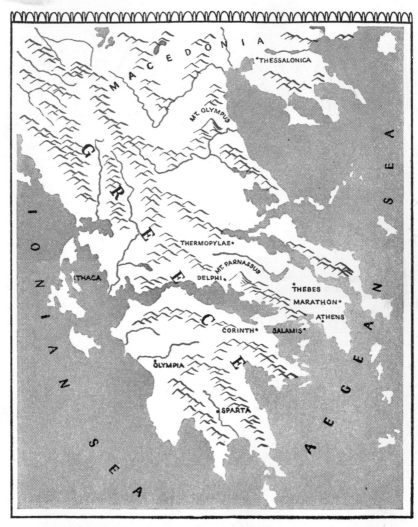

ANCIENT GREECE. *In the city-states of their peninsula the Greek people built a civilization which brought gains in art, science, education, and democracy to many regions.*

GREEK CITIES OF LONG AGO

THE CITY-STATES OF HELLAS

In the southeastern part of Europe is the little country of Greece. Long ago there came to this land a people who called themselves Hellenes and their country Hellas. They came from the grasslands of the north, seeking new pastures for their flocks and herds. When they found fertile places they settled down. Gradually the Greeks spread over the peninsula, to the islands of the Aegean Sea, and even to the coast of Asia. They were the first people in Europe to become civilized, and their civilization was to have a great influence on all the later history of the world.

Greece is a beautiful land. Lofty mountains cross the country in all directions. Between them lie pretty valleys and small plains. Long arms of the sea run far inland in many places.

As their homeland was broken into many small regions by the mountains and the sea, the Greeks were unable to form a single, united nation. It was difficult for the people of one part of the country to get to another. So each city with its surrounding country had its own government. The people of each community came to have their own way of thinking and of doing things and were loyal to their own city-state.

[121]

There were many city-states in Greece, but Sparta and Athens were the most important. It is interesting to know about them because the people of those two cities had entirely different ideas about how they should live and how a state should be governed.

Unlike most Greek cities, which were usually built on hills, Sparta was in a low, broad plain. The Spartans were surrounded by people with whom they fought many wars. Because their neighbors were so hostile, the Spartans always had to be prepared against attacks. There were no walls to protect the city. It was the proud boast of the Spartans that their brave citizens made walls for defense unnecessary.

Every Spartan was a good soldier, ready to fight for his city. The men were formed into soldier companies. They had to live together, eating at the same table and sleeping in the same building. If a warrior died in battle he was carried home on his shield. As a mother bade her son good-by when he went off to war, she might say to him, "Return with your shield or upon it!" She meant that he was not to be a coward and throw away his shield in flight, but was to bring it home honorably or be carried home dead on it.

Duty to the state came before everything. A Greek writer said of the Spartans:

No man was at liberty to live as he pleased, the city being like one great camp where each man thought that he was born, not for himself, but for his country. Like bees they acted with one impulse for the public good. They were possessed with a thirst for honor and had not a wish but for their country.

Athens was near the sea, and was built partly upon a steep hill called the Acropolis. This proved to be an excellent place for defense, and as a result the Athenians did not need to spend so much time preparing for war as did the Spartans.

The Athenians were brave soldiers, but they were interested in many things besides warfare. They had time to listen to beautiful poetry, to see fine plays, and to enjoy the good things of life.

Everywhere the Athenians went they traded with the natives, and their city grew rich and prosperous. In the middle of the city was the market place, an open, paved square. It was noisy and busy. There men met their friends and talked over the affairs of the day. Countrymen sat on the ground with piles of fruit and vegetables. Fishermen offered baskets of fish. Wines and olive oil were displayed, and goat's milk and wild honey from the mountains.

The narrow streets leading from the market place were lined with shops, where craftsmen were busy at their trades. There was a street of potters where the potters' wheels were whirling. Not far from Athens was a kind of clay from which very fine pottery could be made. The

beauty-loving workers of Athens fashioned this into vases so graceful in shape and so beautifully decorated that they are today considered works of art. In another street the woodworkers made graceful tables, chairs, couches, and chests. Sculptors, smiths, shoe-makers, and other work-ers followed their trades in their little shops.

GREEK HOMES AND FARMS

The climate of Greece was so mild that the people were able to spend much of their time out of doors. Their houses were flat-roofed, one-story buildings of sun-baked clay. They had no windows, and the door led into an inner court open to the sky. Here the family spent much of their time. Around the court were the sleeping rooms.

The furnishings of the house were simple—just a few couches, tables, and chairs. Pans of burning charcoal on the floor were used for heating. There was no running water in the houses. Here and there along the streets were fountains. Maids carried the water for their households in jars, which they sometimes balanced on their heads.

All but the poorest families had slaves who did most of the work. For the most part the slaves were kindly treated and were like members of the family. Among the slaves was one called a pedagogue. He watched over the children and taught them good manners. He took the boys to school and sat in the schoolroom while they worked until it was time for them to go home.

Around the cities the farming country stretched on all sides, with here and there a tiny village. In the valleys the farmers had olive groves and fields of grain. The growing of olives was very important, for the Greeks used olive oil in many ways. In preparing food it was used instead of butter; it was used for bathing instead of soap; and it was burned in shallow lamps for lighting the house.

On the hillsides, terraced so as to make use of every bit of ground, grapes were grown. In September the grapes were gathered and dropped into huge vats. There they were crushed to let the juice run out. Then the juice was poured into large jars and left to ferment into wine.

GROWING UP IN SPARTA AND ATHENS

The education of boys and girls in Sparta was quite different from that in Athens, as may be imagined. The life of a boy in Sparta was very severe. When a baby was born, a committee of wise men examined it. If it seemed to be weak and feeble, it was taken to a lonely mountainside and left there to die. A strong, well-formed infant was handed back to its parents with the order, "Bring up this child for Sparta."

When a boy was seven years old he was taken away from his parents, and was put with other boys in a public training house. There the boys lived until they became men. They were drilled in everything that would make them strong, and were taught to undergo all kinds of hardships. They swam in the cold, rushing river, and slept on reeds which they gathered from the river bank. They were taught to endure pain without murmuring, to despise cowards, and to admire brave men. Most of their education was given to gymnastic training that would fit them to become good soldiers. At eighteen a boy was considered grown up. From that time on he was ready to give his life for Sparta.

Spartan girls were trained almost as severely as boys. They engaged in many gymnastic exercises—running, wrestling, boxing, and so on. They were to become good wives and mothers, and if they could not themselves die for their city, they were to be willing to sacrifice those whom they loved best.

The first things boys in both Sparta and Athens learned were reading, writing, and arithmetic. Instead of writing on paper, they used tablets covered with a thin layer of wax. On these they made marks with a sharp-pointed bone tool called a stylus.

If they made a mistake it could be erased by smoothing the wax. When the work was finished the whole tablet could be smoothed so that it could be used for writing another time.

Athenian boys, like the boys of Sparta, began school when they were seven years old. The Spartans trained the body more than the mind. The Athenians believed in training the mind as well as the body. The people of Athens

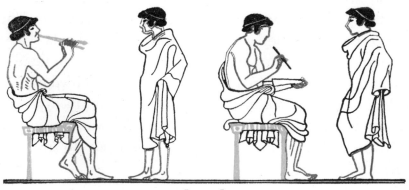

thought that a knowledge of
poetry and music could help a
boy to live a better and happier
life. In school the boy learned
to recite poetry, to sing, to play
the lyre or flute, and to dance.

The teachers worked hard to
build up healthy bodies as well
as to train the minds of their
pupils. The whole afternoon
was given up to many kinds of
gymnastic exercises on beauti-
ful playing fields outside the city. This physical training
made the boys strong and healthy future warriors.

When Athenian boys were eighteen they became citizens.
Before the shrine of Athena they pledged themselves to the
service of their city in this solemn oath:

> We will never bring disgrace to this our city by any act of
> dishonesty or cowardice. We will fight for the ideals and
> sacred things of the city, both alone and with our companions.
> We will revere and obey the city's laws. We will try unceas-
> ingly to quicken the sense of civic duty in others. In every way
> we will strive to pass on the city to our sons greater and better
> than it was when our fathers passed it on to us.

The girls were kept at home. Most of their time was
spent in learning to cook, spin, weave, and take care of
the house. Greek women were expected to spend nearly
all their time in their homes attending to the duties of their
households.

[129]

ZEYC

ΔEMETEP

The Greeks, like most early peoples, believed in many gods. The most important gods were supposed to dwell on Mount Olympus, a lofty, cloud-tipped mountain in northern Greece.

Rule over the world was thought to be divided among three great gods. Zeus ruled the heavens and the earth; Poseidon was the ruler of the seas; and Pluto was the god of the underworld, a dark region beneath the surface of the earth where dwelt the spirits of the dead.

The gods brought all things to pass on the earth. Every day Apollo, the sun god, drove his golden chariot across the sky to light the world and warm it. Zeus sent the rain from heaven to water the earth. Poseidon stirred up storms on the sea and calmed them. Demeter, the goddess of the soil, made all the flowers and grains spring from the fertile earth. Dionysus guarded the vineyards and filled the grapes with sweet juice.

The gods also directed the affairs of men, punishing them for evil deeds and helping them in their daily work. Almost every Greek worker had some special god or goddess to whom he prayed and made gifts. A shepherd prayed to Pan, asking for good flocks with thick, fleecy wool. Before starting out on a voyage, a sailor prayed to Poseidon for favorable winds. The farmer offered a prayer to Demeter for good crops. The potter prayed as he shaped his vase, and the smith as he wrought his metal.

The people of Athens thought that Athena was the greatest of the goddesses. It was for her that their city

was named. Every four years a wonderful festival was held in her honor. It lasted for days, and on the last day there was a magnificent procession in which all the people of Athens took part. Through the principal streets of the city the procession went, and then up the Acropolis. At the head of the procession was a ship on wheels. On the ship's mast was draped, like a sail, a beautiful new robe for the goddess, which had been woven with loving care by maidens of Athens. Then came snow-white cattle and sheep for the sacrifice, followed by the priests in their long robes. Behind them came the people, many of them bearing gifts—maidens with vases containing oil and wine, others carrying baskets of flowers and fruit. The robe was laid before the goddess, and the offerings were placed upon the altar. As the smoke curled up from the sacrifice, the people prayed.

The best way to learn the will of the gods was to consult an oracle. Of all the gods no one could see so far into the future as Apollo. Almost all Greeks sought his advice before taking any important step. At Delphi, high up on the bare, gray rocky side of Mount Parnassus, was Apollo's shrine. It was built over a deep cleft in the rock, from which rose a mysterious vapor. When a person came to consult Apollo, the priestess of the temple seated herself on a three-legged stool over the crack in the rock. The clouds of vapor rolled up about her, and soon she began to utter strange words. A priest wrote down the words of the priestess and explained them. These were thought to be the advice of the god Apollo.

Believing that the gods liked to see men using strength and skill to do them honor, the Greeks often held festivals in which they engaged in different kinds of athletic contests. The most important festival was that held once in every four years at beautiful Olympia in southwestern Greece in honor of Zeus, the greatest of the gods.

Months before the festival, heralds traveled all over the Greek world announcing the date on which it was to begin. If there happened to be a war between some of the city-states at the time, a truce was declared for a month, so that people could go to the celebration and return to their homes in safety.

On the first day of the games people thronged into the stadium where all the best athletes were to contest in races and other forms of sport. Suddenly there was silence as the judges, clothed in purple, took their places at a long table. On it lay the precious crowns made from branches of the sacred olive tree which shaded the altar of Zeus. These were to be given to the victors in the races. Now came those who were to take part in the contests—tall, straight youths; young boys; full-grown men, muscular and tanned.

A trumpet sounded and the first race began. Runners sprang forward and sped with quick, rhythmic pace down the stadium. Twelve times they must go around the course. The people shouted joyously as one of the runners dashed in first at the goal.

[133]

Proudly the victor advanced to the table, where one of the judges placed on his head the olive wreath. The herald called out his name, and the name of his father, and the city from which he came. The people cheered and showered him with garlands of flowers.

All day long there were races—short races and long races, races for boys, and races for soldiers wearing heavy armor and carrying heavy shields.

Then came the discus-throwers. These were very strong young athletes. The discus was a round plate made of stone or metal. The thrower stood holding the discus in his left hand. When the time for throwing it came, he changed it to his right hand. Stooping to take aim, he turned

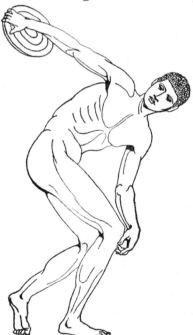

his body around on his right foot, one knee slightly bent, and swung the heavy weight far behind him. Then straightening up he rose to his full height and sprang into the air as he cast the discus into space.

The next day there were jumping contests. Running forward at lightning speed, the jumpers, one after another, leaped into soft sand. An attendant measured the distance each contestant had jumped.

Now it was time for the wrestling matches. Pairs of celebrated wrestlers faced each other. They seized each other and struggled back and forth, their bodies twisting and turning until one, by his skill, suddenly succeeded in throwing the other in a sprawling heap on the sand of the arena. Then they renewed the contest. A second time the two strong wrestlers seized each other. Again they struggled. A third time they matched their strength. The one who threw his opponent three times was the victor.

On the last day the games took place in the hippodrome, where the contests of horses and chariots were held. These were the most exciting events of all. The rich nobles put their swiftest horses in the chariot races, and engaged professional charioteers to drive them.

The trumpet sounded, and forty four-horsed chariots started, a hundred and sixty fleet horses dashing along the course. There was the din of rattling chariots and beating hoofs. The horses flew along, their bodies covered with foam. Each charioteer, urging his horses forward, tried to pass his rivals.

At each end of the track was a pillar to mark the place where the chariots were to turn. They must go twelve times around the course. The turning places were the most dangerous, especially when one charioteer tried to pass his rival there. Chariots were overturned, horses fell, wheels flew off, and the occupants of the chariots were hurled to the ground. A storm of cheers greeted the driver who, with a headlong dash, drove his horses in first at the goal.

The great week of the games ended with a day of joyous celebration.

When a victor returned to his home, more honors awaited him. Riding in a splendid chariot and escorted by hundreds of other chariots, the returning hero approached the city. Part of the city wall had been torn down so that the procession might pass through. "What use of walls of defense for a city that has such brave sons?" cried the people.

The Greeks loved to tell stories of the adventures of their early heroes. These tales were not written down for many years, but were sung by bards who traveled about from place to place. In the early days there lived a blind poet named Homer, who gathered together into two great poems, the *Iliad* and the *Odyssey*, many tales of the exploits of early Greek heroes. Homer was poor and unhonored while he lived, but after his death those who had paid little attention to him realized his greatness. Then people in different cities said that he was their poet. An old rhyme says:

> Seven cities claimed great Homer dead,
> Through which the living Homer begged his bread.

The *Iliad* tells a part of the story of the long war between the Greeks and the inhabitants of Troy. Paris, one of the sons of King Priam of Troy, had run away with Helen, the beautiful wife of Menelaus, a Greek king, and had taken her to Troy in Asia Minor. King Menelaus called upon all the warriors of Greece to join him in trying to get Helen back.

For nine long years the Greek warriors besieged Troy, and many battles were fought on the plain outside the city. But in spite of everything they did, the Greeks were unable to force their way through the well-guarded walls. Then, in the tenth year of the war, they decided to try a trick. They built a huge wooden horse and left it on the plain outside the city. Then they went on board their ships and sailed away. It looked as if they were tired of fighting and had gone home.

Great was the joy of the Trojans when they saw that the Greek ships had gone. At last the long war was over! The gates of the city were thrown wide open and the people streamed out on the broad plain where so many battles had been fought. There, to their astonishment, they discovered the enormous horse. What could it mean? Some feared the wooden horse and wanted to burn it, but others said they should take it into the city and keep it as a reminder of their victory. So the Trojans pulled it into the city. There was feasting in Troy that night and much drinking of wine.

Now the Greeks had only pretended to go home. Their ships were hidden behind an island not far from the Trojan coast. Within the hollow horse they had placed a number of soldiers. Late that night, while the Trojans slept, the

Greek soldiers quietly came out of the horse. With a gleaming torch they signaled to the Greek ships. In a very short time their companions returned. The city gates were opened for them and in they rushed. They slaughtered the sleeping Trojans and burned the city.

Thus, after ten years, Troy was taken, Menelaus got back his beautiful Helen, and the Greek warriors returned to their homes.

Among the Greek kings who had fought in the war was Odysseus, king of the little island of Ithaca off the west coast of Greece. Troy was not far from Greece and most of the Greek warriors reached their homes in a short time, but the ships of Odysseus and his companions were blown out of their course. For ten years they sailed in strange seas and landed on unknown shores. Tales of these Greek heroes tell about their fights with giants, miraculous escapes from monsters, and strange meetings with gods and goddesses. It is the story of these adventures which Homer tells in the *Odyssey*.

At last, weather-beaten and ragged, Odysseus reached his kingdom. But his troubles were not over. During his absence many princes had come from neighboring islands to woo his wife, Penelope. For years they had stayed at the palace, feasting and drinking, and demanding that she should marry one of them. Penelope had put them off by saying that she would do so when she had finished weaving a robe for her father-in-law.

Day after day the suitors watched Penelope weaving. But the queen's weaving was never finished, for every night she unraveled all that she had woven during the day. The princes saw that something was wrong. One night they surprised her and discovered the trick. Then they refused to be put off longer and insisted that Penelope choose one of them at once for a husband.

Penelope said, "Hear me, ye lordly wooers, who have vexed this house that ye might eat and drink evermore. I will set forth for you the great bow of Odysseus, and whoso shall bend it and send a shaft through twelve rings, with him will I go and forsake this house."

Then the contest began. Each suitor tried in vain to bend the mighty bow.

Now Odysseus had entered the hall, disguised as a beggar, and he demanded that he should be allowed to take part in the contest. He took the stout bow, bent it with ease, and skillfully sent an arrow through all twelve rings. Then he turned the terrible bow on the suitors, and not one of them escaped with his life.

Odysseus made himself known to his lovely Penelope. With his faithful queen he lived happily for a long time in his island kingdom.

Greece was the first country in the world in which the citizens had a part in their government. In the early days each little Greek community had a king. In some city-states the nobles later became powerful enough to abolish the kings. Then there were quarrels among the nobles, and one leader would come into control of the state. The Greeks called such a man a tyrant. Some of the tyrants were excellent rulers, but their rule was based on force.

The Greek people came to see that it was not wise to allow one man to have complete control over them. In nearly every Greek state the tyrants were overthrown in time, and it was declared that all the citizens should have a share in the government. This kind of government was called a democracy from the Greek word *demos,* meaning "people," and the word *kratos,* meaning "power."

The greatest of the democracies was Athens. On the sides of a hill called the Pnyx, the freeborn men of Athens assembled four times each month. They made laws, elected officers, levied taxes, and decided other matters.

The president of the assembly brought forward the first business for the day. "Who wishes to speak?" called the herald. Then whoever wanted to address the meeting mounted a platform hewn from the rock. Speeches were followed with close attention. When the speaking was over, the vote was taken. This was the way the people of Athens managed their affairs. They believed that every free man should attend the meetings and take part in the government.

The democracy of Greece did not extend to all the people. There were hundreds of thousands of slaves, who had no rights as citizens. In Greece, however, the first large group of men learned how to govern themselves. They had a share in deciding questions on affairs of state.

THE GREEKS DEFEND THEIR FREEDOM

The Greeks were a seafaring people, whose ships sailed to countries bordering the Aegean, the Mediterranean, and the Black seas. Traders told interesting tales which made some people in Greece eager to go to the new lands to live. Greek colonies grew up on the islands and shores of the Aegean Sea, along the Black Sea coast, in southern Italy, on the island of Sicily, and in other places around the Mediterranean. Greek colonists carried with them the learning and culture of their homeland.

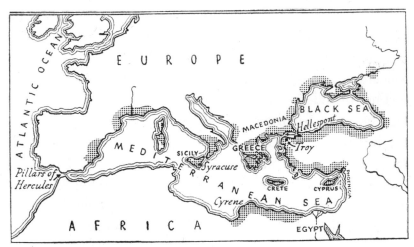

GREEK COLONIES

By the year 490 B.C. Persia had become the largest empire in the world. The king, Darius, had conquered some of the Greek cities in western Asia, but the people soon rebelled and sent messengers to Athens and Sparta asking for help. The Athenians gladly sent them ships and soldiers to fight their powerful enemy.

When news of this came to Darius, he asked, "The Athenians, who are they?" He had never heard of them.

After hearing who the Athenians were, Darius called for his bow, and placing an arrow on the string, shot it high into the air and prayed, "Grant me, O God, that I may revenge myself on the Athenians!" Every day after that, Darius had one of his slaves stand before him as he sat at dinner and repeat three times, "Master, remember the Athenians!"

According to the custom of the day, Darius sent messengers to the different Greek cities demanding that they send him gifts of earth and water. To give earth to a king was to acknowledge him as ruler of the land. To give water meant that he was ruler of the sea.

Some of the Greek states were afraid of Persia and sent earth and water as Darius demanded. Some proudly refused to yield to these unjust demands. When the messenger arrived in Athens he was tossed into a deep pit. The Spartans threw the messenger who came to their city into a well, saying, "There you will find both earth and water for your master."

This made Darius so angry that he sent his ships with an army of a hundred thousand men to conquer Greece.

When the Athenians heard that the Persian army was advancing against them, they were much alarmed, for their army was very small. They sent Pheidippides, a swift runner, with a message imploring the Spartans to help them.

"Men of Sparta," Pheidippides cried, "the Athenians beseech you to hasten to their aid and not allow their state, which is the most ancient in all Greece, to be enslaved by the barbarians."

The Spartans promised help but said they must wait five days till the moon was full, when it was their custom to sacrifice to Apollo. To break this custom would be to insult the god.

Then came grave news. The Persians were only a few miles from Athens. The Athenians could not wait for the Spartans; they must meet the invaders alone. The battle took place on a narrow plain called Marathon. It was a glorious victory for the Athenians.

Immediately after the battle Pheidippides was sent to carry the news of the victory to Athens. Although he was worn out with fighting, he ran over the bad roads without stopping to rest, and in a short time he reached the city.

As the people gathered eagerly about him, the exhausted runner gasped, "Rejoice! Victory is ours!" Then, overcome by his tremendous exertion, he sank dying to the ground.

The battle of Marathon in 490 B.C. ended the first attempt of the Persians to conquer the Greeks. But this was not the last the Greeks were to see of the Persians.

Just ten years after the battle of Marathon, Xerxes, the son of Darius, decided that he would lead an army to conquer Greece. It took him four years to get his army ready for the invasion.

At a place called the Hellespont, only a narrow strait separates Europe from Asia. On modern maps this strait is called the Dardanelles. Here engineers were ordered to construct a bridge so that the army could pass over it.

The engineers had just completed their task when a storm dashed the bridge to pieces. When Xerxes heard what had happened he ordered the engineers beheaded, and he sent men to lash the water three hundred times, saying as they did so: "Thou bitter water, thy lord lays on thee this punishment because thou hast wronged him without cause. Verily, King Xerxes will cross thee, whether thou wilt or not!"

Before long a new bridge was built, stronger than the first one. When all was ready for the army to cross, the king poured wine from a golden goblet into the sea with the prayer: "O Ormuzd, I pray thee that no misfortune may befall me or stay my conquest until I have made my way to the uttermost boundaries of Europe." Then he cast the golden goblet and a scimitar into the sea as gifts to the god of the waters.

Soon the Persians occupied all northern Greece. To reach Athens and Sparta they had to go through a narrow passage, called Thermopylae, where the mountains came

[145]

down almost to the sea. The Spartans sent a force of three hundred men under King Leonidas to defend this pass.

For four days Xerxes waited, expecting the Greeks to flee. On the fifth day he sent a messenger demanding that they give up their arms. The Spartans answered, "Come and take them."

A Spartan was told that the Persians were "so numerous that when they shoot their arrows into the air the very sun will be darkened." He replied, "Our friend brings us excellent news. If the arrows darken the sun, we shall fight in the shade."

For two days the Spartan army held back the invaders. Then at the end of the second day a Greek traitor offered to show the Persians a secret path over the mountain so

that they could attack the Spartans from the rear. During the night Xerxes moved part of his army over this pass. So the little army of Leonidas was trapped, and the Persians won the battle.

Great honor belongs to Leonidas and his three hundred Spartans. The Greeks placed a pillar on a mound where the Spartans made their last stand at Thermopylae. It bears this simple inscription:

> Go, thou that passeth by, and to Sparta tell
> That here, obedient to her laws, we fell.

THE WOODEN WALLS SAVE ATHENS

The taking of the pass of Thermopylae gave Xerxes an open road to Athens. When news of the approach of the Persian army reached Athens, the people sent messengers to Delphi to ask the oracle what they should do. The priestess replied:

> "Safe shall the wooden walls continue for thee and thy children.
> Wait not the tramp of the horse, nor the footmen mightily
>   moving
> Over the land, but turn your back on the foe and retire ye.
> Yet shall the day arrive when ye shall meet him in battle.
> Holy Salamis, thou shalt destroy the offspring of women,
> When men scatter the seed or when they gather the harvest."

The Athenians were greatly puzzled by this strange answer. Some people thought the "wooden walls" meant one thing, and some another. And what did the oracle mean by "holy Salamis"?

At that time the leading statesman of Athens was a general named Themistocles. He declared that the "wooden walls" were the wooden sides of the Athenian ships, and he commanded the people to leave Athens and sail across to the island of Salamis.

The warships of the Persians sailed into the Bay of Salamis. Some of the Greek leaders were unwilling to risk a battle in the narrow strait between the island and the mainland and wanted to retreat. Themistocles, however, believed that the Athenians would have the advantage in the strait. Secretly he sent a message to the Persians: "The Athenian commander bids me tell you that fear has seized the Greeks and they meditate a hasty flight. Now it is open to you to achieve the best work you ever wrought if only you will hinder their escaping. They no longer agree among themselves, so they will not make any resistance."

In the dead of night the Persians moved part of their fleet to one end of the strait and another part to the other end, hoping to bottle up the Greek fleet.

On a tall cliff overlooking the strait Xerxes sat on a throne of gold, watching the battle. It looked like an easy victory for the Persians. But the ships of the Persians were big and clumsy. The strait was so narrow that the ships were jammed together and got in each other's way. Many of them were disabled and drifted about helplessly with broken oars and rudders gone. Proud Xerxes saw one ship after another of his great fleet destroyed.

The words of the oracle had come true. The "wooden walls" of Athens had saved Greece. Sadly Xerxes returned to Persia, which he had left eight months before, expecting to conquer the western world.

The defeat of the Persians at the battle of Salamis in the year 480 B.C. was a turning point in history. If the Persians had been successful and the Persian empire had spread over Europe, the later history of the world would have been very different. Instead, there was peace in Greece for forty years, and during that time the civilization of Greece rose to its greatest height.

[149]

THE GOLDEN AGE OF PERICLES

When the Persians entered Athens before the battle of Salamis, they burned the city to the ground. This seemed like a terrible calamity to the Athenians at first. But as things turned out the burning of the old city made the people set to work to build a finer and more beautiful city.

At that time a great citizen, Pericles, arose in Athens. The years from 461 to 429 B.C., when he was at the head of affairs, have been called the Golden Age of Pericles.

Pericles believed in democracy. What he thought about it was expressed in a speech he once made:

> Our government is called a democracy because it is carried on for the benefit of many, not for a few. All have a share in the laws which give equal justice to all. Neither poverty nor obscure position will keep a man from doing the state any good service of which he is capable.

[150]

The same free spirit with which we carry on the government is to be found in our daily life also. We have no black looks nor angry words for our neighbor if he enjoys himself in his own way. We abstain from little acts which cause annoyance.

It was the dream of Pericles to make Athens the most beautiful city in the world. Near the city was an abundance of creamy-white marble. Great sculptors carved from it statues of gods and goddesses. Beautiful temples and monuments were built with it.

The center of the adornment of the city was the Acropolis. Up one side was built a broad stairway of marble. At the top was placed a bronze statue of Athena, the guardian of the city. High on a pedestal she stood, in full armor, with upraised spear. Its tip, glistening in the sun, could be seen from far out at sea, and it welcomed the sailors returning from long voyages.

Near by was the Parthenon, a temple built to Athena. This temple had many stately columns around the outside to hold up the roof. Inside these, high up on the walls, Phidias, the greatest sculptor the world has ever known, carved a long band of marble figures showing the

procession of Athenians on their way to worship the goddess at the time of the festival held in her honor.

Within the temple was another statue of Athena, made by Phidias. Her head and hands and feet were of ivory, perfectly carved, her eyes of precious jewels, and she was clad in a long, straight-falling robe of gold. In her left hand she held a shield and spear, and in her right hand a small golden statue of victory. Coiled at her feet lay a serpent, which represented wisdom.

In the stony side of the Acropolis was cut a huge half-circle, where rows of stone seats rose, tier upon tier, around a small stage at the base of the hill. In this open-air theater plays were given. There were serious plays called tragedies,

and lighter plays called comedies, in which the writers made fun of the foolish things that men do. In the tragedies the actors wished to be as tall as possible, and they wore heavy-soled boots with high heels. They covered their faces with masks. If the play was a comedy, the mask had a queer face to amuse the people. If the play was sad, the mask was serious.

Even the poorest citizens were able to see plays, for the government gave tickets to those who could not pay for them. So all the people of Athens came to know the plays of their greatest playwriters.

For thirty years Athens was the center of Greek culture. Then the Golden Age of Pericles came to an end. A terrible plague spread through the city and Pericles was stricken. As he lay dying, his friends gathered around him. They spoke of his greatness and praised his many glorious achievements.

Much to their surprise, Pericles suddenly roused himself and spoke. "What you praise in me," he said, "is partly the result of good fortune. What I am most proud of, you have not noticed. No Athenian ever put on mourning for an act of mine."

After the death of its wise counselor, Athens had no great leader and was no longer the strong power she once had been. When Athens was great and powerful, Sparta grew jealous of her. This jealousy finally led to a war between the two cities. Most of the other cities of Greece took part in the war, some on one side and some on the other. For years there was almost continual warfare between Sparta and her allies, and Athens and hers.

LOVERS OF WISDOM

What is truth? What is right? What is justice? The Greeks thought much about such things as these. They wanted to know how to be happy and how they could live best in society. Teachers arose among them who tried to help them answer such questions. We call such people philosophers. This word comes from two Greek words which mean "lovers of wisdom."

One of the wisest of the Greek teachers was Socrates. Day after day he could be seen walking in the market place of Athens questioning the people he met and trying to lead them toward better ways of living. Eager crowds of listeners gathered around this odd-looking philosopher with the bulging forehead, snub nose, and thick lips.

At the time of Socrates, Greek ideas about the gods were changing. Thoughtful men were beginning to give up the beliefs of earlier days. Socrates believed that there was only one God, the wise and just ruler of the universe. To many Athenians who clung to the old beliefs, Socrates seemed to be a dangerous man. They feared that he was leading the young men of Athens astray.

In 399 B.C., when Socrates was an old man, he was brought to trial for his teachings. After setting forth the principles that had guided him, he turned to his judges and said: "If you propose to acquit me on condition that I abandon my search for the truth, I will say: 'I thank you, O Athenians, but I will obey God, who, as I believe, set me this task, and so long as I have life and strength, I will

[154]

continue the practice of accosting anyone I meet, saying to him, "O my friend, why do you, who are a citizen of the great and mighty and wise city of Athens, care so much about laying up the greatest amount of money and honor and reputation, and so little about wisdom and truth and the greatest improvement of the soul, which you never regard or heed at all? Are you not ashamed of this?" ' "

Socrates was condemned to die by drinking hemlock, the juice of a deadly plant. For thirty days he remained in prison. Some of his friends bribed the jailer and made preparations to smuggle him over the frontier. Crito, one of his followers, tried to persuade him to go.

To this plan Socrates replied: "For us, I think the only question is whether it would be right for us to pay money to these men to take us away, right for you to take me, and right for me to let myself be taken.

"Suppose we were to run away and the laws of the state were to come and stand over us and say to me: 'Tell me, Socrates, what is it you mean to do? To overthrow the laws and the whole commonwealth so far as in you lies? Do you imagine that a city can stand and not be overthrown when the decisions of the judges have no power, when they are made of no effect and destroyed by private persons?

" 'We brought you up, we taught you, we gave you of our fairest and best, and we offer full liberty to any Athenian, after he has seen and tested us and all that is done in our city, to take his goods and leave us, if we do not please him, and go wherever he will. Only if he stays with us, after he has seen how we judge our cases and how we rule our city, then we hold that he has pledged himself to do our bidding.'

"Crito, my dear Crito, believe me, this is what I seem to hear, and the sound of those words rings and echoes in my ears and I can listen to nothing else. If you have aught to say, say on."

"No, Socrates," replied Crito, "there is nothing to say."

Quietly Socrates took the cup of hemlock and drank the poison as if it were wine. Bidding his friends good-by, he lay down on his hard prison bed and calmly awaited death. Soon he ceased to breathe.

Plato, one of his pupils, said, "Such was the end of our friend, concerning whom I may truly say that of all the men I have known he was in death the noblest, and in life the wisest and the most righteous."

Socrates died for the right of men to think freely and to act as they think best. He was one of the great figures in the forward march of man in his search for a higher and better life.

GREECE LOSES HER FREEDOM

At the time when all the cities were exhausted through years of fighting, grave danger threatened the Greeks. To the north of them lived the Macedonians. They were a warlike people and they had a strong king, Philip, to lead them. Philip built up a powerful army and planned to make Greece a part of his kingdom.

Most of the people of Greece were so taken up with their quarrels that they paid little attention to what was going on in Macedonia. There was one Athenian, however, who saw more clearly than the others that Philip was planning to make himself master of Greece. This was Demosthenes, one of the greatest orators and defenders of liberty the world has ever known.

As a youth Demosthenes longed to be an orator. He often listened with close attention to public speakers, 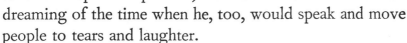 dreaming of the time when he, too, would speak and move people to tears and laughter.

But Demosthenes was greatly handicapped as a speaker. His voice was not strong, and he stammered and could not get out his words clearly. The first time he spoke in public he could not be heard, and he made odd faces and awkward gestures. The people laughed at him so that he was forced to sit down.

There are many stories telling how the youth struggled to overcome his handicaps. He practiced speaking with pebbles in his mouth to cure himself of stammering. He observed himself in a mirror to correct his facial expression. To accustom himself to a noisy audience, he practiced reciting on the seashore amid the roar of the waves.

The hard work and perseverance of Demosthenes were rewarded, for the awkward youth who had at first been ridiculed became the greatest orator of Athens.

Demosthenes warned the Athenians that they were in danger of being conquered by King Philip. "Let the Greeks cease their quarrels with one another," he said, "and unite to preserve the liberty which is their birthright against the despot who seeks to enslave them all.

"Surely," he continued, "though all other people consent to be slaves, we, at least, ought to struggle for freedom. This work belongs to you. This privilege your ancestors have bequeathed to you."

At first Demosthenes pleaded in vain. Many of the people of Athens had lost their public spirit. They were too much concerned with their own affairs. Finally they were roused to unite with the people of Thebes against Philip. In a decisive battle they were the losers. Philip became master of the country.

After Philip's death, his son Alexander became king of Macedonia and ruler of Greece in 336 B.C. As time went on, Alexander became a great general. He conquered many nations and was soon the head of a vast empire.

Alexander the Great admired the Greeks. He founded many cities, which became centers of Greek learning and culture. Thus the civilization of the Greeks spread throughout the known world.

Today there are only the ruined remains of what was once the glory of Greece. Her masterpieces of sculpture are shattered and broken, her beautiful temples are in ruins, but Greece the glorious still lives in the minds of men.

Greek knowledge and wisdom were passed on to other people and so were handed down to us through the ages. The Greeks taught the world to love the beautiful. The statues they carved, the temples they built, have been admired and studied for centuries. Many buildings in American cities—banks, city halls, libraries, schools, and houses —have Greek columns and other Greek decorations.

The poems of the Greeks have given inspiration to many poets of later days. The great Greek dramas are still being read and acted. The ideas of Greek thinkers have influenced the thoughts of men ever since their time. What the Greeks discovered about the best way to live is full of meaning for people today. In their country, for the first time, freedom of thought and expression was encouraged.

The great and precious gifts which Greece made to the world will never die.

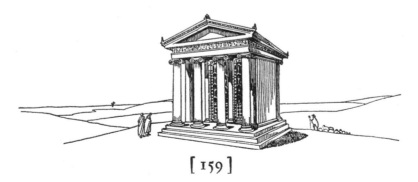

[159]

TALKING TOGETHER

1. If you had been in Greece long ago, would you have preferred to live in Athens or in Sparta?

2. The map on page 120 helps you to see why it was difficult for the Greek city-states to be united. What other influences did the geography of Greece have upon her people?

3. Which of the ancient Greeks do you most admire?

4. Where were Olympic games held in modern days? How often were these held and who took part?

5. Discuss the bravery and courage of the Greek heroes in the past as an influence on the Greek people.

6. What evidence do you find here in America of the contributions of the Greeks?

INTERESTING THINGS TO TRY

1. Choose a committee from your class to make a large map of Greece and place on it pictures to locate the important places.

2. Paint panels to contrast the life of boys and girls in ancient Greece with that of children in the United States today.

3. Show in pantomime scenes of Greek life. Use as a background a scene of Athens painted to show the Acropolis and the Parthenon.

4. Read to your class some of the fables written by Aesop, the Greek slave.

5. Dramatize the story of the return of Odysseus to Ithaca. His appearance in disguise before Penelope would be an exciting part.

6. Name all the buildings in your community which have evidences of Greek architecture. Bring to class pictures of national buildings, such as the Lincoln Memorial, which show the influence of the architecture of the Greeks.

7. Your class would be interested in the motion picture "Demosthenes' Fight for Freedom." Ask your teacher to secure this for you. After seeing the film, note the points you would like to talk about.

Stories of the Gods and Heroes, by Sally Benson. If you like myths and fables, you will enjoy this book.

In the Beginning, by Eva Erleigh. Read the chapter on Greece to learn more about this interesting country.

The Trojan War, by Olivia E. Coolidge. Among the stories read "The Golden Apple" and "The Adventures of Menelaus."

Alexander the Great, by John Gunther. A moving story of this colorful character from the days of "The Boy and His Giant Horse" to "Alexander, the Conqueror."

History Can Be Fun, by Munro Leaf. This story is amusingly told and has many pictures you will enjoy.

A Child's History of the World, by Virgil M. Hillyer. The stories "Hard As Nails" and "The Golden Age" make interesting reading.

Theras and His Town, by Caroline D. Snedeker. This is a story telling about the life and adventures of an Athenian boy.

Can You Use the Card File?

The books in libraries are listed on separate cards showing the subject, author, title, and number of each book. These cards are filed alphabetically in the card file. Imagine you are in a library and are looking at a section of the files containing cards A to S.

1	A – C	D – F	2
3	G – I	J – M	4
5	N – P	Q – S	6

Drawer No. 1 contains cards A to C. If you are looking for *Alexander the Great,* by John Gunther, look for the title in drawer No. 1. The card shows this book to be under the subject of *biography* and the number on the card shows the location of the book in the biography section. Jot down the number on your note pad and ask the librarian to show you the location of the biographies in the library. From the number you should be able to find the book.

Tell in which drawer of this imaginary card file you would find titles of other books listed under "Let's Read."

Quiz Yourself

A Choosing Game

In this exercise after each of the ten sentences there are three possible endings, only one of which is correct. On a separate sheet of paper write the numbers 1 to 10. After each number write the ending that will make the sentence that has the same number complete and true. Then read the sentence with the ending you selected. *Remember that you must not write in this book.*

1. It was difficult for Greece to be united because (a) the people were jealous (b) the country was divided by mountains and by the sea (c) the people were very different.
2. Sparta was protected by (a) the walls of the city (b) slaves (c) her brave citizens.
3. The Trojan War was won by (a) a siege (b) a trick (c) over-powering numbers of Greeks.
4. Penelope's weaving was never finished because she (a) un-raveled at night what she had woven during the day (b) grew ill (c) pined for Odysseus.
5. The Parthenon is (a) by the sea (b) on the Acropolis in Athens (c) on an island in the Aegean Sea.
6. Athens gave to civilization valuable contributions in (a) religion (b) farming (c) architecture and sculpture.
7. The Greek citizens were in advance of other people in the world because they had a large part in (a) ruling the state (b) group manufacturing (c) exploring other countries.
8. The greatest of the Greek city-states in its contribution to the rest of the world was (a) Troy (b) Sparta (c) Athens.
9. Pericles sought to make Athens (a) the center of trade (b) the most beautiful city in the world (c) a military stronghold.
10. The Greeks were finally overcome by the (a) Persians (b) Romans (c) Macedonians.

V

ROME WINS AND
LOSES AN EMPIRE

ANCIENT ITALY. *The people of Rome developed the resources of this peninsula and carried to other lands their ideas and achievements.*

ROME WINS AND LOSES AN EMPIRE

THE CITY OF THE SEVEN HILLS

During the time when Greece was reaching the height of her glory, another power was rising to the west along the Mediterranean Sea in the long, slender peninsula now called Italy. Halfway down the peninsula is a small river named the Tiber. Near its mouth lie seven low hills.

In the early days, when the peoples of the world were wandering about in search of better places in which to live, shepherds made their way into Italy seeking good pastures for their flocks. About the year 753 B.C. some of them settled down on one of the hills near the mouth of the Tiber River. This settlement was the beginning of Rome. In later times it grew into a city and became the center of a vast empire.

The Romans told many tales about the beginning of their city. One old story was that Rome was built by Romulus and Remus, twin brothers, who were the sons of a princess. When they were babies their wicked grandfather put them in a basket and set them afloat on the river Tiber.

Down the stream floated the basket with its tiny passengers. Finally it drifted into shallow water and was washed up on the shore at a place where the seven hills rose near the bank of the river. An old mother wolf who lived in a cave near by came to the river to drink. She found the infants, and with her strong teeth she lifted them out of the basket and carried them to her den.

One day a shepherd who was trying to find a wolf that had stolen one of his sheep happened to come to the cave. Great was his surprise when he saw two baby boys with the mother wolf. The shepherd carried the boys home, and his wife fed them and cared for them.

When the boys were grown they heard the story of their strange childhood, and they decided to form a kingdom for themselves. They planned to build a city on one of the hills near the place where they had been thrown into the river. The sides of the hill were steep, but they decided to build a wall around their city to make it still safer from enemies.

One day, while the brothers were building the wall, they quarreled.

"This is the way your enemies will leap over your wall," cried Remus scornfully, climbing over the half-built wall.

"And this is what I shall do to them when they do," replied Romulus, striking his brother such a mighty blow that he fell down dead.

All the rest of his life Romulus grieved for the brother he had slain in a moment of anger.

The walls of the city were completed and the city was named Rome after Romulus. Romulus became its king. He called together the people he was to govern and said:

"We have now completed the walls of our city. But our walls, we must remember, are not what we rely on. No walls can be so high that an enemy cannot scale them. It is the courage and energy of the people, not the strength of its outward defenses, on which the safety and prosperity of a state depend."

Romulus reigned for many years. One day when he was an old man he called his people together for a sacred festival. In the midst of it there was a terrible thunderstorm. When the storm cleared, Romulus had vanished. The story spread that he had been taken up to heaven.

Later, one of the most respected citizens declared that he had seen Romulus after his disappearance and that Romulus had given him a message for the people of Rome.

"Why did you leave us so suddenly?" the citizen asked.

"I left," answered Romulus, "because it pleased the gods to call me back to heaven. It was no longer necessary for me to remain on earth, for Rome is now established. Her future greatness is assured. Go back and tell the people that if they continue to be industrious and brave, the time will come when Rome will be the mistress of the world."

Other peoples settled on the other six hills near the settlement of Rome. To the north, across the Tiber River, lived the Etruscans. Toward the end of the seventh century B.C. the Etruscans were at the height of their power. An Etruscan ruler led an army across the Tiber and took possession of Rome. For more than one hundred years after this invasion from the north Rome was governed by Etruscan kings.

Under the Etruscans Rome grew steadily in size and power. The Etruscan kings conquered the people living on the other hills near Rome and united them all under one rule. In later days, Rome was often spoken of as the "City of the Seven Hills."

EARLY ROMAN HEROES

Seven kings ruled Rome. The last of these was Tarquin, an Etruscan so tyrannical that the people rose against him and drove him from the city.

The banished king persuaded Lars Porsena, another powerful Etruscan, to become his ally. Together these two Etruscans with a strong army marched against Rome.

An interesting story about the battle has often been told since early Roman days. The invaders had marched so close to the city that only a wooden bridge over the Tiber River separated them from Rome. The Romans feared that Tarquin might once again get possession of their city. Their only hope was to destroy the bridge before the armies of their enemies could reach it.

A brave noble named Horatius offered to hold off the enemy while the others cut down the bridge behind him. Herminius and Lartius, two other warriors, volunteered to help Horatius.

With axes the Romans hewed away at the beams and posts of the bridge and loosened its foundations. The bridge trembled and was tottering. Horatius ordered Lartius and Herminius to go back to safety. He himself kept his place on the bridge until it fell with a crash.

Horatius uttered a prayer to the Tiber, saying, "Tiber, Father Tiber, I pray thee to receive unto thy holy stream these arms and this, thy warrior." And in all his heavy armor he plunged into the rushing waters of the river. It seemed a miracle that he did not drown but was able to swim back in safety to Rome.

As the invaders were unable to cross the river, they gave up their attempt to capture Rome. By his brave deed Horatius had saved the city. Roman mothers never tired of telling their children his story. Always they hoped

> For boys with hearts as bold
> As his who kept the bridge so well
> In the brave days of old.

A few years after Horatius there lived another famous Roman, named Cincinnatus. Cincinnatus belonged to a noble family, and he and his wife lived contentedly on their little farm just beyond the Tiber. Like many another noble in the early days of Rome, Cincinnatus worked on his estate and cultivated his own fields. He was wise and good and the people of Rome honored and trusted him.

In a war with the tribes east of Rome the Roman army
was surrounded and was in danger of being destroyed.
The Senate was hurriedly called together. The only thing
to do was to appoint a dictator who should have supreme
authority until the country was out of danger. The Senate
thought of Cincinnatus and sent messengers to him to
ask him to take charge of affairs. It was early morning when
the messengers arrived at the farm.

"Listen to the commands of the Senate," said the messengers, "for we are its ambassadors."

"Is not all well?" asked Cincinnatus. Then he heard the
message.

Leaving his plow in the field, Cincinnatus speedily made
his way to Rome and lost no time in forming a new army.
All able-bodied men were told to assemble without delay.
Each was to bring with him twelve stakes for ramparts.

That same evening, before the sun had set, the new army
set out, and by midnight they reached a place close to the
enemy's camp.

"When the signal is given," commanded Cincinnatus,
"let each man dig a trench in front of him."

Noiselessly the men dug trenches around the camp of the enemy and drove into the ground the stakes they had brought with them. In the morning the enemy, finding that they were surrounded, were forced to surrender.

Great was the rejoicing in Rome at the news of the victory. The returning army marched through the streets in a triumphal procession amid the shouts and cheers of the people. Cincinnatus rode in a splendid chariot drawn by six horses.

Cincinnatus was so beloved for his brave deed that he might have made himself ruler of Rome if he had so wished. But he cared nothing for honors or wealth. He was happy that he had been able to serve his country.

As soon as Cincinnatus was able to do so, he returned to his farm. Soon he was to be seen contentedly plowing his fields once more.

It is not certain that these stories which the Romans told about their early heroes are true, but they suggest the kind of person the Romans admired. They respected men of wisdom and courage.

ROME BECOMES A REPUBLIC

When the Romans drove out Tarquin in about 500 B.C., they declared that never again should a king rule them. After that Rome became a republic. A republic is a state in which the people have a part in ruling themselves and where officers are elected by the people, as they are in the United States.

The heads of their government the Romans called consuls. Each year the people elected two consuls. They thought that if there were two, each one would watch the other and keep him from trying to be king.

Each consul had a bodyguard of twelve men called lictors. A lictor carried over his left shoulder a battle-ax tied in a bundle of sticks. This symbol was known as the *fasces* and signified that the consul had the power to punish by whipping with the sticks or by chopping off a man's head with the ax.

The Romans also had a Senate. The senators were the oldest and wisest men of Rome, and it was their business to advise the consuls.

Although Rome was a republic, all the citizens did not have equal rights. The Romans, like most ancient peoples, were divided into two classes, nobles and common people. The nobles were called the patricians and the common people were called the plebeians.

The nobles, who were members of famous old families, were the leading people. They were proud of their rank and thought themselves much better than the common people.

The plebeians did not have the same rights and privileges as the patricians. The laws of Rome had never been written down. An unjust judge could declare the law to be whatever he wished it to be, and there was no way of proving that he was wrong.

The common people believed that the patricians changed the laws to suit themselves. Therefore the plebeians demanded written laws so that everyone could know what kinds of laws had been made affecting their rights. Finally twelve bronze tablets were set up where all could see the laws engraved upon them.

The plebeians thought that all Romans should have equal rights. Many and long were the struggles between them and the patricians. At one time the plebeians decided to leave Rome and found a city of their own. They left the city and encamped on a hill not far away.

The patricians saw that they could not get along without the plebeians and sent messengers to persuade them to return. The plebeians agreed to return only if the patricians would grant them more privileges. Laws were made to give fuller rights to the common people. Thus the plebeians gradually increased their power.

The early Romans lived very simply. Their houses resembled those of the Greeks. The central part was left unroofed. In this court, known as the *atrium,* the life of the family was carried on. There the women spun and wove wool into cloth for the family. There was the altar where the household gods were worshiped. Around the court were other rooms. However, even well-to-do families had only a few rooms in their houses. Couches, tables, and a few stools were the only furniture.

The dress of the Romans was as simple as their houses. Their chief garment was a short-sleeved woolen shirt or tunic, reaching to the knees. When a Roman appeared in public, he threw about him a blanket of white wool called a toga. Slaves wore tunics but were not allowed to wear the toga. That was the special dress of a Roman citizen.

Ten great aqueducts made possible an abundant supply of water for the people of Rome. Some of this water came from lakes sixty miles from the city. The aqueducts were stone pipes. If an aqueduct had to cross a river or a low valley, the Romans built stone arches to hold it up.

The Romans worshiped many of the same gods as the Greeks did, but the Romans had different names for them. Zeus was called Jupiter, Demeter was Ceres, Dionysus was Bacchus. The favorite god was Mars, the god of battle.

Their gods, the Romans believed, watched over everything. There was Janus, a god with two faces, who guarded the door of every home. One of his faces looked out and the other looked in. The spirit of the hearth was Vesta. Watching over the storeroom were the penates, who blessed the supplies of the family. The gods of the fields were the lares. Before sitting down to a meal a Roman threw a little food into the fire. That was his way of giving thanks to the household gods, the lares and penates.

In the center of Rome was an open space called the Forum. This was the market place, where all kinds of things were sold. It was also a place where citizens met and talked over the affairs of the city and the latest news. Affairs of state were carried on there also. At the entrance to the Forum was the shrine of Janus. The doors of the shrine stood open in time of war but were shut when Rome was at peace.

The most interesting building in the Forum was the small round temple of Vesta, the goddess of the home. On the temple altar burned a sacred fire. Six noble maidens, called the Vestal Virgins, were chosen to guard the fire and keep it burning day and night. The welfare of the city was thought to depend on the fire's never going out.

Until a boy was six years old, his training was carried on at home. He was told stories of the Roman heroes and of his own ancestors, and taught to be modest, brave, and obedient.

Young children learned to read and write on waxed tablets similar to those used by Greek children. They also learned arithmetic.

Because of the difficulty of calculating with the Roman numerals, the pupils used counting-frames. These were oblong wooden frames divided into columns. A Roman boy worked his problems with little pebbles which he put in the different columns representing different denominations.

When a boy was fifteen or sixteen years old, there came a great day in his life. With his father and friends he went to the Forum and wrote his name on the list of Roman citizens. Then he went to a temple to offer sacrifices to the gods. After that ceremony he could proudly call himself a Roman citizen. He was allowed to give up the boy's toga with its narrow purple border and put on for the first time the "manly toga," as it was called. Then he had the right to do everything that grown men were allowed to do when they were Roman citizens.

Usually a girl did not remain many years in school. She spent most of her time at home with her mother, learning the duties of the household. She was taught how to cook, weave, sew, and care for a house. She was being fitted for her duty in life, the management of her own household.

[177]

The Romans were a warlike people. Their army was their great pride. Every Roman citizen between the ages of eighteen and forty-five was obliged to serve in it.

There was no gunpowder in those days, but the Romans had a number of ingenious war machines. One of these was a movable tower, or shed, several stories high and set on rollers. The soldiers pushed the tower close to the enemy's wall. Then they ran up a stairway to the top and shot arrows or hurled stones down on the enemy. Sometimes they dropped a swinging bridge from the top of the tower to the wall and rushed over it into the town they were attacking.

Another device was a battering-ram, a long, very heavy post. Men ran with it up to a wall and beat again and again at the same spot, trying to make a hole in the wall through which the soldiers could enter. There were other machines called catapults for hurling stones or pieces of red-hot iron a great distance.

Rome was almost constantly at war with her neighbors and won victory after victory over the other little states of Italy. Thus she forced the conquered peoples to come under her rule.

When a victorious general returned from a war, a triumphal arch was built to honor him and a great celebration was held for him and his army. Through the gaily decorated streets, crowded with shouting people, passed a splendid procession headed by the Senate and the chief officers of the city.

In a chariot of gold drawn by four horses stood the victorious general. In his right hand he held a branch of laurel, the symbol of victory, and in his left hand an ivory scepter with an eagle at its end, the symbol of power. Behind the general came the army which had helped him to gain his victory, and at the end sadly walked the captives taken in the war.

The power of Rome was constantly growing. By the year 275 B.C. the city on the Tiber had become the mistress of all Italy.

Just across the Mediterranean Sea from Italy, on the
northern coast of Africa, was the city of Carthage, the
most famous trading city on the Mediterranean. Her ships
went from one end of that great sea to the other, and she
ruled over many countries along its shores. The people of
Carthage regarded the Mediterranean as their sea. They
are said to have boasted that a Roman could not even wash
his hands in its waters without their consent. Carthage did
not like to see Rome becoming so powerful.

At last a series of wars broke out between Rome and
Carthage. In the second war the Carthaginians were led
by a great general named Hannibal.

When Hannibal was a boy,
he had been taken by his
father to a temple. There he
had been told, "Lay your

hand upon the sacrifice and swear that you will never be a friend to the Roman people."

"I swear that I will never be a friend to the Roman people," the boy had repeated. He never forgot his promise.

Hannibal determined to conquer Rome. He knew that he would be defeated if he sailed directly across the Mediterranean to Italy. Instead, he decided to march overland to Rome. Through Spain and across Gaul marched Hannibal and his army of about forty thousand men. Hundreds of mules and horses and thirty-seven war elephants went with the army.

At the north of Italy are the high Alps mountains. Their peaks, covered with snow, formed the natural defense of Rome. The Romans thought that no enemy could cross this mountain barrier.

When Hannibal and his army reached the Alps, the greatest difficulties of his march on Rome began. Every step over the mountains was dangerous. For more than two weeks the army climbed the ice-covered trails. Many of the horses and elephants slipped down the steep cliffs and were killed.

"Yonder lies Italy and the way to Rome!" cried Hannibal joyfully as his army reached the summit.

There were new difficulties ahead. The way down was more dangerous than the way up had been. At last, however, the great feat of crossing the mountains was successfully accomplished by Hannibal's army.

The Romans were astonished and alarmed when news came that the Carthaginian army was in Italy. They

[181]

hurriedly gathered together their forces and sent them on to meet the enemy. Hannibal defeated them at first in battle after battle.

After sixteen years of almost constant fighting, Hannibal was called back to Africa to defend Carthage. There he was defeated and forced to accept a harsh treaty of peace.

In a third and final war, Carthage was burned to the ground. Then the Romans plowed the land on which their rival city had been. They sowed the ground with salt so that nothing would grow there. This was in 146 B.C.

By this victory Rome gained the land which had belonged to Carthage. The Romans also sent powerful armies to conquer other lands. They fought Macedonia, which still held Greece, and Greece came under the rule of Rome. In the course of time Rome gained control of all the lands bordering on the Mediterranean Sea. Thus for several centuries the boundaries of the Roman Empire were extended in Europe, Africa, and Asia.

HOW THE LATER ROMANS LIVED

The conquest of these many lands brought power and wealth to Rome. All the conquered countries were obliged to pay tribute to her, and riches poured into the city. During this time great changes came over the Roman people. Those who had become rich were no longer satisfied to live simply, like Cincinnatus and other fine Romans of the early days. Besides their city homes they had large estates, called villas, in the country. Lovely frescoes adorned the walls of their houses. Floors were often fine mosaics made by putting many little pieces of colored marble or glass together to make pictures or beautiful designs. Around the houses spread parklike grounds, with marble statues gleaming through the trees, with fish ponds and playing fountains, and with ornamental shrubbery. As there were many slaves to do the work, wealthy people lived lives of luxury and ease. When they traveled, they were carried in litters

by four or more slaves, or rode in chariots drawn by high-bred horses.

Rome had conquered so many nations that slaves were very numerous. Free farmers therefore found it hard to make a living. They became very poor. Many were forced to sell their farms. They drifted into Rome, hoping to find work there. In time there was not enough work in Rome for the poor people, so they had to be supported by the state. Food was given to them free. This was better than letting them starve, but it was bad for the people not to be able to earn a living. They would not work when they could get food for nothing. Soon a large part of the population of Rome was living in idleness at the public expense.

The Romans loved shows. They had great amphitheaters, somewhat like our stadiums. The shows which delighted the Romans most were chariot races and gladiatorial fights.

Gladiators were powerful men who were made to fight with wild animals or with each other for the amusement of the people. Often they were slaves or captives.

These fights were extremely cruel. Usually the gladiators fought until one was killed. When one was wounded, the victor stopped fighting and waited for the people to let him know whether he was to continue. If the crowd stretched out their hands with their thumbs up, it meant that the wounded man was to be spared. If they turned their thumbs down, it meant that the fight was to go on.

Many of the poor people sold their votes to officials who gave them free food and provided them with free shows to keep them amused. A Roman writer of the time said sadly: "This majestic people, which once controlled armies, high offices, and everything else, now limits its desires and its eager longing to two things only—bread and circus games!"

Some good men in Rome saw that things must be changed. Two of these men belonged to a family named the Gracchi. Their mother was Cornelia, a lady of a noble family who had married a man of the common people. Her husband died not long after their marriage and Cornelia was left to bring up her two boys. Tiberius was the older and Gaius the younger.

One day, while the boys were still young, a rich lady came to see Cornelia. The guest was proud of her wealth and her jewels. Cornelia listened while her friend described her precious stones. Then the guest asked to see Cornelia's rare jewels.

Cornelia led the way into another room. There in bed lay her two sons fast asleep. Their mother smiled and, pointing to them, said, "These are my jewels, the only ones of which I am proud."

As the boys grew to manhood, their mother urged them to do something worthy of their country. "I have been called the daughter of Scipio," she said, "but in the days to come I shall be known as the mother of the Gracchi."

Tiberius, the older son, was greatly stirred by conditions among the poor people of Rome. He tried to get a law passed to take some of the land away from the nobles and give it to the poorer people.

In pleading for the poor, he said: "The wild beasts of Italy have their caves and lairs, but the brave men who spill their blood in her cause are without home or settled habitations. They wander from place to place with their wives and children. They fight and die to advance the luxury of the rich, and they do not possess a foot of earth they may call their own."

Tiberius made many enemies, and one day, in a riot, he was killed. A few years later Gaius Gracchus took up the cause for which his brother had given his life. Gaius was hated by the rich as his brother had been. Another riot broke out in which Gaius met the same fate as his brother.

Two noble sons of a noble mother lost their lives in trying to make their people happier and their country better.

To the end of her life the mother of Tiberius and Gaius mourned the loss of her two sons. While she was still living, a bronze statue was set up in Rome on which were inscribed the words, "To Cornelia, Mother of the Gracchi."

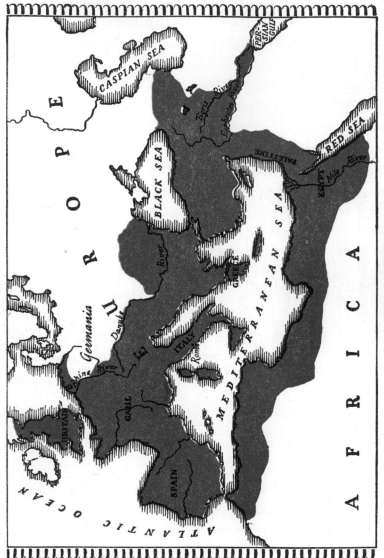

The Roman Empire

For years the Romans were content with the lands which bordered the Mediterranean Sea. Then they began extending their conquests over the continent of Europe. The man who was responsible for these new conquests in Europe was a great general named Julius Caesar.

When Caesar was about forty years old, he was made governor of a province in the northern part of the Roman lands. The land of the Gauls bordered his province. Caesar decided that he would conquer the Gauls and add their land to his.

In the year 58 B.C. Caesar's army entered Gaul. Though the Gauls fought bravely, they were no match for the well-trained soldiers in the Roman army. Caesar soon conquered the country and made it a Roman province.

While Caesar was winning glory for himself and Rome, the government was growing steadily worse. Most of the citizens did not care who governed them, and the Senate was governing to suit the interests of its members. When the citizens of a republic do not take part in their government, the republic becomes a failure.

The news of Caesar's victories reached Rome and some of the Roman leaders were jealous of him. They persuaded the Senate to command him to give up his army and return to Rome. Caesar knew that if he went back to Rome without an army to protect him, he would be in the power of his enemies. So he set out for Rome at the head of his faithful soldiers.

[189]

The southern boundary of Caesar's province was the little river Rubicon. For Caesar to cross it with his army meant disobedience to the Senate. When Caesar reached the Rubicon he hesitated for a short time. Then he plunged his horse into the shallow river, exclaiming, "The die is cast!" and marched his men to Rome. So important was Caesar's decision that today the expression "to cross the Rubicon" means to make some great decision.

After Caesar returned to Rome, five years of warfare followed in which Caesar was successful. He not only destroyed his enemies, but he put down rebellions which they had stirred up in other lands.

Caesar now had all power in Rome. He set about making the government better and carried out many reforms. He gave land to needy families, he cut down taxes, and he remedied many abuses from which Rome was suffering.

CAESAR MAKES A NEW CALENDAR

Caesar introduced the Egyptian calendar into Rome after he had made some changes in it. It is interesting to know that the names of the months of the Roman calendar are still in use. January is named for the god Janus. February

[190]

comes from the Roman name of a feast. March is named for Mars, the god of war. April is from a Latin word which means "to open," for in that month came the opening of flowers and plants. May comes from Maia, a Roman goddess. June is from Juno, the wife of Jupiter. July is from Julius, in honor of Julius Caesar. August was named for the emperor Augustus. The Latin words meaning seven, eight, nine, and ten give us the names of September, October, November, and December, for the Roman year began in March.

The months of the Egyptian calendar were all thirty days long, with five extra days at the end of the year. In rearranging this calendar, Caesar decided to have thirty-one days in every other month. There were, however, only enough days in the year to have five months with thirty-one days. Caesar took a day from February, the last month in the Roman year, and left it with twenty-nine days, the only short month of the year.

Some years later, when Augustus was emperor of Rome, the number of days in August was changed because there were thirty-one days in July, which was named for Caesar, and it would never do to have fewer days in the month named for the emperor! So a day was taken from February, leaving it with twenty-eight days, and given to August, making it thirty-one days long.

This change made three months in succession with thirty-one days, and so September was given thirty days and the months following were rearranged as they appear on the calendar today.

Many of the men of Rome feared Caesar's power. Some were opposed to him because they were jealous of him; others thought that Caesar was trying to make himself a dictator and that the liberties of the people were in danger.

It was the year 44 B.C. An important meeting of the Senate was to be held on March fifteenth—the Ides of March, as the Romans called that day. A few days before, Caesar had had a strange warning of danger. A soothsayer, an old man who was supposed to be able to tell things that were about to happen, had called out to Caesar, "Beware the Ides of March!"

The fifteenth of March came. Caesar set out for the Senate as usual. On his way he passed the soothsayer and called to him lightly, "The Ides of March have come."

"Yes," replied the old man, "but they are not past."

As soon as Caesar entered the Senate, conspirators crowded around him as if they were presenting a petition to him. Suddenly, on a signal from their leader, they drew their daggers, which they had concealed under their togas, and fell upon him. Caesar defended himself for a short time. Then he saw his trusted friend, Brutus, among his foes. This was a terrible shock to him. He cried out, "*Et tu, Brute!*" meaning "You too, Brutus!" Then, drawing his toga over his face, he fell, pierced with many wounds.

Great was the excitement in Rome when the murder of Caesar became known. People rushed through the streets shouting for vengeance. Soon there was civil war.

ROME, MISTRESS OF THE ANCIENT WORLD

Those who had expected to bring back the republic by killing Caesar were sadly mistaken. The republic of the old days was gone forever. After the death of Caesar three men ruled Rome for a while. One of them was Octavius, Caesar's adopted son. In the year 31 B.C., Octavius became the only ruler. His name was then changed to Augustus. The Roman Republic had become the Roman Empire. This lasted for four hundred years.

All the people in the Empire had to pay taxes to Rome. Much of this money was spent for splendid buildings. In the Forum the market stalls of earlier days were replaced by temples and civic buildings, by noble statues and grand monuments. It was at that time that the largest amphitheater, the Colosseum, was built. It seated fifty thousand people. There shows were given in which both men and

[193]

wild beasts fought for the amusement of the people. Large public baths were built where thousands of people could bathe at one time. Many people spent a large part of their spare time in these buildings, which were like public clubhouses with libraries and reading rooms.

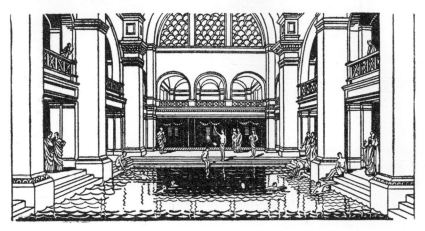

At the height of her power, Rome's far-flung Empire included the whole civilized world of that time. Northward it stretched to the Rhine and Danube rivers, and even the far northern island of Britain belonged to it. Eastward, Rome had all Asia Minor. To the south she had Egypt and a fringe of land along the northern coast of Africa. To the west it included Spain and France.

The most northern point of the Empire was more than two thousand miles north of the most southern point. The distance from the farthest western point of Spain to the farthest eastern point of Asia Minor was about three thousand miles. A hundred or more nations were included in that vast Empire.

The Romans were skillful road builders. When a country came under their rule, one of the first things they did was to build a direct road from that country to Rome. With such roads an army could be moved quickly from one place to another to keep order. From the many gates in the walls of Rome, wide, hard, smooth roads branched off in all directions to the distant corners of the Empire. The saying grew up, "All roads lead to Rome." The roads helped to tie the Empire together.

Rome developed a system of laws which was put into operation everywhere in the realm. Roman laws were strict but they were fair. It was these laws, binding the Empire together, and Roman soldiers, enforcing the laws, that made it possible for Rome to govern her great territory.

Throughout all the lands of the Empire the Latin language and the customs and institutions of Rome gradually spread. The people of the conquered countries were usually contented to live under Roman rule because Rome gave them peace and protection. The extension of Roman influence had a lasting effect on the Western world.

In the reign of Augustus, the first emperor, something happened far off in a distant part of the Empire which was to be the most important event of his reign, though the people living at the time did not realize it. In Bethlehem, a tiny village of Palestine, was born Jesus Christ, the founder of a new religion.

All the things that have happened since the birth of Christ are now reckoned from that date in our calendars. Before a date we write A.D., which means "in the year of our Lord." After the date of things which happened before the birth of Christ we put B.C., meaning "before Christ."

Jesus went about doing good among the poor and lowly. He healed the sick, fed the hungry, and comforted those who were in trouble. He believed that rich people or people of noble birth were no better than poor people. The thing that really counted, he thought, was living a good life and being kind to others.

Often Jesus taught the people by means of stories, or parables. At one time, when he was trying to teach a man how to be a good neighbor, he told the following story:

A certain man went down from Jerusalem to Jericho and fell among thieves, which stripped him of his raiment, and wounded him, and departed, leaving him half dead.

And by chance there came down a certain priest that way; and when he saw him, he passed by on the other side.

And likewise a Levite, when he was at the place, came and looked on him, and passed by on the other side.

[196]

But a certain Samaritan, as he journeyed, came to where he was; and when he saw him he had compassion on him,

And went to him, and bound up his wounds, pouring in oil and wine, and set him on his own beast, and brought him to an inn, and took care of him.

And on the morrow when he departed, he took out two pence, and gave them to the host, and said unto him: Take care of him; and whatsoever thou spendest more, when I come again, I will repay thee.

When Jesus had finished the story, he asked the man, "Which now of these three, thinkest thou, was neighbor unto him that fell among the thieves?"

The man answered, "He that showed mercy on him."

Then said Jesus, "Go, and do thou likewise."

Thus Jesus taught that men should be kind to one another and help one another.

Many of the Hebrews listened to Jesus and believed what he taught. They thought that he was the leader for whom the Hebrews had been looking. There were some, however, who feared that he was turning the people away from the old religion. They went to the Roman governor,

Pontius Pilate, and accused Jesus of refusing to obey the Roman laws and trying to make himself king of the Jews. Jesus was arrested and brought to trial before Pilate. Finally he was put to death on the cross.

Christians were eager to teach their religion to other people. Many of them traveled about from town to town preaching to the people, and the people listened to the new teaching and became Christians. Paul, who was the greatest preacher of them all, did more than any other one man to spread the new religion through the Roman world. For thirty years he traveled far and wide, carrying the teachings of Christ to many parts of the Empire and helping people to live Christian lives.

At first the Roman government paid little attention to the followers of the new faith. But the Christians refused to join in the worship of the Roman gods or to take part in festivals in their honor. They continued to follow the new teaching and to worship in their own way.

The Romans who believed in the old faith came to fear the followers of Christ. If any misfortune came to the Romans, they thought it was due to neglect of the gods and blamed the Christians. The emperors tried to make the Christians give up their religion. Many Christians were tortured and burned at the stake. When the people were gathered to see the games, Christians were driven into the arena. Lions and leopards were turned loose upon them while the people watched.

One of the early Christian writers said: "If the Tiber rises, if the Nile does not rise, if the heavens give no rain, if there is an earthquake, famine, or pestilence, straightway the cry is, 'The Christians to the lions!' "

During the reign of Nero, one of the most cruel of the Roman emperors, the city was almost destroyed by fire. Some thought that Nero himself started the fire so that he could rebuild Rome in a more magnificent way. There was a rumor that the Emperor Nero amused himself by playing music as he watched the great blaze from the roof of his palace. The Roman people were up in arms at the burning of the city. Nero had it reported that the Christians had started the fire. That turned the people's wrath from the emperor to the Christians.

The Christians were ready to suffer for their religion. They willingly and even joyously gave their lives for their faith. In spite of all kinds of persecution they increased rapidly in numbers.

[199]

For several centuries the Empire continued to be strong and prosperous. Then, slowly, its strength gave way. There were many reasons for this. One Roman emperor after another was placed on the throne by the army. Many of the later emperors were weak. There seemed to be no one capable of ruling Rome's vast realm. The people themselves seemed to care little whether one man or another was their ruler. They had no interest in a government in which they had no voice.

The army was no longer made up of patriotic Roman citizens who fought for love of their country, but was a band of paid soldiers. Many of the soldiers had come from foreign lands.

The emperors built costly palaces, temples, and baths, many of which were not needed. All of this extravagance increased taxes. The burden fell heaviest on the poor. As time went on, a worker paid to the government nearly every cent he made above a bare living, and he was compelled by law to labor at his trade. The amount of work a man did was regulated by an overseer. If the workman failed to do it in the appointed time, he was punished. The law, in fact, regulated everything. A man could not set a price on his own goods; the government did it for him. These oppressions destroyed all public spirit among the common people.

The Rhine and the Danube rivers formed the northern boundary of the Empire. Beyond these rivers stretched a vast region of dense forest land which the Romans called Germania. This land was inhabited by warlike tribes who knew little about the ways of civilization. Rome, which had conquered many nations, had never been able to conquer these German tribes. From time to time some of them tried to break through the northern frontier of the Empire. To keep them out, Rome had built all along the frontier many forts, which were manned by Roman legions. This army was not strong enough to keep out the German tribes. About the year 400 some of these tribes burst through the northern defenses. From that time on, the invasion of German tribes gradually weakened the Roman Empire.

By the latter part of the fifth century, the Roman Empire had come to an end. In the year 476, the last weak Roman emperor was driven out. Instead of one far-spreading empire, regulated by Roman law and protected by Roman power, the land of the once proud Empire was divided by the invading tribes into a number of kingdoms, each one ruled by a Germanic king.

TALKING TOGETHER

1. What advantage was it to Rome, for both health and protection, that the city was built on hills? Is this as great an advantage today? Looking at the map on page 164 you will notice other good features about the location of Rome.

2. What are some of the evils which slavery brings to a country? In your book find ways slavery helped to cause Rome's fall.

3. Discuss the disadvantages of a nation in which most of the people live in cities.

4. Rome is today the capital of Italy. Do you know anyone from that country? Can you think of names of Italians who have made great contributions to present-day life?

5. We speak now of good neighbors among nations. Was this ever thought of in the days of the Roman Empire?

INTERESTING THINGS TO TRY

1. Your group is sure to enjoy reading together Macaulay's "Horatius at the Bridge." Then the class may want to dramatize this famous scene.

2. Perhaps your class can secure slides which would show some of the buildings and places of interest in old Rome. Some boys and girls make their own slides.

3. A tapestry showing life in Rome could be made upon cloth with wax crayon. This process gives the effect of a woven tapestry. "A Day in the Forum" and "The Return of the Victor" would make interesting scenes.

4. Your class might give a program of living pictures having as a title "Heroes from the Past." In such a program whom would you include from Rome?

5. Choose some high spots from the history of Rome and picture these scenes in drawings.

6. The saying is often used today, "All roads lead to Rome." Can you explain this?

LET'S READ

The Stolen Oracle, by Jay Williams. Two boys in the time of Emperor Augustus solve a mystery connected with state secrets.

How the World Is Ruled, by Carrie L. George. This book tells of the first government in the Old World.

In Bible Days, by Gertrude Hartman. In this book you will find more about the beginning of Christianity.

Augustus Caesar's World, by Genevieve Foster. Here the glorious days of Rome are pictured.

The Golden Encyclopedia, by Dorothy Bennett. You will find here many facts about history.

Exploring the Old World, by Hamer, Oliver S. and others. The story of "Italy—Where Past and Present Meet" gives glimpses of old and new Italy and raises some interesting questions.

The Story of Ancient Civilizations, by Donald Culross Peattie. The attractive illustrations help to make Roman life more real and give to your group ideas for their pictures and plays.

EXPLORING OTHER BOOKS

Can you easily locate information for your reports? To do this you must be able to use the card catalogue in your library, and the table of contents and the index of any books to which you refer.

When you studied Greece, you located in an imaginary card catalogue the titles of books listed in your text. Library card catalogues also contain cards filed alphabetically by authors. Read over the list of books about Rome listed above. See if you can locate any of these books in your library by looking for the name of the author in the card file.

Besides the books listed above, there are many others which will give you information, such as your geography, other history texts, and reference books. Locate material in these books by using the table of contents, the glossary, and the index.

QUIZ YOURSELF

Choose the Right Word

From the list below choose the word needed to make each of the following sentences complete and true. On a separate sheet of paper write the numbers 1 to 10. After each number place the correct word that will complete the sentence which has the same number. Then read the sentence with the right word in it. *Do not write in this book.*

1. Rome was named for ——.
2. —— saved his country by holding off the enemy while the bridge was destroyed.
3. After the rule of kings, Rome became a ——.
4. —— left his field to save his country.
5. The —— demanded that the laws be written down.
6. In Rome there were many ——.
7. —— attempted to reach Rome by crossing the Alps.
8. ——, the two-faced god, guarded the door of the Roman home.
9. Children in Rome used a —— upon which to calculate their arithmetic.
10. Rome gave us the names of our ——.

<table>
<tr><td>plebeians</td><td>Cincinnatus</td></tr>
<tr><td>Janus</td><td>counting-frame</td></tr>
<tr><td>Romulus</td><td>Horatius</td></tr>
<tr><td>slaves</td><td>republic</td></tr>
<tr><td>months</td><td>Hannibal</td></tr>
</table>

VI

WANDERING TRIBES
BECOME NATIONS

TRIBES OF WESTERN EUROPE. *From north, south, and east, different peoples migrated to western Europe, and their tribal customs combined into new ways of living.*

WANDERING TRIBES BECOME NATIONS

THE GERMAN TRIBES SEEK NEW HOMES

The people of the northern forest land who made their way into the Roman Empire were tall, strong people with blue eyes and long golden or red hair. They dressed in the skins of animals or in coarsely woven, one-piece garments thrown about them. They lived in little round huts which they made of roughly hewn timbers, or by weaving together reeds or branches of trees. These huts were often grouped together in clearings in the forest to form villages. A group of neighboring villages formed a tribe.

For centuries, before they began to overrun the Empire, many of these tribes lived in the region stretching from the Rhine and the Danube to the northern part of Europe. Among them were the Goths, the Vandals, the Burgundians, the Lombards, and the Franks. To the north of these tribes lived the Angles, the Saxons, and the Jutes. Still farther north, in the countries now called Norway and Sweden, lived the Norsemen, men of the north.

All these tribes were related and had similar ways of living. The men spent most of their time hunting and fighting. The women took care of the homes and the children, spun and wove, cared for the cattle, and tilled the fields.

These people loved liberty. The chief of a tribe was chosen at a meeting of the people, or "folk." When important matters were to be decided, the folk met in an assembly. If the warriors liked what their leaders proposed, they struck their weapons against their shields.

Courage and bravery were the two qualities most admired by all the German tribes. "It is shameful for a chief to be outdone in bravery," said a Roman writer in describing them, "and equally shameful for his followers not to match the bravery of their chief. To survive one's chief and return from battle is a disgrace which lasts as long as life. It is unlawful for a man so disgraced to enter the assembly."

About the year 375, hordes of Huns, a fierce Mongolian people from the wildest part of Asia, swept into Europe on their shaggy little horses, destroying everything in their way. As they swept westward, the Huns came to the land of the Goths, not far north of the Roman Empire. Although the Goths were brave, they fled in terror before these fierce, swift-moving invaders.

When the Goths reached the Danube River, they looked across at the protected land of the Empire and thought that there surely was safety. They sent messengers to the emperor and "humbly begged and entreated," says a Roman historian, "to be received by him as his subjects. They promised to live quietly and to furnish troops." Since this was at the time when the Empire was growing weak and needed more men to defend it, the emperor let the Goths come in. Thousands of warriors, with their wives and children, crossed the river on rafts or in boats made from hollowed-out trunks of trees. They "crossed the stream night and day without ceasing," says an old account.

The emperor had promised to treat the Goths well, but the promise was soon broken by his officials, who oppressed the newcomers in many ways. Then the angry Goths rose against the Romans.

The Goths had an able leader named Alaric. Alaric took counsel with his people and they "decided to carve out a new kingdom for themselves, rather than to continue as subjects of others."

In the year 410, Alaric and his army of Goths easily took possession of Rome. Messengers from the frightened Romans asked Alaric what terms he would make.

"Deliver to me all your gold, all your silver, all the treasures that can be moved, all the slaves," said Alaric.

"What, then, do you leave us?" asked the messengers from Rome.

"Your lives," replied Alaric, scornfully.

For six terrible days and nights, the followers of Alaric roved through the streets of Rome ransacking the city.

Other German tribes broke through the Roman frontiers and wandered over the land of the Roman Empire seeking new homes. During this time the cities built by Rome were plundered. Priceless treasures were destroyed. Roman aqueducts, bridges, and roads went unrepaired. Theaters, baths, and other public buildings fell into ruins. Art, literature, and learning declined. This period in which the barbarous tribes were overrunning Europe was called the Dark Ages. It lasted for several centuries.

Yet civilization was moving forward. The people of the German tribes brought new life and vigor to the lands they seized. The kingdoms they established were, in later times, to grow into the important nations of modern Europe. As the tribes settled down, a new society grew up and spread over the land. Then Europe entered upon a new period of history, the later and better half of the Middle Ages.

About the time that Alaric was conquering Italy, other tribes of Goths made their way to Spain and settled down. For three hundred years they remained undisturbed there. Then, in the year 711, their country was invaded by a great army of Arabs who came over from northern Africa.

From very early times the Arabs had lived in Arabia as desert tribes and had taken little part in world history. In the sixth century an Arab named Mohammed became a great religious leader. In early life Mohammed had been a camel driver who conducted caravans across Arabia. As he traveled back and forth across the deserts he met many Jews and Christians. From them he learned about the worship of one God. Mohammed thought that such a religion was much better than the worship of idols, which most of his people practiced.

Mohammed came to believe that he was the prophet chosen by God to spread a new religion. He went about teaching people and saying, "There is but one God, and Mohammed is his prophet." Some people believed in his teachings and became his followers. Other people thought that he was a dangerous man and decided to kill him. But Mohammed heard what his enemies were planning and with a handful of followers fled to Medina in the year 622.

Mohammed won many converts while he stayed in Medina. Then he returned to Mecca, the city from which he had fled, and took possession of it. Mecca became the center of the new religion, which spread rapidly.

[211]

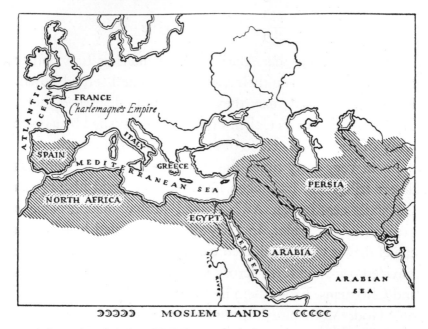

ว ว ว ว ว ว   MOSLEM LANDS   ᑕ ᑕ ᑕ ᑕ ᑕ

After the death of Mohammed, his sayings were written down by his faithful followers and gathered together into a book called the Koran. This became the sacred book of the Mohammedan, or Moslem, people.

The caliphs, who were the rulers after Mohammed, wanted more land. Within a hundred years after the death of Mohammed they had established a vast empire in Asia, and the Arabs had spread over northern Africa.

From Africa it was easy for the Mohammedans to cross the narrow Strait of Gibraltar into Spain. There they found a tribe of Goths who had been living in the country for nearly three hundred years. In 711 the Mohammedans defeated the Goths and established a kingdom which extended north to the Pyrenees Mountains.

In Spain the Moors, as the Arabs who settled there came to be called, built up a great civilization. Under their rule cities grew up which were famous for their beautiful buildings. Some palaces had roofs of gold and silver, and walls of tinted marble. They were surrounded by lovely gardens.

The Mohammedans called their churches mosques. The architecture of the mosques was quite different from that of the Greek and Roman temples or the Christian churches. On the tops were great domes and around the roofs were tall, slender towers called minarets. The Mohammedans did not believe in making pictures of living creatures, but by skillfully putting together bits of colored glass, marble, and other materials they made mosaics in beautiful designs. These were used as wall and floor decorations for their mosques.

According to the rules laid down in the Koran, a good Mohammedan prayed frequently. Five times a day a priest, called a muezzin, climbed a narrow stairway to the top of the minaret and cried, "Come to prayer! Come to prayer!" A faithful Moslem knelt, wherever he was, and prayed with his face toward Mecca.

Cordova was a rich and beautiful city, famed for its learning and its prosperous merchants. There skilled craftsmen made ornamental metalwork in silver, copper, and brass. On their looms the weavers made fine cloths of linen and wool. Traders carried these products to distant markets in other lands.

The Arabs brought to Spain the learning of the East. At Cordova they established a university where Arabian scholars taught the learning of the Egyptians, the Greeks, the Romans, and other ancient peoples. Young men came from other lands to study at this university. They studied astronomy and medicine, mathematics and natural science. Thus new ways of thinking spread from East to West.

From the Chinese the Arabs had learned the art of paper making. Most of the books in the great library at Cordova were written on paper instead of parchment.

Before the Moors came to Spain people in Europe wrote numbers in the Roman way. The Arabs brought with them a simpler way of making numerals. This was found to be so good that it was later adopted by other countries in Europe. The Arabic system of numerals came to be used in many parts of the world.

Granada became the center of government. For protection of the city the Moors built a great fortress high up in the mountains. In it was a palace where the kings lived. The outer walls of this fortress were made of red sundried bricks. For this reason the fortress came to be called the Alhambra. This name comes from Arabic words which mean "the red castle."

The Alhambra still stands as a beautiful example of Moorish architecture.

For seven hundred years the Moors were able to hold the greater part of Spain. During that time a number of small Christian kingdoms had come into existence in the mountains of northern Spain. Gradually they conquered territory from the Moors.

In 1469 an event of great importance occurred. This was the marriage of Princess Isabella of Castile to Prince Ferdinand of Aragon. Since these two kingdoms were then the largest in Spain, the royal marriage united a large part of the country. The new king and queen decided to drive the Moors from Spain. They finally succeeded in doing this after a long war which ended in 1492.

Caesar had conquered Gaul and brought it under Roman rule in 58–51 B.C. Among the Germanic peoples who invaded the Roman Empire several centuries later were the Franks. They crossed the Rhine River and settled in Gaul about A.D. 400. At first they were divided into many small tribes, each ruled by its king. In the year 481, Clovis became king of the Franks and united all the tribes into one nation. Under Clovis the Franks prospered. They imitated the manners of the Romans and used the Latin language.

After Clovis the kingdom of the Franks continued to grow. In time, however, it came to be ruled by weak kings who spent their days in idleness or amusement and left the affairs of government to officials. They accomplished so little that they have been called the "do-nothing kings." Then, in the eighth century, the kingdom once more found a strong and capable ruler.

While the Franks were building up their kingdom, the Moors in Spain, wanting more land, crossed the Pyrenees in the year 732 to conquer the kingdom of the Franks. The Moors fought so fiercely that it looked as if they might conquer all Europe. But an able leader by the name of Charles met the invaders at Tours in central France with a strong host of fighting men from all over the Frankish lands. Charles struck such blows with his great battle-ax that always afterwards he was called Charles Martel, that is, Charles the Hammer. The Moors retreated to Spain and never again tried to conquer the land of the Franks.

After the time of Charles the Hammer the kingdom of the Franks came under his grandson Charles. He was later known as Charlemagne, which means Charles the Great. While Charlemagne reigned, many lands were brought under the rule of the Franks.

The great fame of Charlemagne as a warrior is shown in an old story told by a monk of his time. One day when Charles and his army were advancing in an enemy country, two of the defenders climbed a high tower where they could see in all directions. When some of the Frankish soldiers appeared, one of the defenders said to the other: "Is Charles with this army?"

"Not yet," said the other.

More soldiers appeared. The first man said, "Surely Charles is with these hosts."

"Not yet," replied his companion. "When you see a harvest of steel waving in the fields, and the rivers dashing steel-black waves against the city walls, then you may believe that Charles is coming."

Scarcely had the words been spoken when a dark cloud appeared in the north far in the distance.

[217]

As the cloud drew nearer, the defenders saw Charles, the man of steel, his arms covered with plates of steel, his iron breast and his broad shoulders protected by steel armor. His left hand caried aloft the iron lance, for his right was always ready with the victorious sword. His thighs were covered with iron scales. His shield was of steel and his horse was iron in color and in spirit.

His whole army tried to imitate Charles as closely as possible. Steel filled the fields and roads. The rays of the sun were reflected from the gleaming steel. The people of the invaded country did homage to the bristling steel. The mighty walls trembled before Charlemagne's army. The bravest youths fled before the terrible weapons.

The conquests of Charlemagne gave the Franks a larger empire than any in Europe since the days of the Roman Empire. What later became France, Belgium, Holland, and Switzerland, more than half of Germany and Italy, and parts of Spain were included in it by the year 800, when Charlemagne, king of the Franks, was crowned emperor.

Charlemagne made good laws for his empire and saw that they were carried out. He did all he could to make his people more civilized. In those days few people could read or write. In most places there were no schools. Charlemagne himself could not read until he was a grown man, and he never learned to write, although he kept tablets under his pillow and at night often drew them out and practiced his letters. Charlemagne, however, wanted children to learn to read and write. In his palace he had a school for them conducted by a learned teacher, Alcuin.

Alcuin taught his pupils by a series of questions and answers. The pupils would ask him the questions and he would answer them until they knew the answers perfectly.

"What is the mouth?" a pupil might ask.

Alcuin would answer, "The nourisher of the body because all food comes through it."

"What is the stomach?" asked the pupil.

"The cook of the food," was the answer.

The scholars learned that the hands were the workmen of the body, the bones the strength of the body, and the legs the columns of the body.

There were other schools, too. "Let every monastery have its school, where boys may be taught the Psalms, the system of musical notation, singing, arithmetic, and grammar," said one of Charlemagne's orders.

All books at that time were written by hand and Charlemagne knew that some books had errors in them. "Let the books which are given the boys be free from faults, and let care be taken that the boys do not spoil them when reading or writing," he said.

The fighting nobles of the day often looked upon learning with contempt. The sons of nobles thought that as their fathers were of high rank they need not work hard, and so they often neglected their books. At one time Charlemagne sent for a group of boys and asked them to show him their work. The boys from poorer families had done their work well, and Charlemagne was much pleased.

"I can see that you have taken pains," he said. "Try now to reach perfection and you shall be highly honored."

The sons of some of the nobles had no good work to show the king. Charlemagne scolded them roundly.

"You sons of princes," he said to them, "you pretty and dainty little gentlemen who count upon your birth and wealth! You have disregarded my orders, you have neglected your studies, and spent your time in idleness or in foolish occupations.

"I care little for your noble birth and your pretty looks, though others think them so fine. And let me promise you this: If you do not make haste to recover what you have lost by your neglect, you need never think to get favors from Charles!"

After the death of Charlemagne it proved impossible to hold his vast empire together. By the middle of the ninth century the land over which he had ruled was divided. The eastern part was to grow into Germany, the western part became France, and another part became Italy. Each country had its own ruler and developed in its own way as an independent kingdom.

During the centuries when the Franks were changing Gaul into France, Britain was slowly being changed into England. Britain had been a Roman province, but when the barbarian tribes were overrunning the Empire the Roman legions in Britain were recalled to Rome.

The Britons had grown used to having the Romans protect them. Now they were left undefended. Their old enemies, the Picts and Scots, wild tribes from Scotland and Ireland, swept down upon them. The unhappy Britons sent an appeal to Rome: "The barbarians drive us into the sea; the sea throws us back on the barbarians. Our only choice is whether we shall be slain or drowned."

Rome was not able to send help. She needed all her soldiers to defend her own city.

Then the Britons called upon the Angles and Saxons and Jutes who lived along the shores of the North Sea and the Baltic Sea to help them. This brought new trouble.

From 449 on, for nearly two hundred years, Angles and Saxons kept pouring into Britain. At first they made short raids to steal and plunder. Making their way up the rivers, they robbed and burned the villages of the Britons and stole the crops, the sheep, and the cattle.

"Foes are they, fierce beyond other foes, and cunning as they are fierce," says an old writer. "The sea is their school, war and storm their friends. They are the sea wolves that live on the pillage of the world."

Each year more Angles and Saxons came, and in time they drove the Britons westward and became the masters of the whole country.

The Angles and Saxons settled down by tribes into several small kingdoms, each under its own leader. For a long time these kingdoms fought one another, but in the ninth century they were all united into a single kingdom.

Thus Britain came to be known as Angleland, which gradually changed to England. The people were called Anglo-Saxons.

Like the other Germanic tribes, the Anglo-Saxons loved freedom and independence. No one dared cross the threshold of a man's house without first calling out to the owner. If he entered without permission the owner had the right to kill him. There grew up an old saying among them, "Every man's house is his castle."

The Anglo-Saxons lived in small villages. Each village and its land formed a township. The townships were grouped into larger districts called hundreds. Each village had a special meeting place called a moot. Whenever it

was necessary, all the freemen of the village met there to talk over the affairs of the village. Every man at this meeting, or town-moot, as it was called, had a right to say what he thought and to vote as he wished.

Once a month there was a hundred-moot for the people of several villages. To this assembly each village in a region sent representatives. As the hundred bound together several villages, so the "folk," or tribe, bound together several hundreds. The folk-moot discussed matters that were of importance to all the hundreds.

When the tribes had been united into one kingdom, it was customary for the king to call together the chief men from all the folk-moots to give him advice. This gathering was called the witan or witenagemot, which means "assembly of the wise men." The laws were made by the older men and put before the assembly. A clashing of spears against shields meant that a law was pleasing. A murmur of discontent caused a law to be put aside.

Thus the Anglo-Saxons from the earliest times took part in their government.

KING ALFRED THE GREAT

In the ninth century bands of fierce warriors from Denmark swept down upon the English coasts, burning and plundering. It looked as if they were going to conquer the whole island. Then in the year 871 an able leader, King Alfred, came to the throne. This young king of the Anglo-Saxons helped his people to defend their land.

At one time the king, disguised as a wandering minstrel, stole into the camp of the Danes and strolled about playing and singing. He could play well on the harp and the Danish warriors were delighted with his sweet music. The commander of the Danes heard it and ordered the minstrel brought to his tent. So Alfred played and sang for him. While he played and while the Danes drank and made merry, Alfred kept his ears open and overheard the Danish plan of campaign. Then he slipped away and, collecting his men, made a sudden attack upon the Danes, whom he defeated. After the battle Alfred took his harp and played for the Danish commander a tune which he recognized.

When the commander heard the tune he exclaimed, "Then you, King Alfred, were the wandering minstrel!"

"Yes," said Alfred, "I was the musician whom you received so kindly. I will give you your liberty if you will promise never more to make war on my people."

The Danish leader promised and he and his men were set free.

King Alfred was a wise and good king. Before his time few laws were written down. People remembered what their fathers had done and called that the law. Alfred had all these old customs written down. Then he chose what was best from them and added a few laws of his own. Here is what he said about these laws:

> I, Alfred, gathered these laws together and commanded many of them to be written which our forefathers held, those which seemed to me good. And many of them which seemed to me not so good I rejected. I durst not venture to set down in writing much of my own, for it was unknown to me what of them would please those who should come after me.

First he submitted his laws to the assembly. "I, Alfred, King of the Saxons, showed them all to my Witan and they said they approved them all and would observe them," he wrote.

Toward the end of his life Alfred said: "It has ever been my desire to live worthily while I am alive, and after my death to leave to those that should come after me a remembrance of me in good works."

When the great king lay dying he called his son to him. "My dear son," said the king, "sit thee now beside me and I will deliver to thee true counsel.

"I go to another world and thou art left alone to hold to all that which I have held to in my time. I pray thee, my child, be a father to thy people. Comfort the poor, protect and shelter the weak, and with all thy might, right that which is wrong."

For a time after Alfred's death the kingdom that he had made strong continued united. Then a weak king lost it to a new swarm of Danes, and a Danish warrior by the name of Canute came to the throne.

There is an interesting story about Canute. His courtiers tried to flatter him by saying that so great was his power that if he commanded the waves they would obey him. Disliking such flattery, Canute ordered a chair placed near the ocean's edge when the tide was rising.

Seating himself, he looked over the water and said, "O sea, I am thy lord. My ships sail over thee whither I will, and the land against which thou dashest is mine. Stay, then, thy waves, and dare not to wet the feet of thy lord and master."

Of course the waves continued to come in, and as the water washed around his chair, Canute said to his courtiers, "See how weak is the power of kings and of all men, for ye see that the waves will not hearken to my voice. Let all men know how empty and worthless is the power of kings, for there is none worthy of the name but Him whom heaven, earth, and the sea obey."

VOYAGES OF THE VIKINGS

THE VIKINGS SAIL THE NORTHERN SEAS

In the far north of Europe, in the countries now known as Denmark, Norway, and Sweden, lived hardy tribes of people called Norsemen, men of the North. As the coasts of their land were indented by many long narrow inlets, the Norsemen were sometimes called Vikings. This name comes from the word *vic*, meaning a "bay" or "fiord."

Inland the country of the Vikings was so wild and rugged that most of them lived along the coast. The forests supplied plenty of wood for ships. In early days the men spent most of their time on the sea fishing. Later the Vikings learned to build sturdy, seagoing ships, and became daring sea rovers. They raided the coasts of western Europe.

Their ships were long and narrow, each with forty to fifty oars and a large square sail woven in stripes of gay colors—in red and white, or blue and green. On the sails were painted devices like the eagle or the wolf. The prows

were gilded and carved to look like huge dragon
heads, stretching far above the water. The
sterns were like dragon tails, curling upward.
Around the ships' sides hung the gaily painted
shields of the warriors, ready for use. The
steering was done by means of a large oar
fastened to the right side of the ship.

The Norse sea rovers spent the long, cold
winter evenings in feasting and song in the long
hall, lighted chiefly by flames from the large
fire burning in the middle of the floor. The
walls were hung with swords and helmets, their
polished steel gleaming in the light of the fire.

Bison horns filled with foaming mead were passed up and down the long table. Then the skald, or minstrel, took his harp and sang of brave heroes and great voyages.

> Our sea-steed through the foam goes prancing,
> While shields and spears and helms are glancing.
> From fiord to sea,
> Our ships ride free,
> And down the wind, with swelling sail,
> We scud before the gathering gale.

In clear weather the Norse sailors guided their ships by the sun in the daytime and by the North Star at night. But when the weather was stormy and the sky overcast, it was hard for the Vikings to know where they were. The sailors often carried with them a number of ravens which they let loose when they thought they might be nearing land. If the ravens returned, the sailors knew that they were still far from land. If the ravens did not come back, the sailors steered in the direction which the birds had taken. The men knew that land must be near if the birds had found a resting place and did not return to the ship.

How the Vikings loved their ships! They often gave them interesting names—*Deer of the Surf, Reindeer of the Breezes, Raven of the Wind*. When a Viking chieftain died, he was laid to rest in his ship, with his shield and spear. A funeral pyre was built upon it. Then the fire was lighted and the ship was set adrift to float out to sea.

In the ninth century the Vikings set out in their long, many-oared dragon ships to explore the gray, stormy waters of the North Atlantic. They discovered an island which they named Iceland and made settlements there.

One of the chief men of Iceland was a fierce young warrior, Eric the Red. Eric got into trouble and was banished from Iceland. With some of his followers he sailed westward seeking a new home.

After three years Eric returned to Iceland with a wonderful tale. He had found, he said, not an ice land but a green land. Most of the land was covered with ice and snow, but it was green along the coast. Eric called it Greenland, hoping to persuade other people to settle in the new land he had discovered.

Eric had a son Leif, who was one of the best navigators in Greenland. On a voyage which he made in the year 1000, Leif Ericsson and his men were blown far out of their course by storms. It is believed that the voyagers reached the coast of North America. The land they found was covered with trees and vines and flowers. Great quantities of wild grapes grew everywhere. Leif called the land Vinland, or Wineland.

About a hundred years after the death of Charlemagne a band of Vikings made their way to the northern coast of France and forced the king to give them a stretch of land bordering on the English Channel. They settled down, and as time passed they gave up their rough manners and customs and adopted those of the Frankish people among whom they had settled. They called their new homeland Normandy.

WILLIAM THE CONQUEROR

When the Northmen had been settled in Normandy for about a hundred years, Duke William ruled over the country. He had visited England and was a friend of King Edward. When King Edward died the people of England chose Harold, a Saxon earl, as their new king. William declared that Edward had promised the throne to him.

"Edward dead?" he said. "Then England is mine." And he decided to invade the country. He gathered together an army and built a fleet of ships to carry his men across the English Channel.

On October 14, 1066, the fleet reached the English shore. William was the first to set foot on English soil. As he jumped out of his boat he slipped and fell forward. Some of his followers thought this was a bad sign and meant that he would be beaten. Grasping a handful of earth William cried out, "Nay, I have taken this land with my two hands, and by the splendor of God, it is mine."

The Normans met the English forces under Harold at Hastings in the south of England.

Before going into battle William addressed his soldiers: "Make up your minds to fight valiantly. A great booty is before us, for if we conquer, we shall all be rich. What I gain, you gain. If I take this land, you will have it in lots among you."

In the midst of the battle William was struck from his horse, and his soldiers thought that he had been killed. "Our leader is down!" The cry of alarm spread and the soldiers began to retreat.

William threw himself in front of the fleeing soldiers. Tearing off his helmet so that his men might see his face, he shouted, "Here I am! Look at me! I am still alive and I will conquer by God's help. What madness is driving you to flight? You are deserting victory and everlasting honor. You are going to destruction and everlasting disgrace."

At these words the Normans recovered their courage and won the battle.

On Christmas Day in 1066, William was crowned king of England. Thus the rule of the old Anglo-Saxon kings came to an end. To the knights who had helped him win

England, William gave large stretches of land and the Normans became the ruling class in the country.

William had been strong enough to conquer England. He also showed himself wise enough to rule it. He made stern laws, but he was fair and just. An old account of the time says:

> Amongst other things is not to be forgotten the good peace that he made in this land, so that a man of any account might go over his kingdom unhurt with his bosom full of gold. No man durst slay another, no matter how great might be the wrong done him.

The coming of the Normans made great changes in England. The Normans carried to England their customs and language. At first, two languages were spoken. The king and nobles spoke Norman-French; the plain people clung to their own language, Anglo-Saxon. The Anglo-Saxon farmers called their animals by their Anglo-Saxon names: pig, cow, calf, sheep. When the meats were served on the tables of the Norman nobles, these foods were called by the Norman-French names: pork, beef, veal, mutton. Gradually the two languages were combined and both peoples spoke English. There are many words in the English language which have come down from the Anglo-Saxon people, and many which have come down from the Norman-French.

LORDS AND VASSALS

The people of Europe were divided into various nations, but their ways of living were similar. All the land in a kingdom belonged to the king. As he was unable to defend the whole of it, he gave large stretches of land to the leading warriors who had helped him win it. They promised that they would help him defend the kingdom in case of attack. These men became the higher nobles. They, in turn, gave parts of their land to other men who promised to be loyal to them and help them defend their land in time of attack.

In a time when men's lives were always in danger, weaker men were glad to put themselves under the protection of more powerful leaders. A man who received land from another noble was called his vassal.

When a man wished to become the vassal of another he took a solemn oath: "I promise on my faith that I will in future be faithful to my lord and will observe my homage to him completely in good faith and without deceit." The lord kissed his new vassal and answered: "And I receive you and take you to be my man and give you this kiss as a sign of faith."

This new way of living, known as feudalism, spread over Europe. Society seemed to be like a vast pyramid. At the top was the king. Below him were the powerful nobles who had sworn to serve the king. Below these were the lesser nobles, each of whom had their vassals. The broad base of the pyramid was made up of the mass of the common people.

Although the king was supposed to be the head of the kingdom, his power extended only to the parts of it he reserved for himself. Sometimes the nobles in a kingdom had more power than the king.

There was almost constant fighting among the nobles. Not content with the land they had, they tried to get more by attacking their neighbors. A noble who was successful in such an attack added the land of the defeated noble to his own. Sometimes a great lord, more powerful than the king, rose against him and threw off the rule of the king entirely, setting up a kingdom of his own.

In the early days of each nation which grew out of the wandering tribes, the people were not Christians. They believed in the old pagan gods whom their forest ancestors had worshiped for centuries.

Woden, or Odin, as he was sometimes called, was the chief god. He directed the affairs of the world. He had two ravens which flew over the earth each day and brought back news of what was happening.

Thor was Odin's oldest son. He had a great hammer with which he slew giants, and a belt which doubled his strength when he wore it, and a pair of iron gloves. When it thundered, the people thought that Thor was hurling his hammer across the heavens.

There were many other pagan gods and there were spirits that dwelt in the wild mountains and forests.

The old Norse gods were thought to live in Asgard, which was connected with the earth by a rainbow bridge called Byfrost. In Asgard were many beautiful palaces.

The most splendid was Valhalla, the home of Odin. He feasted in his great hall with the heroes from earth who had died gloriously on the battlefield.

It was the duty of warlike maidens, called Valkyries, to bring to Odin all the brave warriors who had been slain. The Valkyries were armed with spears and shields and could speed through the air on powerful horses.

The names of some of the days of the week come from the names of the old Germanic gods. Wednesday is Woden's day; Thursday is Thor's day; Tuesday is Tieu's day; and Friday is named after Freya, the Norse goddess of love and beauty.

After the fall of the Roman Empire, zealous Christian missionaries journeyed all over Europe to spread the Christian religion. An old story relates how Clovis and the Franks became Christians. When Clovis first became king, the Franks worshiped Woden, Thor, and the other pagan gods.

Clotilda, the wife of Clovis, had become a Christian. She pleaded with her husband to give up the old gods, but she was unable to persuade him to follow the new religion. Then, one day, in a battle, everything seemed to be going against Clovis and his men. It seemed to him that his army surely would be defeated.

Suddenly Clovis thought of the Christian God, and cried out, "O Jesus Christ, Son of the living God, who art said to give victory to those who put their hope in thee, I beseech the glory of thine aid. If thou wilt grant me victory over these enemies, I will believe in thee and be baptized in thy name."

Clovis won the battle and Clotilda sent for a bishop and asked him to teach her husband the true religion. Clovis said, "I am glad to listen to you, but my people will not leave their gods." Yet after Clovis became a Christian he said to the missionaries, "I will go forth and tell my people what you have told me."

He went among his people, and almost before he had spoken a word the people cried out, "We are ready to follow the immortal God."

About a hundred years after the time of Clovis, a band of missionaries under a famous monk, Augustine, landed on the shores of Britain. An interesting old story tells how these missionaries happened to go to England. One day a monk named Gregory was passing through the market place in Rome. There he saw a group of boys waiting to be sold as slaves. Gregory asked from what land they came.

"They are Angles," was the slave-dealer's reply.

"Rather should they be called angels," replied Gregory, "for they have the faces of angels."

The monk then asked whether they were Christians and was told that they were heathens.

"They should be Christians. I will myself go to their land and save their people from the wrath of God."

"What is the name of their king?" then asked the monk.

"Aella," was the answer.

"Alleluia!" cried Gregory. "The praise of God, the Creator, must be sung in those parts."

It is not known whether Gregory was able to do anything for the poor little boys he saw in the market place, but he did not forget about them. When he became Pope he sent Augustine to England with a band of missionaries.

The monks landed and sent word to the king that they had come. The king said that he would hear what they had to say. When he had heard them he said: "Your words and promises sound very good to me, but they are new and strange and I cannot believe them all at once. Nor can I leave all that my fathers and the whole English folk have believed so long. But I see that you have come from a far country to tell us what ye yourselves hold truth. So ye may stay in the land and I will give you a house to dwell in and food to eat, and ye may preach to my folk and if any man of them will believe as ye believe, I will hinder him not."

The monks remained, and in time most of the people of England became Christians.

Christian missionaries carried their message to other parts of Europe. "Though I wear a coat of mail always on my breast, I have found a man whose words pierce like an arrow to my heart," said one king after a missionary had talked with him.

By the eleventh century most of the people in the western part of Europe had become Christians.

The head of the Church was the Pope, who lived in Rome. Under him were the clergy all over Europe. In every village there was a priest who had charge of the services in the village church. There were bishops, whose duty it was to oversee the priests of their districts. The bishops in the more important towns came to have certain powers over the bishops of the smaller towns about them. These were called archbishops.

In all the churches there was the same service and the same teaching about how people ought to live. Everyone was subject to the rules of the Church, for the Pope's authority was above that of the greatest nobles and even that of kings.

Talking Together

1. Looking at the map on page 206 you find the names of the early tribes. Discuss the way nations gradually developed in Europe.

2. What contribution did the Moors make to Spain? What did Spain gain when the Moors were expelled?

3. Do you think it was wise for King Canute to rebuke his people for their flattery?

4. What qualities do you admire in Charlemagne? In King Alfred?

5. Are the people of Norway and Sweden, like the Vikings of old, still seafaring people?

Interesting Things to Try

1. A group of your classmates might read some of the stories from *The Arabian Nights* and tell them to the class.

2. For your classroom print and decorate one of Charlemagne's favorite mottoes, "He that ruleth his spirit is better than he that taketh a city."

3. Choose scenes to dramatize from the life of Alfred the Great.

4. If you made models of Egyptian and Phoenician boats, you might wish to add models of the Viking boats. Which kind of boat is best suited to sail rough seas?

5. Ask your teacher to read to you some of the famous stories of Siegfried.

6. Plan and make a time line or time chart with important events from early days to the beginning of the new nations.

Let's Read

Sticks across the Chimney, by Nora Burglon. This is a gripping story in which a boy and a girl of today share in finding a Viking mound stored with relics of these bold people.

In Norway, by Gudrun Thorne-Thomsen. Read the "Vikings" and other "Old, Old Stories."

The Picture Story of Norway, by Hester O'Neill. Pictures by Ursula O'Neill Koering. A colorful story beginning with the nine hundredth celebration of the founding of Oslo, in 1950.

In France, by Marguerite Clément. France had great men in the past. She has great men today. What will her future be?

Leif the Lucky, by Ingri and Edgar d'Aulaire. Everyone likes this strikingly illustrated story of the Vikings.

The Land of the English People, by Alicia Street. The chapters "How England Became English" and "England in the Middle Ages" show the struggles and courage of the English people.

Page, Esquire, and Knight, by Marion F. Lansing. In the chapters "Roland, a Knight of France" and "Tales of King Arthur" you find out more about these two famous historical characters.

The Story Book of Ships, by Maud and Miska Petersham. You may enjoy this well-illustrated story of ships from the early days to the present.

The Romance of Discovery, by Hendrik W. Van Loon. This is another story of the Vikings that tells you more about these interesting sea rovers.

The Sword with the Golden Hilt, by Margery Evernden. The sword is the prize for which two cousins in Norway are rivals. Great adventures take place.

SEEING AND LEARNING

You may learn from seeing just as you do from reading. But if you wish to get the most from seeing a movie in your classroom, you must follow a plan as you do when studying history.

Preparing for the Film. In selecting your movie, see that you already know something about the subject of the picture. While you are studying this unit, you have read not only the text but probably *The Land of the English People* by Alicia Street and other books on England. With what you have learned from these, you are well prepared to enjoy the film "London, City of Tradition," which shows buildings and other places of historic interest.

[243]

Before seeing a movie in school, make a list of questions you would like to have answered, or of points upon which you wish information. For example, prepare in advance a list of places you will look for in the picture "London, City of Tradition."

Seeing the Film. After the movie has been shown, other questions may arise. To answer these, you will want to look at the picture again.

Follow-up Period. At this time, check your questions and see whether they have been answered. Have a class discussion on these. Perhaps you may want more information from books about places shown in the movie. Some boys and girls will gather this material and give a report. Others may make paintings of pictures suggested to them by the movie, while still others may wish to write stories or poems based on the film they have seen.

QUIZ YOURSELF

A Matching Game

In column A are the names of some of the persons and places mentioned in this unit. Write these names on a separate sheet of paper. Then for each name select from column B the group of words that tell something about that person or place. *Be sure that you do not write in this book.*

A	B
Mohammed	was a fortress in Spain
Moors	commanded the waters
Alhambra	were Mohammedans in Spain
Gaul	became England
Charlemagne	landed in Greenland
Britain	became France
Normandy	became King of England
William the Conqueror	is on the northern coast of France
Canute	was the greatest king of the Franks
Eric the Red	founded the Mohammedan religion

VII

NEW WAYS OF LIVING

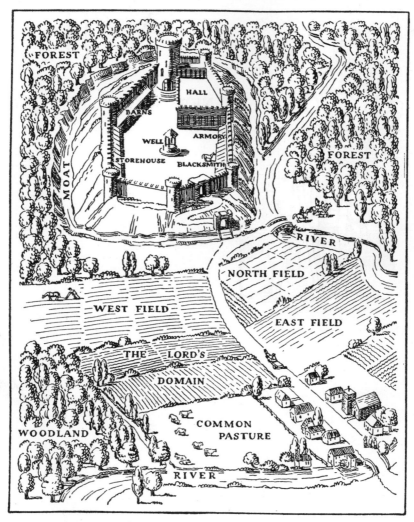

A MEDIEVAL MANOR. *In the Middle Ages the lords lived in walled castles on large estates, and the peasants dwelt in cottages near the fields which they cultivated for the landowners.*

NEW WAYS OF LIVING

IN A MEDIEVAL CASTLE

With warlike enemies on every side, the nobles had to live in strongly fortified castles. In many places castles were built on steep, rocky cliffs, on islands far out on lakes, or in some other places hard to attack. The castle and its grounds were surrounded by massive stone walls, sometimes eight feet thick. High towers were at every corner of a castle wall, where sentinels were on constant watch for the approach of an enemy.

If a castle was built in a place where there were no strong natural defenses, a deep ditch called a moat was dug around the outer wall and filled with water. The only entrance was a drawbridge which could be drawn up at a moment's notice. That made it very difficult for enemies to cross the moat.

When a castle was attacked, battering-rams and hurling-engines, very much like those of the Romans, were used. Perhaps the enemy might creep up to the wall and put up ladders, or roll up a movable tower to the wall and so climb over it. The castle defenders on the wall shot arrows, or threw down huge stones and burning pitch.

The nobles and their fighting men protected their bodies with heavy steel armor. Their heads and faces were covered

with steel helmets, with only little slits to see and breathe through. They carried long lances and shields. When they sallied forth from their castles they rode on strong horses also protected by heavy armor.

As the helmet hid the face of a knight, he had on his shield some special mark to show who he was. Perhaps it was the picture of a lion or some other animal. Sometimes it was a design which showed a deed for which he was famous.

The most important room in the castle was the hall. This was a large rectangular room, lofty and spacious.

The walls were usually of rough stone. In the winter the cold floors were covered with rushes or the furry skins of animals. Instead of a ceiling there were usually rafters of wood, often richly carved and painted. At one end of the room was a stone fireplace where a roaring fire could be kept burning during the long winter months.

The whole household gathered in the hall at mealtime. Across one end was a raised platform on which was a long, high table for the lord, his family, and the most honored guests. Long boards set on trestles were arranged down the whole length of the hall, with benches along each side, for the rest of the household. All through the meal the "fool," or jester, provided entertainment with his joking. He wore a costume half of one color and half of another.

After the evening meal the hall was cleared for dancing, or tables and chairs were brought in for checkers, chess, backgammon, and other games. Perhaps a wandering minstrel would arrive at the castle and sing songs of love and tales of knightly adventure, accompanying himself on the lute. Sometimes the minstrels recited long poems about a favorite hero, like King Arthur, who helped to defend the Britons, or Roland, the nephew of Charlemagne.

LEARNING TO BE A KNIGHT

In every castle were a number of boys of noble birth who were learning to be knights. Until he was fourteen years of age a boy served as a page. There was much for him to learn. One of the ladies of the castle had particular charge over each page. She told him stories of the saints and brave knights. She taught him good manners and the rules of knighthood. Perhaps she taught him to dance and play the lute. She made sure that her page went frequently to church. Thus a lady at the castle trained her page to be an honorable, Christian knight.

Always the page was looking forward to the time when he should become a squire. This came when he was about fourteen years old. The squire led a busy life. He must be up early and late, always ready to answer his lord's call. He polished his lord's armor, helped care for his horses, and waited upon him at mealtime. When the lord went into battle, the squire must stay near, holding a spare horse and fresh weapons ready for his master at any moment they might be needed.

When he was twenty or twenty-one, the squire, if he was deemed worthy, was made a knight. The ceremony was long and solemn, and every part of it had a special meaning. First, the squire bathed and put on a snow-white tunic, for he was to begin a new, clean life. Then he put on a red robe, representing the blood he might be called upon to shed in defense of the oppressed. Over this went a tight-fitting black coat, representing death, which comes to all men.

The whole night before he was knighted the young squire spent in the chapel of the castle before the altar, upon which lay his sword, his shield, and his lance. Alone in the dark church, lighted only by a few candles, he prayed, for he had been taught that "he ought to pray much that

God give him his blessing, by which he may be a good knight all the days of his life."

When day dawned a priest came, and the young squire solemnly vowed to be brave and honorable, to maintain right, to redress wrong, to protect women, to give help to those in trouble, and to show mercy to the weak and defenseless. Taking the squire's sword from the altar, the priest said, "Receive this in the name of the Father. Use it for your own defense and that of God's Holy Church, and wound no one unjustly with it."

By this time the members of the household and many guests had gathered in the courtyard of the castle. Knights and ladies belted on the squire's sword, buckled on his golden spurs, and presented him with his shield. Then came the great moment of the ceremony. The young squire knelt, and his lord, touching him on the shoulder with a sword, proclaimed, "In the name of God and Saint Michael and Saint George, I dub thee knight. Be brave and loyal."

The nobles loved feasting. The marriage of a lord's daughter, the knighting of his son, in fact almost any unusual event was accompanied by a banquet at which a gay company of richly dressed knights and ladies gathered. At the tables everyone was carefully seated according to his rank. Course after course of rich food was brought in by servingmen, while musicians played on harps or lutes.

The Christmas season especially was a time of feasting and revelry. A great yule log, sometimes the whole trunk of a tree, was dragged into the hall and placed in the fireplace. The lord kindled it from the dying embers and soon the flames were roaring up the chimney. A big bowl with little red apples floating in it was passed, and everyone drank to his neighbor's health.

Then the feasting began. The boar's head was brought in, borne shoulder-high on a broad silver platter. In the mouth of the boar was a roasted apple and in its ears were sprigs of rosemary. Perhaps two servants together would

[252]

carry in a platter on which was a roast peacock, its beautiful feathers so arranged over the roasted body that the bird seemed alive. Sometimes there was a surprise, when the crust of a huge pie was cut open by the master of the house and out fluttered many small birds, which flew up to the rafters of the hall.

After the feasting there was fun of all sorts. There were games of blindman's buff, hunt the slipper, bob for apples, and forfeits. One of the company, called the Lord of Misrule, went about amusing people with his jokes and seeing that everyone had a good time. Sometimes a band of mummers would sweep in and take part in the merriment. These were poor men and women who disguised themselves and went about from castle to castle, singing, dancing, and acting little plays.

For miles about every castle there were great stretches of wild forest land, in which there were many deer, bears, wild hogs, and other animals. The castle folk were very fond of the meat of these animals and they loved the sport of hunting them.

On a fine day a party of nobles, armed with stout hunting spears or bows and arrows, would ride out from the castle at dawn, accompanied by a pack of hunting dogs and their keepers.

Over hills, across streams, through meadows, the gay party of hunters rode to the woods. The dogs were un-leashed and bounded away on the trail of some animal. The hunters dashed after them. Often throughout a whole day they scoured the woods, covering many miles of country in tracking the game.

Another favorite sport was hawking, which was the method by which pheasants, quail, and other game birds were caught. Ladies, as well as gentlemen, engaged in this sport. On the wrist of every member of a hawking party perched a hawk, or falcon, which had been carefully trained from the time it was a tiny bird to obey instantly the whistles or calls of its owner. Its head was covered with a little hood and it was held fast to the wrist of its master or mistress by a chain attached to its leg.

When someone caught sight of a bird, he quickly whipped off his hawk's hood and turned it loose. The hawk soared high into the air, then suddenly whirled and

swooped down on the bird.
The hawk's master blew on
his whistle and the hawk
flew back to him and was
chained and hooded until
another bird was sighted.

Sometimes all the hawks
were sent up at the same
time. Then there was great
excitement, and bets were
made as to whose hawk
would get the bird.

A TOURNAMENT

The most exciting event at a castle was a tournament.
This was a mock battle in which the nobles exhibited their
skill in fighting. Months before the event, the noble who
was to give a tournament sent messengers to all the castles
for miles around, telling when it was to be held. "Let all
come who love to see or to join in deeds of valor," read
the announcement.

The place where a tournament was held was called the
lists. A level grassy space in a meadow was fenced off into
a long oblong, with rows of seats and richly canopied
pavilions decorated with shields and banners and bright
with colored hangings. At the center of one of the longer
sides of the lists was a special gallery for the ladies, and in
this was the throne for the Queen of Love and Beauty.

[255]

The ladies who attended the tournament were richly dressed in long robes of beautifully hued silks, some wrought with gold and silver threads, with long flowing sleeves and embroidered girdles. The gentlemen were scarcely less brilliant in their long cloaks with rich ermine at the neck and wrists, with heavy gold chains around their necks, and jeweled rings on their fingers.

When it was time for the contest to begin, a gay procession made its way to the lists. First came the heralds in their bright uniforms. Behind them rode the knights, two by two, their highly polished armor gleaming in the bright sunlight. Tall plumes nodded from the tops of some of the helmets. Gay ribbons or perhaps a richly embroidered scarf streamed from the lances of many knights, for ladies gave their favorites some token to wear.

[256]

The riders took their places, half at one end of the lists, half at the other, to await the signal to begin the tournament. Then came a blare of trumpets. The marshal cried, "In the name of God and Saint Michael, do your battle." The heralds shouted, "Go!"

Instantly the two sets of horsemen dashed to the center of the field, each knight with his lance raised to strike his opponent's shield. There was the thundering sound of galloping hoofs, the deafening clang of shields and lances. There were wild shouts from the excited onlookers. "Brave knight! Fight for your lady's favor!" came from one side. "Remember whose son you are! Be worthy of your ancestry!" came from another.

Many knights on both sides were flung from their horses and lay sprawled on the ground until their squires ran to pick them up. But many others still sat proudly on their horses as the trumpets sounded, marking the end of the first contest.

The knights went back to their stations at the ends of the lists. They took fresh weapons and were ready for a second tilt. Again and again the knights charged. At length the heralds cried, "Fold your banners," and the tournament came to an end.

In the evening there was a feast in the great hall of the castle. The knight who had broken the most lances received the first prize. He knelt before the Queen of Love and Beauty, who placed a wreath of flowers on his head, saying, "Sir Knight, I bestow upon thee this chaplet, assigned to this day's victor for deeds of valor."

The people of each castle-community had to provide themselves with all the things they needed. Someone had to raise food for the nobles and their fighting men. Someone had to make clothes for them to wear. Someone had to make the armor of the lord and his knights, and care for the horses.

The people who did all the work of the castles were called peasants. They were not exactly slaves, for they could not be bought and sold. Yet they were not free. They were serfs. When a noble received a piece of land, the serfs living on it became his, like the trees that grew on it.

The serfs were not paid for their work. Instead, they were given the use of a certain number of strips of land on which they could raise crops for their families. In return for the use of the land, the peasant owed his lord many services. A portion of the estate or manor, called the lord's domain, was reserved by the lord for his own use. For at least three days a week every peasant had to work on his lord's land. The peasant was required to bring his grain to his lord's mill to be ground and his flour to his lord's oven to be baked. He had to leave part of the ground grain for his lord, and a loaf of bread for his lord out of each baking. At Easter and other special times of the year he had to take gifts of eggs or chickens to his lord, and at harvest time a portion of the grain he had raised. In such ways the peasants paid for their own use of the land.

HOW THE LAND WAS DIVIDED

The fertile land of each manor was divided into three
big fields. In the fall one field was planted with wheat or
some other grain. In the spring the second field was planted
with oats or barley. The third field was unplanted. The
next year the empty field of the year before was seeded
with wheat, and the old wheat field with oats, while the
oat field was left unplanted.

The farmers of the Middle Ages knew very little about
soil. They had learned, however, that when land was used
year after year it produced poor crops. So they worked out
the plan of always letting one field "lie fallow" for a season
so that nature might make it fertile again.

Each field was divided into many long strips, separated
from one another by narrow lines of sod. Every peasant
had several of these strips in each field. The strange thing
was that his strips, even in one field, were scattered about,
a strip here and a strip there, instead of lying next to one
another. In this way no one serf had all good land or all
poor land. This may seem like a fair arrangement, but in

some ways it was not a good one. A serf's strips of land were so scattered that he wasted much time going from one strip to another.

In the spring the peasants plowed their land with big, clumsy plows drawn by slow-moving oxen; then they harrowed it and sowed it. In the fall they reaped the grain with sickles, bound it into sheaves, piled these high on their two-wheeled carts, and hauled them to the lord's barn. There they spread the grain thinly over the floor and beat out the seeds with long, jointed clubs called flails.

HOW THE PEASANTS LIVED

The peasant workers lived in little villages just outside the castle walls. Their homes were one-roomed houses, thatched with straw, with floors of packed earth and with perhaps a single small window. A fire burned on the floor, and the only chimney was a hole in the roof.

The peasants usually wore rough garments tied with rope belts. Their clothes were made from the wool of their own sheep. They wrapped pieces of cloth around their legs to keep them warm in winter. Instead of wearing shoes they wound their feet in heavy cloth and strapped on wooden soles to make walking easier.

Their food was poor and coarse: mainly porridge, soup, salt pork, fish, and black bread. According to a twelfth century writer "the peasant never drinks the fruit of his vine, nor tastes a scrap of good food. Only too happy is he if he can keep his black bread and some of his butter and cheese."

The peasants had little freedom. They had to obey their lord in all things. They could not leave the manor without his permission. They had to get his consent before they could marry. They could not leave the service of their lord. If they tried to run away they would very likely be caught and severely punished. Their life was indeed hard. One peasant said:

> I go at dawn to drive the oxen to the field and yoke them to the plow. However hard the winter may be, I dare not stay at home for fear of my master. When I have yoked the oxen, I have to plow a whole acre or more every day. I have also to fill the oxen's mangers with hay and give them water. It is very hard work, for I am not free.

Such was the life of most of the people of Europe during the early Middle Ages. Of course, life varied in different places, and the lot of some peasants was much better than that of others. If the lord of a manor was kind and just, his peasants were treated well. But the serfs were almost entirely in their lord's power, and he could treat them as he wished.

HOLY MEN HELP THE PEOPLE

During this period there were men who thought that
the best way to live really Christian lives was to get away
from the wickedness of the world to a lonely place where
they could pray and think holy thoughts. These men were
called hermits.

A few years after the barbarians drove the last Roman
emperor from Rome, a young Italian nobleman named
Benedict decided to become a hermit. In time other men
joined him and Benedict became the head of a monastery.
He worked out a set of rules which came to be followed by
the monks in most monasteries.

When a man thought that he wanted to become a monk,
he stayed in a monastery for a year to find out whether
he really wished to be a monk for his whole life. If at the
end of that time he decided that he was willing to give up
all the pleasures of the world, he was admitted to the
monastery. "From that day forth," said the rule of Benedict, "he shall not be allowed to depart from the monastery,
nor to shake from his neck the yoke of the rule."

Every man who became a monk had to promise three things: to obey the head of the monastery, to have no money, and never to marry. "A monk," said Benedict, "should have absolutely nothing, neither a book, nor a tablet, nor a pen."

A monastery was usually built around an enclosed square. All around the four sides of this open court, which had a garden in the center, was a covered passageway, called a cloister, where the monks could come for quiet walks.

On one side of the court was the part of the monastery where the monks slept. They had very small rooms, or cells. On another side of the court was the long dining room where they all ate together. On another side was the library and reading room, and on the fourth side was the chapel of the monastery.

In contrast to the rich dress of most men of the time, the monks wore long robes of coarse stuff, tied around the waist with a cord, with hoods which could be pulled up over the head when necessary. They had only the simplest food, and ate their meals either in complete silence, or listening as one of their members read aloud from some religious book.

Long before the sun was up, the monks began their devotions in the chapel of the monastery, and several times during the day the chapel bell rang, summoning them to Mass or to prayer and meditation.

Benedict wanted monasteries to be places where everyone worked. "They are truly monks," he wrote, "if they live by the labor of their hands as did our Father and his disciples." There was plenty of work to be done, for the monks made everything they needed. Outside the walls of the monasteries lay the fields where they raised their grain. In their gardens they raised vegetables and herbs which were useful in treating the sick. They cared for their flocks and herds. Food had to be cooked, clothes had to be washed, and the monastery had to be kept clean.

Although the monks in monasteries lived apart from the world, they were very valuable members of society and played an important part in the lives of the people of the Middle Ages.

The monks helped the poor and needy and they gave food to the hungry people of the neighborhood. So it became the custom for all people who were in trouble or who needed help to go to the nearest monastery. The sick also came there to be treated.

In the monasteries were schools where boys were taught to read, write, and speak Latin, the language of learning and the Church. The monks were the best-educated men of the Middle Ages. What they knew they gladly taught the boys who came to study with them. For centuries, almost the only schools in existence were those kept by the monks.

At that time there were no inns where travelers could stop and rest, but every monastery had a guest house and gave shelter to all who came to the gate. Anyone who asked for lodging was received and given food and a place to sleep whether he had money to pay or not. The prior invited guests to his own table, for Benedict's rule said: "All guests who come shall be received as though they were Christ, for he said, 'I was a stranger and ye took me in.' When, therefore, a guest is announced, the prior, or the brothers, shall run to meet him and treat him with every office of love."

MAKING BOOKS IN A MONASTERY

One of the most important things the monks did was to make books, or manuscripts, as they were called at that time. All books had to be written by hand, for the printing press had not yet been invented. During hundreds of years the monks made the only books there were.

The pages of the books were not made of paper as are those of modern books, for paper was not known in Europe during the Middle Ages. The monks wrote their books on calfskin or sheepskin, which they prepared themselves. First they soaked the hide in limewater to loosen the hair. Then they spread it on boards and cleaned it of the hair and flesh and washed it thoroughly. Then they stretched it on a frame to dry. Finally they washed it thoroughly once more and rubbed it smooth with pumice.

At last there was a beautiful creamy-white piece of parchment or vellum ready for the writing. From soot, mixed with gum, the monks made their ink; from berries and flowers which grew in their gardens they made colors; and they made pens from birds' quills or from reeds.

With all the things necessary for his work about him, the monk began slowly, carefully, making the big black

letters of his text. When he began a new chapter, he made a beautiful initial letter, rich in gold and color. Here and there throughout the text he scattered pictures of angels and saints, or scenes from the life he saw about him. Every page was made gay with color. Even the margins of some books were decorated with garlands, or with birds and butterflies, bees and ladybugs, flying in and out among the flowers.

The making of such a book was a long, tiring task, as can well be imagined. Day after day, from early morning till late at night, the patient monk bent over his work. It might take a year to make a single book. Little comments at the end of some books show how the monk felt when at last his work was finished. One monk wrote: "You do not know what it is to write. It cramps your back, it obscures your eyes, it breaks your sides and stomach."

The books were bound in leather, beautifully decorated, or in ivory, delicately carved. They had silver corners, and clasps of silver to keep them shut. The most precious books had covers of beaten gold, with jewels and colored enamel set in.

On the top of a steep hill in the central part of Italy is the little town of Assisi. There, near the end of the twelfth century, lived a wealthy merchant by the name of Pietro Bernardone. He had a son, Francesco, or Francis. Of all the gay youths of Assisi, the gayest was Francis. As his father was rich, Francis had plenty of money to spend and was always ready for a good time. He led a happy, carefree life.

One day, in church, Francis suddenly thought of the words of Christ when he told his disciples to preach the gospel and to "carry neither gold nor silver, nor money in their girdles, nor bag, nor two coats, nor sandals, nor staff." It seemed to Francis that these words were spoken to him. So he decided to give up his gay life and live as Christ had lived when he was on earth.

His father cast him off, but Francis gladly gave up all his money. From that time on, he said, he was wedded to Lady Poverty. After that, the young man who had always been so splendidly dressed wore only a rough brown gown with a rope tied around his waist. He went about tending the sick and helping those who were in trouble. So kind and gentle was he that everyone was his friend.

Some young men—among the richest and noblest of Assisi—believed that Francis had learned the secret of happiness and wished to join him and live as he did.

"Early tomorrow we will go to the church to learn from the Book of the Gospels what the Lord means us to do," said Francis.

Near the altar of the church was the Book of the Gospels on the stand, for all to read who wished. Kneeling before the altar, Francis prayed to God to show His will. When Francis opened the Bible, the first passage his eyes fell upon was: "If thou wilt be perfect, go, and sell all that thou hast and give to the poor and thou shalt have treasure in heaven."

A second time he opened the book. This time the first passage he read was: "Take nothing with you for your journey, neither staff, nor scrip, nor bread, nor money, neither have two coats." The third time Francis opened the book, he read: "If any man will come after me, let him deny himself and take up his cross, and follow me."

Closing the Bible, Francis cried, "Brothers, here is the rule of life for us and for all who join us. Let us go forth at once in the name of God and fulfill what we have heard."

Then those who had joined Francis went out and gave away all they had to the sick, to orphans and widows and old people. Clad in coarse gowns, they journeyed about among the towns of Italy preaching to the poor. Francis and his followers were called friars, which means "brothers."

Francis loved not only people but all living creatures. One day, it is said, when he came to a little town, he thought he would stop a while and preach to the people. The swallows made such noise singing in the near-by bushes that the people could not hear. "Our sisters the birds are praising their Maker," said the good friar. He listened to them for a while, then said gently, "Swallows,

my sisters, you have had all the morning for speaking and now it is my turn. Be silent for a little while until I have finished my preaching and then you can go on talking." The swallows ceased their twittering and were silent until Francis finished.

Year after year the influence of Francis spread, and the number of his followers grew greatly. They called themselves Little Brothers of the Poor. They taught people not to care for riches or power, but to love God and to help one another. Their days were filled with labors of love.

Not long after his death Francis was called St. Francis. Whenever a very holy man died, the Pope looked into his deeds, and if his life had been worthy, he was declared a saint. Many holy men and women were made saints during the Middle Ages. The places where they were buried became shrines. Throngs of people visited the shrines every year to pray and worship.

Devout Christians traveled to the shrines of St. Francis and other saints to offer up their prayers, but the shrine they most wanted to visit was the tomb of Christ in Jerusalem, for the place where Christ had lived and died was considered the most sacred in the world. Jerusalem was called the Holy City.

For centuries Palestine belonged to the Arabs. Although they were Mohammedans they treated the Christian pilgrims kindly. Then the Arabs were conquered by other Mohammedans, the Turks. The Turks in those days were cruel and barbaric. Pilgrims returning from Jerusalem told terrible tales of how they had been treated.

The Turks were growing steadily more powerful. They overran Asia almost to Constantinople. The emperor, who lived at Constantinople, was afraid that they would capture the city. He sent an urgent message to the Pope, Urban II, appealing for help. Pope Urban was alarmed. What if the Mohammedan conquerors should come over into Europe and crush Christianity?

The Pope called a meeting at Clermont in France in 1095. The wide plain around the town was dotted with tents, for the town itself could not accommodate the throngs who came to hear the Pope.

"Christian warriors," said the Pope, "on whom is the labor of avenging these wrongs and recovering this territory, if not upon you? Take ye the road to Jerusalem for the remission of your sins.

"If ye are hindered by love of children, parents, or wives, let none of your possessions detain you, no solicitude for your family affairs. Remember what the Lord says in the Gospel, 'He that loveth father or mother more than me is not worthy of me.' And again, 'Everyone that hath forsaken houses, or brethren, or sisters, or father, or mother, or wife, or children, or lands, for my sake, shall receive a hundredfold and shall inherit everlasting life.'"

All were deeply moved by the Pope's message.

"It is the will of God! It is the will of God!" rang out from all sides.

When the venerable Pope heard that, he said, "Most beloved brethren, today it is manifest in you what the Lord says in the Gospel, 'Where two or three are gathered together in my name, there am I in the midst of them.' Unless the Lord God had been present in your spirits you would not have uttered the same cry. Therefore I say to you, let this be your war cry, because the word is given to you by God. When an armed attack is made upon the enemy, let this one cry be raised by all the soldiers of God: 'It is the will of God! It is the will of God!'

"Whoever shall determine upon this holy pilgrimage and shall make his vow to God to that effect, shall wear the sign of the cross of the Lord on his forehead or on his breast. When, having fulfilled his vow, he wishes to return, let him place the cross on his back."

"The cross! The cross! Give us the cross!" came the cry from all sides, and the nobles pressed forward to receive a red cross of silk or cloth.

[271]

Soon people all over Europe were preparing for the journey to Jerusalem. The nobles took a long time getting ready, and many of the poor people decided to set out by themselves. They were unorganized, they had not enough food for the journey, and they had no money to buy any. Some of them plundered the people through whose lands they passed. This roused the anger of the people and they rose against these first-comers, killing many. Others died from sickness or the hardships of the trip. The real army of the Crusaders was made up of well-armed men led by some of the greatest nobles of Europe.

On a beautiful June morning in 1099 the walls of the Holy City came in sight. For three long years the Crusaders had toiled and suffered in the hope of reaching it. Now it lay before them. The flat white roofs of the houses shone in the bright sunlight. The round domes and the tall, slender minarets of the Mohammedan mosques stood out against the clear blue sky.

With battering-rams the Crusaders broke great holes in the walls of the city; with hurling-machines they threw showers of stones; their archers shot sheaves of arrows. Above all the din could be heard shouts, "It is the will of God! It is the will of God!" At last high wooden towers were pushed up against the walls, and the Crusaders swarmed over the top and took possession of the city. When the conquest was complete, they knelt at the tomb of Christ and gave thanks for their victory. Thus ended the First Crusade.

After about a hundred years the Turks took the Holy City again. Then for another hundred years kings and nobles led armies to the East to regain it, but they were not successful. By the middle of the thirteenth century the series of Crusades came to an end.

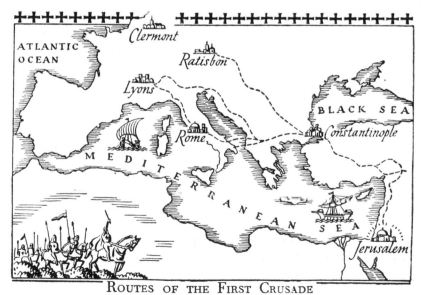

ROUTES OF THE FIRST CRUSADE

IN A MEDIEVAL TOWN

During the centuries when the tribes of barbarians were swarming over Europe there were almost no European towns. Many towns that had grown up under Roman rule had fallen into ruins. Most of the people lived in or near the castle-strongholds. Gradually little settlements began growing up at some place like the crossing of two roads, or a favorable spot on a river where trade could be carried on. Wandering merchants were glad to settle down in a place where they could sell their goods instead of having to travel around all the time. Some of these settlements gradually grew into towns.

Most of the towns were surrounded by high stone walls and moats, just as the castles were. They could be entered only through big gateways, where watchmen were on guard day and night to give the alarm at the approach of an enemy. In towers on each side of a gateway were narrow windows from which the people could shoot arrows. At nightfall the gates were closed and no one was allowed to go in or out of the town without special permission.

The towns were usually small and crowded. The narrow, winding streets had rows of high-peaked houses on both sides, some with their fronts quaintly carved and decorated. There were few of the conveniences we have today. There was no water system, no fire department, and no system of lighting. Most people did not go out after dark, but anyone who did had to carry a torch to light his footsteps and had to explain to the night watch why he was out.

THE CATHEDRAL BUILDERS

Every village and town had its church. In certain towns beautiful cathedrals were built. These were great churches with high, tapering spires. At first many pillars were needed to hold up the heavy roofs. It was also necessary to make the walls very thick, and the windows had to be quite small. As a result, the churches were dark and gloomy.

The architects of France were not satisfied with this way of building. To help the walls bear the weight, they were braced at certain points outside the church with solid masses of stonework called buttresses. In later buildings, masses of stonework, called flying buttresses, were separated slightly from the wall of the church and connected only at the top to the arches of the roof. The new way of building spread from France to many other countries.

[275]

Buttresses supported the roof of the church, and the wall spaces could be used for high, wide windows. The windows were made with tiny pieces of colored glass fitted together to make pictures of Bible stories or beautiful designs. When the bright sunlight came through the windows they glowed like colored jewels—deep red like rubies, blue like sapphires, green like emeralds.

How proud the people of a town were of their cathedral! With what love and devotion they worked to build and beautify it! Everyone joined in the task. The wealthy gave money; the poor gave their labor.

A writer tells about the building of one cathedral:

> Who has ever heard tell in times past that powerful princes of the world, that men brought up in honor and wealth, that noble men and women have bent their proud and haughty necks to the harness of carts, and that like beasts of burden they have dragged stones, cement, wood, to build the abode of Christ?
>
> And while men drag the heavy loads—so great is the weight that sometimes a thousand are attached to each wagon—they march in such silence that not a murmur is heard.

The cathedral was usually built in the form of a cross. At one end of the long part of the cross was the high altar. At the other end were the great entrance doors, carved with saints and angels. Above the doors there was often a stained-glass "rose window," beautifully designed. The altar and the pulpit were lovingly carved by hand. In the open places of the church were tombs of lords and ladies. High on the roof, outside, queer figures of beasts or odd looking human beings formed the waterspouts. These figures were called gargoyles.

So the house of God grew in beauty. When the cathedral was finished, its tall spires rose high above every other building in the town.

Every day the doors of the church were open. On weekdays anyone might enter for quiet meditation and prayer. On Sundays and holy days the high altar was ablaze with lights from the many tall, tapering candles. Banners and crosses were borne aloft to the altar by a procession of priests in richly embroidered robes, while all the people knelt, humbly worshiping.

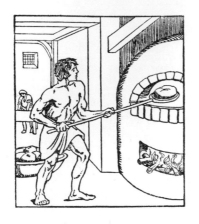

BUTCHER, BAKER
AND CANDLESTICK MAKER

In the towns the tradesmen joined together in guilds. Every man who followed a trade had to belong to the guild of that trade or he was not allowed to work. Most of the leatherworkers lived in one street, most of the goldsmiths in another, and so on. Their wares were displayed in the open windows of their shops, which were the front rooms of their homes.

A boy had to go through a long period of training in order to learn a trade. First he was put to work as an apprentice in the home of a master craftsman. The boy was to obey his master and work for him for seven years. During this time he was fed, clothed, and lodged with his master's family and received no pay. If he misbehaved, the master had the right to punish him. If the boy ran away, his master could go after him and bring him back.

When the years of his apprenticeship were over, the young workman was called a journeyman and could receive wages. For the next few years this new guild member journeyed from town to town working for a few months or years under the most skillful masters he could find in different places. When a journeyman had saved up enough money and had passed an examination to show that he knew his work, he could become a master workman.

The members of a guild decided at what price their goods
should be sold and what wages
their workmen should receive.
Everybody had to sell at what
was called the "just price." No
member was allowed to try to
get a brother member's business away from him by selling
at a lower price, or by buying
up all the material that was for sale, or by inviting his
neighbor's customers to his shop, or by taking his neighbor's workmen from him.

Each guild chose officers and levied dues to pay expenses. Everything made was inspected by guild officers.
They punished severely any shopkeeper or workman who
charged more than the guild price, who put out poor
articles, or who gave short weight. If a baker made his
loaves of bread too small, his oven might be destroyed. If
a shoemaker made shoes of poor leather, he might be put
out of the guild and then he could get no work. Working
at night was forbidden "by reason that no man can work
so neatly by night as by day."

The guild also took care of its members. Here is a rule
made by one of the guilds: "If anyone of the said trade
shall have work in his house that he cannot complete, or
if, for want of help, such work shall be in danger of being
lost, those of the said trade shall aid him, that so the said
work be not lost."

Another rule said: "If anyone of the said trade shall depart this life and have not wherewithal to be buried, he shall be buried at the expense of the common box. If, by chance, anyone of the said trade shall fall into poverty, whether through old age or because he cannot labor or work, and have nothing with which to keep himself, he shall have every week from the box seven pence for his support if he be a man of good repute. And after his decease, if he have a wife, a woman of good repute, she shall have weekly for her support seven pence from the said box, so long as she shall behave herself and keep single."

The different guilds built beautiful guildhalls, where the members held banquets and had many good times together.

On certain festival days the guilds gave plays. These were acted on two-story wagons, which were dragged about from one part of the town to another. The chief scenes from the Bible story were presented. Each guild gave a

single scene. First came the creation of the world, then the flood, then scenes from the lives of Abraham and Isaac, and so on through the Old and New Testaments. The play which the people loved best of all was that of the shepherds watching their flocks and seeing the star which led them to the place where Christ was born.

MARKETS AND FAIRS

On one or two days a week a market was held in the market place. Stalls were set up and the people of the town and the near-by manors sent their wares to be sold. Market days were gay and lively times, for all the good folk for miles around came to the big open space in the middle of the town to buy goods and to gossip.

The most exciting event in the lives of the townspeople was a fair. In an open space outside the town, tents and rows of stalls and booths were set up, and merchants displayed their wares. Soon every road leading to the town was crowded with a throng of travelers, as people from far and near flocked to the fair.

How interesting it must have been to the people of those days, who traveled so little, to see at the fair the many beautiful and unusual things they did not have in the little shops of their town.

There were good times at the fair, for people came to enjoy themselves as well as to buy. On the outskirts of the grounds were all kinds of amusing shows. There were clowns who made people laugh with their funny antics. Jugglers balanced poles on their noses or kept six balls in the air at the same time. Acrobats tumbled and wrestled.

There were strolling players, tightrope walkers, men with trained animals, and a host of other amusement-makers. Peddlers made their way through the jostling, good-natured crowds, loudly calling attention to their wares.

For a week or two the fair continued. Then long lines of merchants with their pack-horses streamed along the roads, the amusement-makers wandered to another place, and the town settled down once more to its customary life.

In the early part of the Middle Ages the towns were on the land owned by the nobles, and the people of each town were subject to their lord. They were compelled to furnish money to him in return for the protection he gave them. He made the laws of any town on his land and appointed the town's officers.

The nobles greatly interfered with the trade of the townspeople who traveled from one place to another with their goods. The nobles set up toll gates at the borders of their lands, and compelled all merchants to pay heavy tolls for the privilege of passing through.

When a bridge over a stream flowing through a noble's land was to be crossed, a toll had to be paid. If a noble lived on a river, all merchants who passed in boats had to pay tolls. Robber barons, who made their living by attacks on traveling merchants, were likely to seize goods on the road.

The people of the towns wanted to be free from the nobles, who were constantly interfering with their progress. They wanted to manage their own affairs and be able to do the things necessary for their success. As the townspeople gained wealth they demanded certain privileges.

Most nobles had plenty of land, but very little money. Sooner or later the noble on whose land a town was located would need money for one purpose or another, and the people of the town would give it to him in return for certain rights and privileges. Sometimes a noble was willing

[283]

to give up the right to tax a town. Instead of a yearly payment he would take a lump sum and free the people of the town from further payments of taxes.

Many of the towns were able to buy their freedom from their lords during the Crusades. It cost the lords a great deal to equip armies and keep them in the Holy Land for a year or two. By one means or another many towns gained their freedom.

The townsmen, when they got their rights, had them set down in a charter. The word *charter* comes from the Latin word *charta*, meaning "sheet of paper." The charter of a town was a paper giving a list of important things which the inhabitants could do without asking permission from a lord or a king. In the free towns the people made their own laws and elected the officials to take charge of the town's affairs.

TRADERS EAST

When the Crusaders were in the East, they saw in the
bazaars there many wonderful things which were unknown
in Europe at that time. They saw lovely fabrics made from
cotton, silk, and camel's hair. In the bazaars there was
carved ivory, brought from India. Traders had rare fruits
and beautiful jewels for sale. Their caravans brought perfume from Arabia and soft rugs from Persia. When the
Crusaders returned to Europe they took back with them
many of these new things.

The lords and ladies of Europe were delighted when
they saw the beautiful Eastern things and were eager to
have them. They wanted the soft materials for their clothes,
the jewels with which to adorn themselves, the sweet-
smelling perfumes, and the rare fruits for the table. To
brighten the stone walls of their gloomy castles, they
wanted gay tapestries, and they wanted carpets and rugs
for their stone floors. More than almost anything else, they
wanted the spices which came from the East—cloves, cinnamon, nutmeg, pepper.

The people of the Middle Ages were eager to have
spices. Since the cooks did not have ice to keep their meat

fresh, they used spices to preserve it. Then, too, food in those days was lacking in variety. Most of the vegetables common today were unknown. There were no green vegetables, no salads, few fruits. It is no wonder that the people enjoyed spiced foods.

Almost all dishes were so spiced that it was almost impossible to tell what they were made of. Here is a recipe found in one of the cookbooks of those times:

> Take one half-pound of figs, one half-pound of raisins; boil in wine, then mash them together. Then take currants, pine-seeds, cloves, mace, sugar of Cypress, and cast them in. Then put in a pot and take a few saunders, pepper, cinnamon, and a little saffron. If it be not thick enough, take a little flour and draw all through the strainer. Cast in salt and serve stiff.

There are many other recipes which show how fond of spices people were in the Middle Ages.

The enterprising merchants of the cities set out to get for their people the longed-for luxuries from the East. The Italian cities, especially Venice and Genoa, were the center of the trade with the East.

The riches of the East were sent to Europe by three routes. Goods went by land and water or by overland routes of thousands of miles across the vast plains and deserts of Asia. For safety, merchants traveled together in caravans, for there were robbers along the routes. The goods changed hands many times on their journey. One caravan carried them for several hundred miles, then they were sold to other merchants. At Constantinople they were sold again to Venetian merchants.

Sometimes the goods were a year or two on their way. The cost of freight of course was high, as each merchant through whose hands they passed had to make a profit. The goods were therefore very expensive when they were sold in Europe and only rich people could afford to have luxuries from the Orient.

For many years the merchants of Venice brought the luxuries of the East to the lords and ladies of Europe, while Venice grew rich and powerful. Along her canals rose the splendid marble palaces of her traders, and the Rialto, the commercial exchange of Venice, became the business center of the world.

TRADE ROUTES FROM THE EAST

While the people of the towns were gaining their freedom, the kings were increasing their power. All through the Middle Ages there was an almost constant struggle between the kings and the nobles. In the early days the kings were weak and the nobles strong. Some of the nobles had more land, more castles, and more men-at-arms than their king. Sometimes a great lord, more powerful than the others, called upon his vassals to rise against the king.

In their struggles with the nobles the kings were greatly aided by the use of gunpowder, which was introduced into Europe about the year 1340. As long as the old weapons like spears and crossbows, the battering-ram, and the movable tower were the only means of attacking castles, the nobles were well protected. As cannon and guns came into use and were improved, the thick walls, deep moats, and other castle defenses were of little value. By means of their armies, equipped with the new firearms and ammunition, kings were able to overthrow many nobles and take possession of their lands.

The people of the towns, engaged in trade, came to see that it was better for them to have one central authority which was strong enough to curb the lawless nobles. They were therefore willing to help the kings extend their power. Wise kings saw that it was to their advantage to favor the towns. The towns paid them taxes, and the richer the towns grew, the more they were able to pay toward the expenses of the government.

[288]

The kings built roads and made them safe for travel from one end of a country to another. Often they granted merchants and traders special privileges. One of the old English laws says:

> All merchants may safely and securely go out of England and come into England, and also delay and pass through England as well by land as by water, for the purpose of buying and selling, free from all evil taxes, subject to the ancient and right customs.

Here is part of a charter granted by a king of England:

> Know that we have granted, and by this our charter have confirmed, that our town of Helleston shall be a free town, and that the burgesses shall be free from tolls throughout our realm; whether the tolls be for crossing a bridge, or using a road, or for having a stall in a market, or for loading a ship, or for the use of the soil. We grant also to the people that their cases concerning the matters and tenures of their town shall be heard only within the walls of their own town.

Thus, with the help of the towns, the kings brought to an end the power of the nobles. Europe was changed from many small areas, each ruled by a lord, into several different nations. In each nation the people were bound together by loyalty to their king and country.

Talking Together

1. In the days when there was no central government in the country, what services did each of these groups of people render: the nobles, the vassals, the serfs?

2. You have read how boys trained to become knights. Discuss ideals of knighthood resembling the aims of good citizenship today.

3. Among the amusements which people enjoyed in medieval days, which would you have enjoyed most?

4. Gunpowder was first used in Europe about 1340. Discuss how this helped to bring about new freedom for the towns.

Interesting Things to Try

1. The group may dramatize the work of the peasants, such as plowing fields, sowing grain, harvesting crops, making flour, baking bread, preparing meat, making cider, and laboring to make the lord's life comfortable and pleasant.

2. Some boys and girls enjoy making illuminated manuscripts, or books, as the monks did. You might choose a poem or a passage from the Bible. Print it and decorate it with designs in color.

3. You might divide your class into groups and become guild workers, weavers, potters, woodworkers, printers, or woodcarvers. Different places in the room could be used for your shops. You could have apprentices, journeymen, and masters.

4. Ask your teacher to secure the motion pictures "St. Francis of Assisi" and "The Crusades." Follow the suggestions given in the section "Seeing and Learning" on page 243, in studying these films.

Let's Read

Man and His Records, by Franklin Barnes. Your group may read "Writing in the Middle Ages," which tells you more about the work of the monks in making their manuscripts.

Words on Wings, by Lillian J. Bragdon. In the chapter on "Poetry and Song" you find stories of minstrels and troubadours.

Medieval Days and Ways, by Gertrude Hartman. When your group reads the chapters "Little Brothers of the Poor," "God Wills It!" "Christmas Revels," and "Guildsmen Give Their Plays," you understand more about life in the Middle Ages.

Great Moments in Freedom, by Marion F. Lansing. The story of St. Francis of Assisi, "A Rich Boy Who Became Poor," is sure to interest you.

The Story of Simpson and Sampson, by Munro Leaf. Everyone enjoys this humorous story.

The Boy Knight of Reims, by Eloise Lownsbery. Some of you may read together this story of cathedral builders.

Marching to Jerusalem, by Ruth Langland Holberg. A story of the Children's Crusade that will interest you.

A Story of the Middle Ages, by Donald Culross Peattie. This book, with its large colored illustrations, gives you a good idea of life in the Middle Ages.

The Crusades, by Anthony West. The stories "Peter the Hermit Sets Out," "Two Kings Turn Crusaders," and "Richard Becomes the Lionhearted" are especially good.

The Story of Peace and War, by Tom Galt. An account of man's attempt to bring world peace through organizations. These efforts date from the early Greeks to the United Nations. Read "Medieval Wars and Peace Plans."

MAKING A BIBLIOGRAPHY

A bibliography is a list of books on a subject such as the Middle Ages. An annotated bibliography is one with a brief note about each book. "Let's Read" is an annotated bibliography giving the titles and authors of books about each unit.

In the list of books in this unit under "Let's Read," you may find the annotations useful.

Your class may begin a list by finding books on the Middle Ages. Write the title, author, publisher, and two or three sentences which tell something important about each book. You might put your list together on the blackboard or on a chart. Keep a card file of the books you find. You then have an annotated bibliography which helps you in the study of this unit.

QUIZ YOURSELF

How Carefully Did You Read?

Below is a list of terms used in talking about the Middle Ages. Write the numbers 1 to 10 on a separate sheet of paper. After each number place the correct word or words that will complete the sentence that has the same number. Then read the sentence with the right word in it. *Do not write in this book.*

1. During the Middle Ages members of trades formed themselves into ——.
2. A lord's estate was called a ——.
3. Nobles exhibited their skill in fighting in mock battles called ——.
4. Monks lived in ——.
5. In the Middle Ages books were written on ——.
6. —— journeyed about doing good.
7. The —— —— grew rich by seizing goods and wealth of traveling merchants.
8. The —— belonged to the land of the nobles.
9. The —— gave protection to his people.
10. The —— were holy wars to recover Jerusalem and the tomb of Christ.

tournaments	monasteries
robber barons	parchment
serfs	friars
manor	guilds
lord	Crusades

VIII

FOUNDATIONS
OF FREEDOM

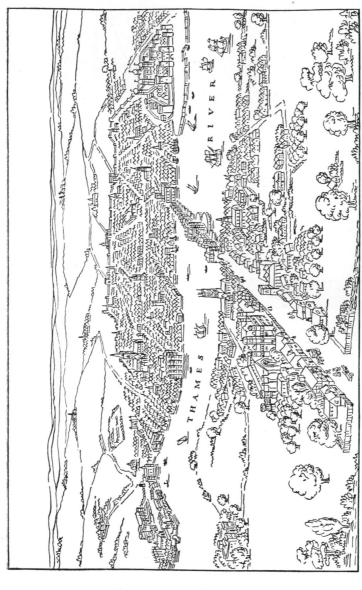

OLD LONDON. London Town grew up along the Thames River with the English House of Parliament as the center of representative government to protect the rights slowly gained by the common people.

FOUNDATIONS OF FREEDOM

GUILTY OR NOT GUILTY?

In the early Middle Ages, when the German tribes were overrunning Europe, the law courts which had been established by the Romans in various places fell into disuse. These tribes had several strange ways of trying people accused of having committed crimes. When the Angles and Saxons came to England, they introduced these methods there.

One way of deciding whether a person was guilty or not guilty was called the ordeal by fire. With a pair of tongs a priest carried a piece of iron to a fire and heated it till it was red hot. The red-hot iron was placed in the hand of the accused, who took three steps carrying it. His hand was bound up for three days. Then the priest examined it. If the sore had healed, the accused person was thought to be innocent. If there was a blister on his hand "half as large as a walnut," he was declared guilty.

Another form of trial was the ordeal by water. In this, an accused person plunged his hand into a pitcher of boiling water to show whether he was innocent or guilty.

The usual method of finding out whether a noble was guilty was called trial by combat. The accused and the accuser met before a judge. After reciting his wrongs, the accuser threw down his glove, or gauntlet. The accused exchanged this for his own glove, showing that he accepted the challenge. Then the two prepared for combat to prove which was in the right.

First they knelt down before a priest and each solemnly swore on the cross and the Bible that he was in the right. The marshal called out, "Let them begin! Let them do their best!" And the fight began. It was thought that God would give victory to the man who was in the right. The noble who was beaten was dragged off in disgrace, and his armor was thrown away.

After trial by combat to settle legal matters had been given up, the method was still used in the form of the duel to settle points of honor.

These methods of trying people were not very good ways of finding out whether people really were guilty of wrongdoing, because there was no attempt to find out

the facts about a crime. In time it was discovered that many wrongdoers whom people knew to be guilty escaped punishment.

THE BEGINNING OF TRIAL BY JURY

King Henry II, who began to rule England in 1154, introduced in his country a better method of trying people. He appointed certain men as judges and sent them to all parts of the country. They had to visit a district at least once a year.

When one of the king's judges came to a district, the persons suspected of having committed crimes were brought before him. He picked out "twelve good men and true" who might know the facts of the crimes to tell what they knew. As they were obliged to swear to "tell the truth, the whole truth, and nothing but the truth," they came to be called jurors, from the Latin word meaning "I swear."

The men composing the jury had to be of the same rank as that of the person being tried. Hence came the expression "a jury of one's peers," meaning a jury of one's equals. This new kind of trial introduced by Henry II was the beginning of trial by jury.

The judges kept a careful record of all the disputes as they arose, time after time, and gave the same punishment for the same kind of crime. Thus, in time, a body of laws developed which came to be called the "common law" because it was common throughout England. The law was the same for the poor and the weak as for the rich and the strong.

The right of trial by jury came to be regarded as one of the most precious rights of English people, for it gave to everyone, even the humblest in the nation, a fair trial.

THE KING MUST OBEY THE LAW

King Henry II was a good king, who ruled according to law, but his son John was one of the worst kings England ever had. He was extravagant and greedy for money. Again and again he demanded immense sums from the people. They dared not refuse to pay, for the king had all sorts of ways of punishing them if they did. Men were thrown into prison and their goods and lands were seized, merely because they were enemies of the king.

Not even the highest nobles were free from fines and taxes of the most tyrannical kind. A chronicle of the time says: "There were at this time in the kingdom of England many nobles whose wives and daughters the king had insulted; others whom he had by unjust exactions reduced to the extreme of poverty; some whose parents and kindred he had exiled, converting their inheritances to his own use."

At last, in 1214, the important barons decided that they would endure John's bad government no longer. They went together to a church and "commencing with those of highest rank, they all swore on the great altar that if the king refused to grant them liberties and laws, they would withdraw all allegiance to him and make war on him until he should, by a charter furnished with his seal, confirm to them all that they required." Then they went to London and demanded that John agree to give them the charter.

Fearing that they would attack him, John put off the nobles by saying, "Your petition contains matter weighty and arduous. You must grant me time till Easter, that with due deliberation I may be able to do justice to myself and satisfy the dignity of the crown."

The barons waited until the spring of the next year. By that time many other nobles had joined them, so that they had a "countless host." When the king learned this he sent a messenger to inquire what "laws and liberties" the barons wanted. The barons gave the messenger the charter they had made, and declared, "These are our claims and if they are not granted, our arms shall do us justice."

One by one the demands of the nobles were read to the king. John listened with a scornful smile on his face. Finally, in a rage he burst out, "Why do not the barons ask me for my crown also? Their demands are vain and visionary and are unsupported by any pleas of reason whatsoever."

The king's followers urged him to yield, but he bade the messenger go back and repeat every word he had said.

Then the barons took up arms against the king and in May they marched on London. They were joyfully welcomed by the people.

John saw that he must yield. So he sent a messenger to assure the barons that for the good of the nation he was ready freely to grant all the rights and liberties they asked. He wished them to name the day and the place of meeting.

"Let the day be the fifteenth of June," said the barons, "and the place, the meadow which is called Runnymede."

Runnymede, which means the "Meadows of Council," was a broad, green meadow on the Thames River not far from London. It was there, in the early days, that the Anglo-Saxons held their councils. On this meadow the nobles were to meet John.

A "multitude of knights, all thoroughly well armed," marched from London, their armor gleaming in the sun, their banners flying, and made their camp at Runnymede. The royal tent was pitched near by. "King John, seeing that he was inferior in strength to his barons, without raising any difficulty, granted the laws and liberties and confirmed them with his charter."

So, on June 15, 1215, in that meadow consecrated to freedom by ancient associations, King John set his seal on Magna Charta, the Great Charter, as it came to be called.

The barons departed, believing that "God had compassionately touched the king's heart." So said Matthew Paris, a writer of the time. "And all and everyone hoped that England, being by the grace of God freed in their time from bondage, would enjoy peace and liberty.

"But far otherwise was it, and far differently from what was expected did events happen. The son of Belial whispered words of discord in the king's ears: 'Alas, wretched man, to what a state of slavery have you fallen! You have been a king, now you are the scum of the people; you have been the greatest, now you are the least.'"

Then the king appealed to the Pope, saying that the barons had won the charter by force. The Pope declared that John need not keep the promises he had made to his rebellious barons and excommunicated "all the disturbers of the king and kingdom of England until the said barons shall give satisfaction to the king for the injuries they have inflicted upon him and shall return to their duty."

John then turned on his nobles with hired soldiers from the continent. Burning, plundering, and laying waste the land, he met with success everywhere until he became ill. In a short time he died, leaving his kingdom to his nine-year-old son, Henry III. He had not been able to abolish the charter or to conquer the nobles.

Johannes dei Gra Rex Angl Dns Hybn Dux
Sciatis nos intuitu dei z p Salute anime nre et omium
cecte Cardinalis Henr Dublin Archiepis itimi London, z Petri
Viroy Willmi Marscall Comitis Pembrok Willmi Comitis Sar z
Thome Basset Alani Basset. Philippi de Albini Robti de Ropp
Sua integra z libertate ssuas illesos z ita Volum observari qd app
him z z eam optimim y dno Papa Innocentio tertio confirmari C

THE GREAT CHARTER OF ENGLISH FREEDOM

Magna Charta was important in the story of English
freedom because it stated in black and white that there
were certain things which a king could not do. A king
could not rule exactly as he pleased; he had to observe the
"law of the land."

There were certain rights included in the charter which
were very important in securing freedom and justice to the
people. One was that no freeman was to be banished, or
thrown into prison, or put to death merely because some
tyrannical king wished to get rid of him. It must first be
proved that he was guilty of breaking a law. One clause
of the charter stated that "no freeman shall be taken, or
imprisoned, or outlawed, or banished, or in any way destroyed, nor will we go upon him, nor will we send against
him save by the legal judgment of his peers, or by the
law of the land." Another clause said, "To no one will
we deny or delay right or justice," which meant that a

person who was accused of having committed a crime had the right to a speedy trial. He could not be thrown into prison and kept there indefinitely.

No longer was a king to demand money from his people. When he wanted money he must call together the Great Council, composed of the important nobles, and they would decide whether they would give it to him, for the charter said: "No scutage [tax] shall be levied except by the general council of the realm."

Twenty-five of the highest nobles in the kingdom were chosen by the barons to see that John kept the promises he had made in the charter. "They have given me five-and-twenty overlords!" cried John when he heard about this.

Many copies of the charter were made and were sent about to the principal churches to be read to the people. There was great rejoicing throughout the country.

The barons who forced John to give them Magna Charta were probably thinking only of their own troubles and were concerned only with preserving their own rights and privileges. The promises made by John in the charter, however, became the foundation upon which, in later days, the people of England built up their freedom.

Long after the names of those who wrote the charter had been forgotten, the people looked back upon Magna Charta with pride. After the time of John and his barons, kings often tried to rule despotically. The people cried out against them and declared that in Magna Charta their ancestors had "gained full protection for property and person to every human being that breathes English air."

Henry III was the king who followed John. In his reign the people of England began working out the new form of government. This was to bring them the freedom and justice which King John had promised them in Magna Charta.

Henry was not cruel and tyrannical as his father had been, but he was weak and extravagant. Magna Charta had said plainly that the Great Council was to give its consent before the king could levy taxes. Although Henry had agreed to keep Magna Charta, he constantly levied taxes without getting the consent of the Great Council. Once again, in spite of what the barons had accomplished at Runnymede, they were suffering from the misrule of a tyrannical king.

At one meeting of the Great Council, all the barons appeared in full armor. Greatly alarmed, the king asked timidly, "Am I, then, your prisoner?"

"No, sire," replied one of the barons, "but your extravagance has brought the country to such a state of misery that we demand reforms."

The barons then drew up a series of new laws, to which the king agreed; but Henry did not keep the new laws any better than he had kept the old ones.

The next time Henry asked the barons for money he was treated with scorn. Then he offered to submit to excommunication if he should fail to keep his word. The Great Council was called together and the meeting was

attended by all the important barons and churchmen. The highest dignitaries of the Church, dressed in their splendid robes and carrying lighted candles in their hands, walked in a procession to the hall of Westminster where the king awaited them. Magna Charta, on which his father, John, had placed his great seal, was read to the king.

When the reading was finished, the bishops and archbishops threatened excommunication to anyone who broke the charter. Then they flung down their lighted candles, crying, "May all those who take away our liberties perish even as these lights perish!"

As the candles were lighted again, Henry declared: "All these promises will I faithfully keep as I am a man, a Christian, a knight, and a crowned king. So help me, God."

In spite of all this, Henry continued doing as he had always done. "The king breaks everything," said one of the barons. "He breaks the laws, his good faith, and his promises."

The Great Council met frequently to discuss the troubles of the barons with their unruly king. During that time it came to be called Parliament.

A CHAMPION OF FREEDOM

In the course of this struggle between the barons and Henry there arose a great champion of freedom, Simon de Montfort. Born in France, he had come to England when he was a young man. He was married to the king's sister, and for many years was Henry's faithful friend. As the king continued to break his promises, however, Simon took the part of the barons.

Henry was very angry when Simon turned against him. Once he called Simon a traitor.

"Traitor!" exclaimed Simon. "If you were not the king, you should soon repent that insult!"

"I shall never repent anything so much as that I allowed you to grow and fatten in my dominions," replied the king.

Henry feared Simon more than he feared any other man. One day the king was overtaken by a terrible thunderstorm and took refuge in a castle where Earl Simon was staying. After a while the storm cleared, but still the king lingered.

"May it please your majesty," said Simon, "the storm is passed. There is no longer anything for you to fear."

"Thunder and lightning I greatly fear," replied Henry, "but I fear thee more than all the thunder and lightning in the world."

"Sire," said Simon, "it is unjust that you should fear me, your friend, faithful to you and to the kingdom of England. It is your enemies and false flatterers that you should fear."

Year after year Henry's rule grew worse. At last affairs came to a crisis. The barons were determined to put an end to the king's bad government. Led by Earl Simon, who "fought stoutly like a giant for the liberties of England," the rebellious barons took up arms against the king. In a great battle they were victorious and King Henry and his son, Prince Edward, were taken prisoners.

After the battle Earl Simon became the real ruler of England.

"Now England breathes in the hope of liberty!" wrote a poet of the time.

Simon at once began making reforms in the government. He realized that in order to rule successfully he must rally to his support all classes of people. To secure the good will of the common people he made a change in Parliament. To a meeting which he held in 1265, he not only called the great lords and churchmen, but requested the counties to send "two knights from the loyal, honest, discreet knights of each shire, and the towns to send two of the discreet, loyal, and honest citizens and burgesses." This was the first time that the plain people were represented in Parliament.

Earl Simon did not rule long, for by a daring trick Prince Edward escaped from prison. A new horse had been given him and he asked to be allowed to ride it. One day he went out with his guards and rode races with them until their horses were tired out. Then he sprang upon a fresh horse and galloped off, calling out, "Farewell to you, gentlemen. I have enjoyed the pleasure of your company long enough."

The king's supporters rallied around the young prince. Many of the barons, who were jealous of Earl Simon's power, deserted him.

"Though all should leave me," declared Simon, "I and my four sons will remain true to the just cause which I have sworn to uphold for the honor of the Church and the good of the realm."

Simon's enemies united against him, and a great battle was fought. When Simon saw how large was the army against him, he said, "Let us commend our souls to God, for our bodies belong to the enemy."

In the battle Simon was wounded. As the great patriot lay dying, he said, "It is God's grace."

GOVERNMENT BY THE PEOPLE

It might seem as if Earl Simon accomplished little, but often in this world the good work begun by one man is carried on by another after the first man's death. So it was in this case. Simon's work was continued by Prince Edward, who became the next king, Edward I.

Edward loved his people and tried to be a good king. "No man ever asked mercy of me and was refused," he once said. He loved truth and justice and tried to be fair to all men.

His motto was "Keep troth," and he was faithful to it. If he said he would do a thing he kept his promise. He did not care for show or fine dress. "I should not be a better king, however splendidly I dressed," he said. For a king he lived a simple life.

The lessons which Edward had learned during the last years of his father's reign helped him to rule wisely. Although he had fought against Earl Simon, he saw that Simon's reforms were good for England and he decided to carry on the good work.

Edward made many changes for the better in the way of carrying out the laws, and made it easier for the people to have justice. He called together many Parliaments during his reign.

At length, in 1295, he called a Parliament in which all classes of people—the church, the nobles, and the common people—had someone to represent them. "It is right," said Edward, "that matters that concern all should be settled by those who can speak for all."

In the changes which Simon de Montfort and King Edward made in Parliament they were following the main principle of representative government.

This is the principle that all who obey the laws should have a voice in the making of the laws. This was the beginning of representative government in England.

PARLIAMENT MAKES THE LAWS

At first Parliament had little power. It did not make
the laws. The right to do that belonged to the king. The
chief business of Parliament was to hear the king's requests
for taxes and grant them. Parliament did not meet regu-
larly. It met only when it was called by the king, and the
king called it only when he needed money.

It was not long, however, before Parliament, in return
for the money it gave the king, began petitioning him for
changes in the laws made by him. If the king decided to
grant a request, he replied to the petition, "The king wills
it," and the petition became law. If he intended to refuse,
he answered, "The king will consider it."

Gradually Parliament began holding back the voting of
taxes until the king promised to correct grievances of which

the members complained. The king had to have the money and found it difficult to refuse whatever Parliament demanded, for if he did, the money he wanted was not forthcoming. In this way Parliament was able to bring about many necessary reforms.

After a while Parliament ceased to petition the king for better laws. It drew up its own laws in the form of bills. If the king approved a bill it became a law. If the king said in Latin, "*Veto*," which means "I forbid," it did not become a law. Thus Parliament began to make the laws of England.

PARLIAMENT IS DIVIDED INTO TWO HOUSES

At first the representatives of the counties and towns merely stood near the entrance of the hall where the nobles and the higher clergy were meeting. The Commons, as the county and town representatives were called, did not take part in the deliberations. They were not consulted about most of the business. They were needed only to give their consent to certain taxes. The king's needs were stated to them and they met by themselves to consider them. Then they returned to Parliament to report. The individual members had no right to speak; their Speaker alone spoke for them all.

If the Commons had continued to report along with the Lords they might not have gained much influence in government; but in 1340 came an important step when, for the first time, the Commons met by themselves. After that, the clergy and the nobility formed the House of Lords, and the representatives of the towns and counties joined to form the House of Commons.

As time passed, the House of Commons grew steadily in importance. The townspeople and all those who engaged in trade were becoming richer, and the taxes they supplied exceeded those of the nobles and clergy. This rapidly increasing wealth raised the middle class to a position of importance. As they grew in importance, they demanded greater political freedom.

In the fifteenth century the House of Commons made a rule that all bills for money must originate with it. The people wanted to control their government, and they knew that they could do this only by controlling the money spent by the government.

THE SERFS SEEK THEIR FREEDOM

The liberties won in the long struggle for representative government were for freemen only; they were not for the serfs, or peasants. Most of the people in England were still serfs, and they had no voice in their government.

For centuries the peasants of England, as well as of other countries of Europe, humbly accepted the fact that the people of higher rank should have more luxuries, more privileges, and greater power. They knew nothing different from the way they lived, and it never occurred to them that any better kind of life was possible for them. Then in the later Middle Ages a new spirit came to the lowly peasants. They wanted better living conditions and they began demanding more freedom and a greater share in the good things of life.

One man of high rank complained thus of this new spirit which was spreading among the peasants: "The world goeth fast from bad to worse. Laborers of old were not wont to eat wheaten bread; their meal was of beans and coarser corn and their drink of water alone. Cheese and milk were a feast to them, and rarely they ate of other dainties. Then the world was ordered aright for folk of this sort."

The towns brought to many serfs the means of breaking their barriers and winning their freedom. The workers in

the towns were much better off than the peasants on the manors. They had better food, better clothes, more comfortable homes. They could marry as they pleased; they could come and go as they wished. "Town air makes a man free," said an old proverb.

Many discontented serfs ran away from the manors and

[313]

took refuge in the towns. When a peasant ran away his lord could go after him, and could severely punish him if he was caught; but if a peasant succeeded in hiding in a town for a year and a day, he might claim his freedom. "If any serf shall dwell unclaimed for a year and a day in a chartered town so that he hath been received into the community or guild of that town as a citizen," said one of the old laws, "that fact shall free him from villeinage." Many peasants were able to secure their freedom by hiding in the towns.

With the growth of trade and industry people began to use money more freely. Some serfs were able to buy their freedom, for the nobles would often accept money payments from the peasants instead of services. Some peasants bought freedom for their sons so that they need not be serfs. In these ways many peasants were able to gain their freedom.

These changes took place slowly. Then came an event which hastened the improvements which might otherwise have taken centuries to bring about.

THE BLACK DEATH

In the year 1348 a terrible plague called the Black Death swept over Europe. The people of those days were not very clean and did not know how to take care of their health as people do today, so the disease spread rapidly. "Advancing from place to place, it attacked men without warning," said an account written by a person who lived at the time.

"Very many of those who were attacked in the morning it carried out of human affairs before noon. And no man whom it had doomed to die did it permit to live more than three days."

Thousands upon thousands of people died. Most of them were peasants. In some places all the families in whole villages were wiped out.

So many serfs died that the nobles had not enough people to do the necessary work. Their lands were left untilled, the crops neglected. "The sheep and cattle went wandering over fields and through crops, and there was none to go and drive or tend them. There was such a scarcity of servants that no one knew what to do. Wherefore many sheep and cattle perished for lack of herdsmen, and crops perished in the fields for want of someone to gather them."

Seeing their lands going to ruin, the nobles made desperate efforts to get workers on almost any terms. The peasants who still lived after the plague refused to work unless they received more pay than the lords had given them in the past. They hired themselves to the landlord who would give them the most money. The nobles were losing their control over the working people.

The nobles were threatened with ruin by the extravagant demands of the peasants. Parliament tried to put an end to this state of affairs by fixing the rate of wages. "Every man or woman of whatever years," said a law passed in 1351, "shall be bound to serve the employer who shall require him to do so, and shall take only the wages which

were accustomed to be taken in the neighborhood two years before the plague began."

Peasants were forbidden by Parliament to leave the place where they had lived in search of better wages elsewhere. Runaway peasants, if caught, were to be severely punished. These laws aroused the peasants, because their former masters were trying to force them back into bondage.

ALL MEN ARE CREATED EQUAL

Among the peasants leaders arose who declared that the poor man was as important as the man of higher birth and that every man had certain rights, no matter how poor or lowly his station. One of these leaders was John Ball, a poor priest. For years he traveled about, talking to the peasants on Sunday as they came out of church.

[316]

At one time John Ball addressed a group of peasants in this fashion:

> My good friends, things will never be well in England so long as there be vassals and lords. By what right are they whom we call lords greater folks than we? On what grounds have they deserved it? For what reason do they hold us in bondage? Are we not all descended from the same parents, Adam and Eve? And what reason do they give why they should be more masters than ourselves, if it be not that they make us gain for them by our toil what they spend in their pride?

There was a low murmuring among the peasants. Some of them said: "What John Ball says is right." Then the peasants became quiet again as John Ball continued:

> They are clothed in velvet, warm in their furs and ermines, while we are forced to wear poor clothing. They have wine, spices, and fine bread, while we have only oat cakes and water to drink. They have leisure and fine castles, while we must brave the wind and the rain in our labors in the fields. And yet it is by our toil that these men have the wherewithal to support their pomp.

Wherever men were oppressed and discontented, they listened eagerly to John Ball's sermons and began to say that there should no longer be lords and serfs. Three times the priest was put in prison for saying that all men should be equal, but as soon as he came out of prison he began preaching again.

Thus things went on for years, with unrest spreading among the peasants.

WAT TYLER LEADS A REVOLT OF THE PEASANTS

In the spring of 1381, some of the peasants decided to go to London and put their grievances before the king, Richard II, a boy of fourteen. The peasants believed that the young king was their best friend and that, if they put their troubles before him, he would help them. So they tramped along the country lanes under the leadership of Wat Tyler, armed with clubs, rusty swords, bows and arrows; farmers with their scythes and pitchforks; blacksmiths with their hammers; woodcutters with their axes. Everywhere, as they passed through villages and towns, other men left their work and joined them until there were about sixty thousand.

In time these rough, wild-looking men reached London. As they assembled in an open space, John Ball preached to them, telling them that they had an opportunity, if they chose to take it, of casting off the yoke they had borne so long and of winning the freedom they had always desired. They should take good courage and behave like the husbandman of Scripture, who gathered the wheat into his barn but uprooted and burned the tares, or weeds, which choked the good grain. The tares of England were her oppressive rulers. Now harvest time had come, in which it was the people's duty to pluck and make way with the tares—the evil lords, unjust judges, and every man who was dangerous to the common good. Then the people would have peace for the present and security for the future. When the great ones had been cut off, all men would enjoy equal freedom, for all would have the same nobility, rank, and power.

Richard II, the young king, was at this time in the Tower of London with his principal advisers. The mob of peasants surrounded the Tower and shouted for him.

The king's advisers, fearing for their lives, said: "Sire, if you can appease them by fair words, it will be so much the better to grant what they ask, for should we begin what we cannot go through with, it will be all over with us and our heirs, and England will be a desert."

The king then promised to meet the peasants the next day at Mile End, an open meadow near London. On his arrival at Mile End he found the peasants assembled. Advancing toward them he said, "My good people, I am your king and lord. What will ye?"

"We will that thou set us free forever," shouted the peasants, "us and our lands, and that we be no longer serfs nor held in bondage."

[319]

The king replied: "I grant your wish. Now, therefore, return to your homes and the places whence you came, leaving two or three men from each village, to whom I will order charters to be given sealed with my seal, which they shall carry back, with every demand you have made fully granted. Go home and dwell in peace and no harm shall come to you."

Many of the peasants set out for their homes, but their leaders, including Wat Tyler, remained behind with about thirty thousand followers. They wanted to wait until the clerks gave them the charters, for they realized that if all the peasants left, there would be no one to see that the king kept his promise.

A few days later about twenty thousand peasants gathered at a place called Smithfield. The king happened to come riding by, and Wat Tyler said to his men, "Here is the king. I will go speak to him. Move not hand nor foot until I give the signal."

Wat rode boldly up to King Richard. "King," he said, "dost thou see all those men out there?"

"I see them," answered Richard, "but why dost thou ask?"

"Because they are all at my will and have sworn by their faith and loyalty to do whatever I should bid them," replied Wat. "Dost thou think that these men ought to go away without your promise in writing to take with them?"

"Tell your companions to go to their homes and the writing shall be given, village by village, and town by town," promised the king.

"Nay, we will take the writings with us," replied Wat in a loud, threatening tone.

While Wat was speaking in his rough way, he played with his dagger and laid hold of the bridle of the king's horse. One of the king's attendants, thinking that Wat intended to kill the king, stepped forward, shouting, "How darest thou so to behave and say such words in the presence of the king? Verily, if I die for it, thou shalt suffer for thy insolence." He drew his sword and struck Wat such a blow that Wat was just able to turn to the people, crying, "Treason!" before he fell to the ground.

[321]

From the mob of peasants there rose a great shout: "We are betrayed! They have slain our captain! Our leader is dead! We will die with our captain or avenge him. Shoot, lads, shoot!" and hundreds of arrows were quickly placed in the bows.

It was a critical moment. The royal party was in danger of being overwhelmed by the angry peasants. But the boy king rode forward fearlessly toward the surging mass, crying out: "What are you doing, my lieges? Will you shoot your king? Never care for Walter's fall. He was a traitor. I will be your chief and your captain. You shall have from me that which you seek."

Then Richard rode back to his lords and asked what he should do next.

"Make for the fields," they said. "If we flee, our ruin is certain. Let us gain a little time and we shall be assisted by our good friends in the city who are preparing and arming their servants."

The king turned his horse toward the open country, and the peasants, not knowing what to do without their leader, obediently followed him. By this time the alarm had spread to London and a great number of citizens came to help the king and his party. They surrounded the peasants, and a proclamation was issued ordering every person who was not an inhabitant of London to leave immediately.

For days clerks were kept busy writing the charters which Richard had promised the peasants. The nobles, however, refused to give up their rights. They said that they **never** did and never would agree to the freeing of their serfs, which would mean their downfall. The king, they said, could not take away their serfs without their consent. "And this consent," they declared, "we have never given and will never give, were we all to die in one day."

Then Richard turned against the peasants and refused **to** grant them the charters which he had promised to them. "Serfs you were, and serfs you are," he said. "In bondage you shall remain." He marched through the country with forty thousand men, executing all the peasant leaders.

So the revolt of the peasants failed. But fear of further uprisings made the nobles grant their workers better conditions. In a short time freemen working for wages **and** farmers renting their farms took the place of serfs.

For several centuries the people of Europe had struggled for greater freedom and justice. But the mass of the people had been powerless in the hands of the kings and a few nobles. As serfs they lived in poverty and misery. They had paid in toil and lack of liberty for food, clothing, shelter, and safety.

In the later Middle Ages a new spirit came to the poor people. They began saying that every man, no matter how humble his station, had certain rights. These were times of slow but steady progress for the plain people, especially those in England. By their efforts they succeeded in lifting themselves out of the bondage in which their forefathers had lived.

In the thirteenth century the foundations of representative government were laid in England. This was a tremendous step forward in the gaining of liberty by the people. In earlier centuries kings and nobles had ruled exactly as they wished. With a parliament made up of their representatives the people of England gained the power to make the laws for their own welfare. No longer could a king or a great noble govern as he pleased. He had to rule in accordance with the laws made by the representatives of the people.

Through representative government the people gained power to rule their own lives. A noted judge of the fifteenth century wrote: "A king of England at his pleasure cannot make any alterations in the laws of the land without the consent of his subjects, nor burden them against their wills with strange impositions. The king is appointed to protect his subjects in their lives, properties, and laws. Every inhabitant of this kingdom enjoys the result which his land and his cattle produce for him. He uses them to please himself and no one can prevent him from doing so. He is not brought to justice except before the common judges and according to the law of the land."

Thus during the Middle Ages the plain people of England slowly gained political liberty. They laid the foundations of democracy and began building the representative government which was to make them a nation of free people. This was England's great contribution to civilization during the Middle Ages.

Talking Together

1. When you trace the steps by which the people in England gained their freedom, discuss the ways different groups won rights for all. How did the serfs, the townspeople, the nobles, and the king contribute to the new ideas of freedom? Read again how laws were made to bring about equality and justice.

2. It is a fortunate thing that our forefathers brought to this country the English idea of freedom. What conditions in the New World have led to greater freedom?

3. The Magna Charta represents a high point in the struggle of the English people for liberty. What event in the history of the United States marks a similar high point in our onward struggle for liberty and freedom?

Interesting Things to Try

1. Make a chart entitled "Freedom and Responsibility in Our School and Classroom." Divide this chart into two parts. On one side plan a list of the privileges your school offers and the freedoms you enjoy. On the other side place the responsibilities you share and the services you render your school and classroom. Which side of your chart has the longer list?

2. Our country is often spoken of as the Land of Liberty and Freedom. Make a list of some of the freedoms we enjoy. Note the freedoms which have come to us from other countries. Make a list of some of the responsibilities we share and the services we should render our country.

3. This unit, "Foundations of Freedom," has two very exciting scenes: King John and the barons, and the Peasants' Revolt. These scenes would be interesting to dramatize.

4. Continue the time line you started in Unit VI. Mark it with important events throughout the Middle Ages. Show the events and dates which trace the steps by which the common people in England gained representative government.

Let's Read

The Magna Charta, by James Daugherty. This book tells of "Living in the Twelfth Century." There are also exciting stories of King Richard and of King John. You will be surprised to find a list of "Children of the Magna Charta."

Democracy, by Ryllis and Omar Goslin. Here the story of democracy is very simply told.

How the World Is Ruled, by Carrie L. George. When you read the chapter "How France and England Were Ruled," you learn more about the early governments of these two countries.

The Story of England, by Beatrice Curtis Brown and Helen Arbuthnot. This is a brief account of English history for young people, with many beautiful illustrations in color.

Put Democracy to Work, by Ruth H. Wagner and Ivah E. Green. Read the chapter which will show you some of your own rights and responsibilities as a young citizen.

Rights We Defend, by Chester S. Williams. The chapters "The Deep Drive," "The Upward Struggle," and "Our English Heritage" help you to understand the long struggle for our rights.

Getting Ready for a Class Discussion

Choose topics or questions in which all are interested. List these on the board in the order in which they will be discussed.

Find out all you can about the questions by getting information from books and other sources before the discussion begins.

Vote for a leader to guide the discussion. A leader does not talk too much. He sees that everyone in the group has a part in the discussion.

Have members of the group arranged so that they can see one another as they talk.

Let the leader introduce the discussion by stating the topic or question. Other members of the class may add their remarks.

Be sure that each person states what he thinks, and always shows respect for the opinions of others.

[327]

Choose the Right Word

From the list below choose the word or group of words needed to make each of the following sentences complete and true. Write the numbers 1 to 10 on a separate sheet of paper. After each number place the correct word or words that will complete the sentence that has the same number. Then read the sentence with the right word in it. *Remember that you must not write in this book.*

1. The right of trial by —— led to greater justice.
2. The body of laws which governed the rich and poor alike became known as the —— ——.
3. The Magna Charta was signed at ——.
4. The people gained —— for their liberties by the Magna Charta.
5. Before the king could levy taxes, the —— —— must give its consent.
6. The Magna Charta was read to King Henry in the hall of ——.
7. In 1295 for the first time —— included representatives of the church, the nobles, and the common people.
8. Representatives in Parliament from counties and towns were called the ——.
9. If a serf succeeded in hiding in a town for a year and a day, he gained his ——.
10. England's great contribution to civilization during the Middle Ages was giving to the people some of the —— formerly in the hands of kings.

Runnymede	Parliament
Commons	power
freedom	jury
common law	Great Council
Westminster	protection

IX

THE GREAT
AWAKENING

WESTERN EUROPE. *Great interest in learning spread through countries and cities of Europe as new ideas and inventions brought changes in ways of living and thinking.*

THE GREAT AWAKENING

THE NEW SPIRIT

Toward the close of the Middle Ages many great changes were taking place in Europe. By the fifteenth century the nobles in many countries had lost most of their power and the old feudal way of life was breaking down. A wonderful new age in the world's history was beginning. This time when men were awakening is called the Renaissance.

During earlier ages the mass of the people had accepted without question what those in authority told them. In the new age which was opening up, the people were beginning to think for themselves. They were beginning to believe that each individual should be free to think as he wished and to act as he thought best. They were beginning to see that many things which had been believed for centuries were not true. There was a great sweep of new ideas over most of Europe. Everywhere people were awakening, eager to study and to learn, and ignorance was giving way to knowledge. As men began giving expression to the many new ideas which were crowding upon them, a new literature and a new art grew up in many countries. All these changes made people's lives very different from those of earlier ages in Europe.

For several hundred years there had been only one form of faith in all western Europe. Then in the latter part of the Middle Ages there arose a feeling among some men that certain practices of the Church should be reformed.

John Wycliffe, a famous scholar in England in the fourteenth century, preached against the evils that had grown up in the Church. He loved the Bible and felt that the reading of it would help people in learning right ways of living. The Bible in those days was written in Latin, which was understood by only a few people. Wycliffe believed that people should read the Bible themselves and learn its teachings from their own reading. He translated the Bible into English so that everyone could understand it, and he organized bands of priests to go about from village to village and read it to the people.

Wycliffe's work brought great opposition. In 1408 the Church passed a resolution which forbade anyone without authority to translate the Holy Scripture "into the English tongue or into any other by way of book or treatise, or to let any such book be read in whole or in part, in public or in private."

Wycliffe's teachings spread to faraway Bohemia. There John Huss, a professor in the university at Prague, took them up and won many followers. Like Wycliffe, Huss declared that everyone should read the Bible and decide religious matters for himself. So Huss translated the Bible into the language of his people.

Church leaders believed that if the views of Huss were accepted, the authority of the Church would be destroyed. They declared that his teachings were heresy. Huss himself was brought before a council of the Church and ordered to give up his teachings. He said that he would gladly change his views if anyone were able to prove to him that the things he said were not true. However, he was de-clared guilty of teaching "many things evil, scan-dalous, seditious, and dan-gerously heretical" and was burned at the stake.

About a hundred years after the death of Wycliffe, there was born in Germany a peasant boy whose name was Martin Luther. When Luther grew up he became a monk and was a professor at the University of Wittenberg.

Luther objected to some of the practices of the Church. In 1517, he wrote out his beliefs and nailed them to the church door at Wittenberg where all might read them.

The Pope sent a message to Luther telling him that he must come to Rome and give an account of what he had done. Instead of going to Rome, Luther went on preaching and writing. This continued for two years. Then the Pope issued a document ordering him to burn his writings and to take back his statements against the Church within six days or be excommunicated as a heretic. Instead of burning his own writings, Luther built a bonfire and burned the Pope's document.

Luther was then summoned by the emperor of Germany to appear before the great Diet, an assembly of all the German rulers and churchmen, which was to be held in the city of Worms. His friends, fearing for his safety, tried to persuade him not to go, but he replied, "I am lawfully summoned to appear in that city and thither I will go in the name of the Lord, though as many devils as there are tiles on the roofs of the houses were there combined against me."

The Diet was an impressive gathering. In the immense hall the emperor, Charles V, sat on a throne. Churchmen

and princes stood near him. Luther was led before his judges. The books he had written lay on a table near by. Would he withdraw what he had written? he was asked.

"If you can convince me from the Holy Scriptures that I am in error, I am ready with my own hands to cast the whole of my writings into the flames," replied the monk.

For two long hours Luther defended his opinions.

"Brother Martin," then said the examiner, "do you or do you not take back your teaching?" He asked for a plain answer.

Luther replied: "If His Imperial Majesty desires a plain answer, I will give it and it is this. It is impossible for me to recant unless I am proved to be in the wrong by the testimony of the Scriptures or by evident reasoning. I believe things contrary to the Pope and Councils because it is as clear as day that they have erred and said things inconsistent with themselves. I am bound by the Scriptures which I have quoted; my conscience is in submission to the word of God. Therefore I may not and will not recant, because to act against conscience is unholy and unsafe. God help me! Amen."

At the next meeting Luther was declared a heretic and an outlaw. He was to be put to death, and his writings were to be burned. The emperor spoke: "A single monk here sets himself against what the Church has believed for a thousand years and more. After his stiff-necked reply of yesterday I am sorry I have bothered with him so long. He shall go free to his home, but after that anyone who finds him is to turn him over to the officers."

"Be it so," replied Luther. "I will bear anything for His Imperial Majesty and the Empire, but the word of God must not be bound."

On his way home, some of Luther's friends had him carried off safely to a castle of a German noble. In this refuge he hid for a year and translated the New Testament into German so that the ordinary person could read it for himself. Luther's teachings spread over northern Germany, and a new church, the Lutheran, was founded on them.

Other reformers appeared. Gradually the new movement spread over a large part of Europe and a number of new religious beliefs grew up. This movement has been called the Reformation, because it had to do with the reforming of the Church. The new churches were called Protestant churches, because they all arose as protests against the Catholic Church. The people of south Germany and most of the countries in the south of Europe remained faithful to the Catholic Church.

Many people were greatly disturbed when they saw others turning away from the Catholic Church. They looked upon such people as heretics and thought that they should be punished. A court called the Inquisition was established to try people accused of heresy. This court was active in southern Europe, particularly in Spain.

Some earnest Catholics saw the need of correcting things that seemed to be harmful to the Church, and they changed many of the practices to which people had objected. These reformers, however, did not want to separate from the Catholic Church.

A young Spanish nobleman, named Ignatius Loyola, decided to give his life to the service of the Catholic Church. In 1540 he formed a society called the Society of Jesus to spread the Catholic faith. Later the members of this society became known as the Jesuits. They promised to spend their lives in the service of others. They established schools and were among the best teachers of the time. They became great missionaries and carried their religion to many lands. The Jesuits won back to the Catholic Church many people who had left it earlier.

The early Protestant reformers did not believe in giving other people religious freedom. The people of each form of faith were so sure that theirs was the only true religion that they would not allow any belief but their own. In every country of Europe people were imprisoned, tortured, and burned at the stake. Catholics imprisoned, banished, and burned Protestants, and Protestants treated Catholics just as harshly. The Protestants even punished other Protestants who differed from them.

Even governments thought it their right to tell their people what to believe. If a ruler was a Catholic, all his subjects had to be Catholics; if he took up one of the new religions, his subjects were forced to adopt it also, and those who did not obey were severely punished.

In England, Henry VIII quarreled with the Pope because the Pope would not grant him a divorce from his queen. Henry decided to break away from the Catholic Church and make himself head of the church in his kingdom. In 1534 he forced Parliament to pass a law making him the "only supreme head on earth of the Church of

England." Henry did not make many changes in the church service, and so the people were allowed to worship very much as they had worshiped before the law was passed.

Henry had three children who became rulers. Edward VI, who followed him on the throne, was a Protestant and tried to make England a Protestant country. His half sister, Mary, who ruled next, was a zealous Catholic. She wished to restore England to the authority of the Pope. After Mary came Elizabeth, who was a Protestant. During her reign the Church of England was established by law, and everyone was required to attend. Those who refused were severely punished.

In spite of persecution, however, people continued to think for themselves in matters of religion. Slowly out of that long struggle came the realization that it was useless to try to force a person to accept a form of religion in which he did not believe. The wisest and best leaders of every sect gave up the idea that persons who differed from them about religion should be punished.

Americans of today believe that people in a democracy should be free to belong to any church they wish. The Bill of Rights, which became part of the Constitution of the United States, declares that "Congress shall make no law respecting an establishment of religion or prohibiting the free exercise thereof."

Freedom of worship is one of the most important of the liberties for which men of the Renaissance struggled. Their struggles helped to lay the foundation of religious freedom for the American people.

MEN CREATE NEW FORMS OF BEAUTY

The growth of trade and industry in Europe during the period of the Renaissance made life more comfortable for many people. They had leisure to enjoy themselves. Rich merchants were often lovers of art and literature and gave money freely to painters and poets so that they might have time to paint and write. A new love of beauty spread over Europe, expressing itself in a great variety of forms. Artists and sculptors, architects and writers, did some of the finest work the world has ever known.

In the rich cities of Italy lived many splendid artists. Like the Greeks of old, the people of Florence were lovers of all kinds of beauty. No other city had so many painters, sculptors, and other artists. They built beautiful palaces and covered the walls of the rooms with frescoes. For the courtyards they made statues and fountains. They set in the outer walls of the palaces plaques of terra cotta in lovely colors. They wanted to make their city the most beautiful city in Italy.

In the center of Florence was built a little eight-sided church, to which the babies of the city were brought to be baptized. For it the sculptor Lorenzo Ghiberti made two sets of bronze doors. He decorated them chiefly with scenes from the Bible set in the midst of exquisite borders. "They are so beautiful," said a great artist when he saw the doors, "that they might be the gates of Paradise."

One of the artists who helped to make Florence beautiful was Giotto. Not only did he adorn his beloved city with pictures, but he carved in stone as well. Of creamy-white marble he built a tall bell tower, slender and graceful, from which the bells pealed, calling the people to church. He decorated it with carvings of shepherds with their sheep, farmers plowing their fields, and other scenes from everyday life.

In the fifteenth century a family of merchants rose to wealth and power in Florence. The most famous member of this family was Lorenzo de' Medici. Lorenzo loved beautiful things. In the gardens surrounding his palace he had many lovely old Greek and Roman statues which he had collected. This rich patron of art invited boys interested in art to study the statues in his garden. Rough marble was there also, so that the young art students could carve anything they chose.

To Lorenzo's garden came a young boy named Michelangelo. He wanted to learn to make statues as beautiful as those of the old Greeks. Three happy years the young artist spent there.

In one of the workshops of Florence there was a huge block of marble. A sculptor had once tried to carve a statue from it but had failed. Michelangelo saw the marble and obtained permission to work on it. For eighteen months he let no one see what he was doing. When at last the work was finished, there was a statue of the young Hebrew shepherd boy, David. This figure is one of the most beloved of all Michelangelo's sculptures.

Like many other artists of the Renaissance period, Michelangelo often chose his subjects from the Bible. His statue of Moses, the great Hebrew leader, is generally considered to be his masterpiece. The huge, impressive figure seems to be teaching his people from the tablets of stone containing the Ten Commandments, which, according to the Bible story, he brought down from Mt. Sinai.

Michelangelo became not only a great sculptor, but a great painter as well. The Pope asked him to paint pictures on the ceiling of the Sistine Chapel in Rome.

"I am not a painter, but a sculptor," said Michelangelo.

"A man such as thou," replied the Pope, "is anything he wishes to be."

The ceiling was arched, and to paint the frescoes the artist had to lie on his back on a high scaffolding. You can imagine how difficult it was to paint in such a position. Yet for four long years Michelangelo had to do that, day after day. There were many days when he did not stop for food. "So weary I am, lying on my back looking upward!" he said. "Pains shoot through my head, my neck, my eyes. In truth, I am getting so I cannot read except when I am lying upon my back."

When the ceiling was finished, there were hundreds of figures representing scenes from the Bible. No other paintings in the world equal these for grandeur.

Another great artist, Leonardo da Vinci, grew up in Florence. He was interested in many things. He was a writer, an engineer, a musician, and a poet, as well as a painter. He seemed to be able to do almost everything wonderfully well. He kept notebooks in which he made sketches and wrote about anything that interested him. Some of these are still in existence.

One of his sketches was a design for a war machine. In this device, sharp blades like sickles were attached front and back to something like a gun carriage. Apparently the blades were supposed to operate like shears when the machine was drawn forward by horses.

The notebooks show that Leonardo had an understanding of engineering and mechanical principles far beyond the general knowledge of his time. He studied the flight of birds, trying to find out what made them able to fly. His sketches show the results of his observations. He invented a machine in which he thought a man could fly through the air. It needed only a motor to make it practical for use.

One of Leonardo's paintings, "The Last Supper," is among the world's greatest masterpieces. The Bible says that shortly before Christ died on the cross, he was at supper with his disciples. As they sat down, Christ said: "Verily, I say unto you that one of you shall betray me." The disciples were startled and each one of them asked, "Lord, is it I?"

Leonardo's great picture shows Christ and his disciples seated at a long table. The words, "Verily, I say unto you that one of you shall betray me," have just been spoken, and the expressions on the faces of the disciples show how they felt when they heard those terrible words.

When Michelangelo and Leonardo were becoming famous, a young painter, Raphael Sanzio, came to Florence. Raphael was soon known and loved by all the great artists of the city. He painted hundreds of pictures but he loved best to paint the Madonna with the Christ child.

The Pope invited Raphael to come to Rome to do some frescoes. One of the pictures Raphael painted in Rome is called "The Madonna of the Chair." In this beautiful picture the Madonna is holding the Christ child just as any mother would hold her baby. Another painting, the familiar "Sistine Madonna," is considered the finest picture Raphael ever painted.

Artists from the northern countries of Europe were attracted to Italy by the renown of the Italian painters and, after learning all that the Italian masters could teach them, returned to practice their art in their own countries.

The paintings of these great artists of the Renaissance are today the priceless treasures of art galleries and churches in Europe, and some of them are to be found in art museums in this country.

BLOCK BOOKS

Through thousands of years people had been making books of one kind or another. In early ages, men expressed their ideas and recorded their thoughts and discoveries on papyrus rolls, or clay tablets, or stone walls. During the Middle Ages, they wrote them out by hand on parchment. But during all those long ages men had been able to produce only one copy of a book at a time. This meant that there were not many books in existence and that those few were very expensive. Only rich people could afford to have them. Then, in the middle of the fifteenth century, men learned how to make books quickly and cheaply.

Fortunately a new material, paper, had come to Europe at that time. Parchment, or vellum, which had been used for centuries, was very expensive. Hundreds of years earlier, the people of China had worked out a way of making paper. They kept it a secret for a long time, but some Arabs learned the secret and brought the idea to Europe.

The first step in papermaking was to beat rags or other fibers to a soft pulp. At first, the Chinese did this by hand, using stone mortars and pestles. Later, they invented a trip hammer which saved much labor. When a workman stepped on the end of the crossbar, he raised a hammer which fell heavily on the material in the mortar.

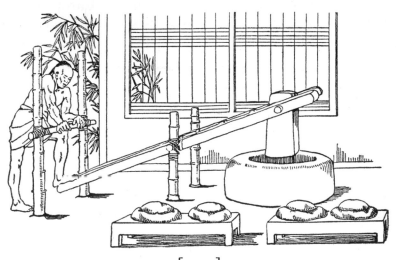

Papermaking became an important craft in Europe. After softening and pounding the rags, the papermaker dipped into the pulp a fine wire sieve of the size which the piece of paper was to be. As he shook the sieve gently to and fro, the water was drained out and the rag pulp was matted together on the sieve. The pulp was put under a heavy press which squeezed out the rest of the water, and the sheet of paper was hung on a line to dry.

Early in the fifteenth century the people of Europe began printing in a simple way. A workman cut a block of wood the size he wished and drew upon it the picture and words he wanted to print. Then he skillfully cut away the wood, leaving the raised outline of the pictures and letters. The carved block was inked, and a sheet of paper was laid on it and pressed down. Thus the picture and words were printed on the paper. These image prints, as they were called, were usually scenes from the Bible. The poor people liked to put them up on the walls of their homes.

From making a single page to making a book by binding together a number of sheets was an easy step.

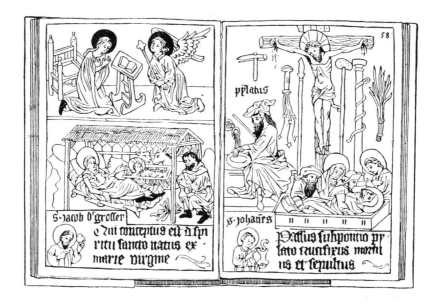

Thus block books, as they were called, came into existence. The poor people could not afford the beautiful books made by the monks, but these simple picture books were cheap and became very popular.

Even with block printing, the making of a book was a long, slow process, as a block had to be carved for each page. When someone thought of a new book, a whole new set of blocks had to be made, one for each page of that book. So up to about the year 1450 the making of books had not made much progress.

Then a way of printing was worked out by someone who, many people think, was Johann Gutenberg, of the city of Mainz, in Germany. In the meantime, other experiments in methods of printing were being made, especially in Holland.

[349]

Gutenberg had made several block books and found the work very slow. He wanted to print the Bible and he knew that he could never print a big book like that from blocks. Surely there must be some quicker way of printing if only he could think of it. Suddenly, one day while he was hard at work, a wonderful idea came to him. Instead of carving the letters of a page all on one block of wood, why not cut each letter of the alphabet separately? He could then put the letters together to form words and sentences just as he wished and could use the same letters over and over again in different combinations to form new words. That would save a great deal of time in the printing of books.

Eagerly Gutenberg set to work. Sawing a big piece of wood into many tiny pieces, he carved a letter on each one. In time he had a pile of all the different letters of the alphabet. He placed several letters together in a row to form words and sentences. He made a little frame to hold the rows of letters together.

[350]

When Gutenberg tried printing with his new letters, he found that great pressure was needed to make a clear impression. He had often seen men making wine by squeezing grapes with a heavy press. He had seen papermakers use a press to expel water from wet sheets of paper. Why not try something like that for printing?

In time Gutenberg had built an upright frame to which was attached a big screw which worked up and down. On the lower end of the screw he fastened a board. He placed the type, set in a little wooden frame, beneath the board. Then he inked the type, laid a piece of paper over it, and worked the screw until the board was forced tightly down on the paper. Then he worked the screw up, and with it the board was lifted. There on the paper was the first printing made with a printing press.

Gutenberg's work was not yet finished. In using the wooden letters over and over again, he found that they soon lost their shape, so that the printing was no longer clear. His type must be made of something harder and more durable than wood. Metalworkers cast small objects in metal. Why not use metal for type? He tried making letters of lead, but he found that it was too soft. Then he tried iron, but that was too hard and cut holes in the paper. Then he decided that he must make a combination of metals, and after much experimenting he succeeded in doing this.

Now a new difficulty arose. The only ink known at the time was that used by the monks. Gutenberg found that when he used this ink with the metal type, it would not stick to the metal letters. It collected in drops and made blots on the paper. What was he to do? Painters had invented a new paint by mixing lampblack and linseed oil. Why not try using that for ink? Again there was much experimenting, which finally resulted in the right kind of ink for the printing press.

Gutenberg had spent years on his experiments, improving this thing and that. At last there came a time when he had no money left to continue his work. A rich businessman, Johann Fust, became interested in his idea. He lent Gutenberg money and went into partnership with him.

Sad to say, after a few years this partnership ended unfortunately for Gutenberg. The work on the Bible which he was printing went slowly. Fust became impatient and said that Gutenberg was wasting money. He demanded that Gutenberg return what had been lent him. But Gutenberg had no money. So Fust took the matter to court, and the judge decided that everything Gutenberg had, even his tools, must be given to Fust in payment of the debt.

This was a terrible blow. It seemed to Gutenberg that all his years of work had come to nothing. What could he do without tools or money? Yet he had faith in his great idea, and he had another thing which everyone needs in order to succeed—courage. And he still had some friends. He appealed to them, and got money to start again.

In 1456, after years of hard work and discouragement, Gutenberg's dream of printing a Bible came true. It is generally considered the first book in the world printed from movable metal type.

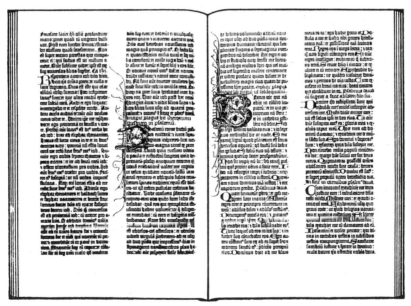

THE MAKING OF MANY BOOKS

The new and better way of printing thus begun by
Gutenberg soon spread all over Europe, and thousands
of books were printed. Sometimes when a printer received
an interesting piece of news, he printed it in the form of
a small pamphlet. These news sheets at first were published
irregularly, and usually dealt with some one current event,
such as a battle, a coronation, or some other important
happening. Many years later, newspapers appearing regu-
larly and containing news of all sorts of current events
came into existence.

When Gutenberg succeeded in inventing the process of
printing, he gave people a most precious gift. Up to this
time the great majority of the people of Europe had not
been able to read or write. To be sure, there had always
been schools in the monasteries, and some kings, like
Charlemagne in France and Alfred in England, encouraged learning, but this education reached only a few

people. The spread of information and ideas was pitifully slow, and most people were very ignorant. The invention of printing made it easy to spread knowledge abroad in every land. As books became cheaper, even people of small means could afford to buy them. Thousands of grown people began learning their letters so that they could find out what was in the new books.

People read eagerly the many pamphlets and news sheets which were now printed. In this way they learned about what went on in other parts of Europe as well as in their own country.

HOW PRINTING HELPED MEN TO BE FREE

Governments soon discovered that printing was a means of affecting other men's thoughts and actions and spreading new ideas and beliefs. They feared this new form of expression and dealt sternly with printers who used the printing press to bring about reforms.

"We must destroy the printing press, or the printing press will destroy us," said one high official in England. It was made a crime to criticize the king, his ministers, or Parliament. The Lord Chief Justice of England declared that it was criminal to "write on the subject of government —whether in terms of praise or censure it is immaterial, for no man has a right to say anything of government." The punishments for doing so were the cutting off of the ears, the slitting of the tongue, and other tortures, and even death itself.

Nevertheless, printers continued to print their ideas on their little presses, for they believed the words of that great teacher who said to his people, "Ye shall know the truth and the truth shall make you free." Many printers suffered at the whipping post, in the pillory, and on the scaffold because they had dared to publish what they believed to be true. "Suffer yourself to be blamed, imprisoned, condemned; suffer yourself even to be hanged; but publish your opinions. It is not a right, it is a duty," said one printer. And said another, "I have twenty-six little lead soldiers with which I shall conquer the world."

One of the most famous of the early printers was an Italian who founded the Aldine press in Venice. Here he printed fine editions of the Latin, Greek, and Italian classics. Another early printer was William Caxton, who was the first to print books written in English.

The people of America should thank the humble printers of those early days who struggled to establish the freedom of the press, which Americans today regard as one of their most precious liberties. The circulation of facts and ideas by books, magazines, and newspapers is one of the greatest means men have of learning the truth about what is going on in the world.

A great eagerness for education spread rapidly over Europe. Schools sprang up in all the larger towns, and they became centers of learning. Scholars traveled about, stopping in one town after another to instruct anyone who cared to listen. Gradually teachers of many different subjects began to gather at a few centers, such as Paris and Oxford. This was a great saving of time for students and masters, because all subjects could be studied at one place. In this way universities grew up, where many teachers and students gathered together.

Young men thronged to the universities. Some of them were very poor and had little to eat but stale bread which they washed down with water. The student's life was a hard one. At first there were no special buildings. Each teacher found a vacant room wherever he could. There were no textbooks. The teacher read his lectures slowly while the students laboriously wrote down what he said, word for word.

As trade grew in the towns, the merchants and their clerks found that they needed to know how to read, write, and keep accounts in order to carry on their business. Rich merchants founded trade schools. Travelers and the Crusaders had learned the Arabic numerals in the East and introduced them into Europe. People found the Arabic numerals much easier to use than the clumsy Roman numerals.

Young children learned to read with a primer called a hornbook. This consisted of a sheet of paper on which were printed the alphabet and the Lord's Prayer. The paper was placed in a frame of wood, and covered with a thin, transparent sheet of horn. Some hornbooks had handles with a hole for a string by which they could be fastened to the girdle.

The Bible also helped to educate the people. Thousands of humble folk learned to read in order that they might study it for themselves. As the various Protestant sects arose, members were anxious to bring up their children in their own faith. So schools were founded to teach children to read the Bible and to instruct them in religion.

In Greece and Rome there had been great poets and prose writers, writers of plays, and historians. During the centuries when tribes of barbarians were overrunning western Europe, all this knowledge and culture of the ancient peoples was forgotten. Only the monks and a few other people knew about it. In Constantinople, also, at the very eastern end of Europe, the ancient learning lived on. This city was full of scholars who loved and studied the old masterpieces. The shelves of its library were filled with priceless manuscripts.

In the year 1453, Constantinople fell into the hands of the Turks. At that time many scholars fled to Italy, carrying with them the precious manuscripts which had been treasured in the library. This aroused interest in Italy in the "new learning," as it was called.

News of this "new learning" spread to other countries, and scholars journeyed to Italy to study. They collected every ancient work they could lay their hands on and had copies made. They ransacked monasteries and cathedral libraries, bringing to light many long-forgotten manuscripts. They read with delight the poems of Homer and Vergil. Scholars studied the stately orations of Demosthenes and Cicero. Once more the wonderful plays of the old Greeks and the histories of Greece and Rome became part of the world's great living literature.

The universities spread the new learning far and wide over Europe. As people wanted to read the old literature in the original languages, Greek and Latin came to be important studies.

Thus the learning of the old Greeks and Romans was brought to life again. This revival of interest in the classics was an important part of the great awakening.

For many a century after the fall of Rome there were almost no poets or writers of plays. During the Renaissance men's minds were greatly stimulated by all the new ideas that were coming to them. They began to feel the need of giving expression to them. These new writers wrote in the language of their own people instead of in Latin, as had been the custom during the Middle Ages. By the fourteenth or fifteenth century every nation was coming to have a literature of its own.

In England, during the reign of Queen Elizabeth, a wonderful literature grew up. Someone has said that England at that time was "a nest of singing birds," for it seemed as if everyone were writing poetry.

The people of Elizabeth's day loved plays. Companies of players traveled about from town to town. All the actors were men or boys. If there were women's parts in the plays, the boys dressed as women. Actors wore the clothes of their own time even if they were acting scenes laid in other times and places. There was no scenery on the stage; there were only curtains. At the beginning of a scene a sign was put up to indicate the place in which the audience were to imagine that the acting was taking place.

The theaters of this time were different from ours. There was a roofed stage at one end and a roofed gallery at the other. The ground space between was open to the sky. Admission to this part of the theater was cheap and it was generally filled with a rough, boisterous crowd. They cheered

when they were pleased, and booed and threw things at the actors when they did not like a play.

Among the actors in London was a poor young man, William Shakespeare. He had come from his home in Stratford-on-Avon to make his fortune. He thought he could write much better plays than those that were being given. One day the queen was present at one of Shakespeare's plays. She liked it so much that she sent for the young playwright and commanded him to write another. After that Shakespeare gave up acting and spent all his time writing plays. Some were comedies, some were tragedies, some were based on history. His characters are so true to life that even today people still enjoy reading his plays or seeing them performed. He is the greatest of our English playwrights.

In the Middle Ages people believed in things which today are considered merely superstitions. Many things were thought to be unlucky. Friday, for instance, was looked upon as an unlucky day, and thirteen as an unlucky number. People wore charms and lucky pieces to keep harm away. Fortunetellers who claimed to have the power to reveal the future abounded. Supernatural beings, it was thought, haunted lonely places. Fairies, gnomes, and goblins lived in the forests; ghosts stalked about at night.

People who were thought to have sold themselves to the devil in return for the power to work magic were called witches. It was believed that they could change themselves or others into animals, that they could raise storms and destroy crops, and that they would stick thorns, pins, and other objects into their victims, thus causing sickness and death. At night they were supposed to ride through the air on broomsticks. At certain times, it was believed, sorcerers and witches met in some lonely place for feasts and wild revels. At these "witches' Sabbaths," as they were called, the devil himself was supposed to be present.

[363]

Medieval people also believed that the lives of men were controlled by the stars. People consulted astrologers about many things—the right time to do business, to get married, to go on a journey.

There were other men, called alchemists, who tried to pry into the secrets of nature. Secretly they worked in their laboratories cluttered up with furnaces, bellows, and odd-shaped bottles filled with colored liquids. They ground powders; burned various substances, making weird and mysterious lights; and mixed fluids, watching the changes that took place in them. These alchemists hoped that they might one day discover a way to change common metals into gold.

The alchemists were never able to discover the secrets for which they looked so eagerly. However, their studies of the changes produced in different substances later developed into the science which we today call chemistry.

Even in those early days there were some men who were real scientists. One of these was Roger Bacon, a Franciscan friar who lived in England in the thirteenth century. He set up a laboratory in an old, deserted monastery and spent years patiently making experiments, trying to understand the laws of nature. He had a magic glass through which, it was said, one could see tiny demons dancing about in a bowl of water. Perhaps this was a microscope. He also had a strange tube through which he could see much farther than ordinary men. Possibly this was a telescope.

An Italian friar who visited Bacon wrote:

> Among other things he showed me a black, ugly stone called a magnet, which has the surprising quality of drawing iron to it; and if a needle be rubbed upon it and afterward fastened to a straw, so that it will swim upon the water, it will instantly turn to the Pole Star. Therefore, be the night ever so dark, with neither moon or stars visible, yet shall the sailor by help of this needle be able to steer his vessel aright.
>
> This discovery, so useful to all who travel by sea, must remain concealed until other times, because no master mariner dare use it, lest he be suspected of being a magician; nor would sailors put to sea with one who carried an instrument so surely constructed by the devil.

This may have been the first compass in Europe.

Roger Bacon was indeed a scientist far ahead of his time. In one of his writings he predicts possible inventions of the future with surprising accuracy.

[365]

Instruments for navigation can be made which will do away with the necessity of rowers, so that great ships in rivers and on the sea shall be borne about with greater speed than if they were full of rowers. Likewise carriages can be constructed so that without animals to draw them they may be moved with incredible speed. Machines can be made in which a man may sit in the middle turning some device by which artificial wings are made to strike the air in the manner of a flying bird.

In these descriptions it is easy to recognize the steamship, the locomotive, and the airplane of today.

In the time of ignorance and superstition in which Bacon lived, it was not safe for anyone to know too much. New ideas were usually considered sinful and dangerous; for how could one person know more than others unless he paid the Evil One to teach him?

Curious neighbors sometimes peeped at Bacon in his laboratory and ran away in terror, declaring that they had seen the devil spouting fire. This early scientist had invented a kind of steam engine; very likely it was this, with its fire and steam, which the people thought was the devil. Bacon also experimented with an explosive much like gunpowder. One day some of this powder exploded with a terrible roar and a blinding flash. After that the neighbors believed more than ever that the friar was in league with the Evil One.

Such things could not be allowed to go on. Bacon was put in prison as a wizard. Twenty-four years of his life he spent there because he tried to advance men's knowledge. But to the end of his life Bacon was faithful to his belief that men should experiment in order to discover the secrets of nature. That idea scientists now know is the very basis of all science.

THE FATHER OF MODERN ASTRONOMY

Toward the end of the fifteenth century came a man named Nicolaus Copernicus, whose ideas were to lay the foundation of astronomy as we know it today.

Copernicus had been interested in the stars from the time he was a boy. Later he studied astronomy with learned men. Often he sat up all night watching the heavenly bodies from the tower of the cathedral in his town.

Most of the people of that time believed that the sun revolved around the earth. After observing the stars for years, Copernicus came to the conclusion that the sun only appears to revolve around the earth. In reality, the earth is spinning about the sun. The earth, declared Copernicus, is one of several stars called planets, and all these planets revolve around the sun.

When Copernicus made known his ideas he was ridiculed. But he decided to write a book about his theory. When at last the book was finished, the astronomer was an old man. He was ill and worn out with work and pain. Two of his friends took his manuscript to a printer.

The news spread that the book was being printed and excitement among those who heard it was great. Some people tried to get to the press to destroy it. The two friends of Copernicus had to guard his manuscript day and night.

In May, 1543, as Copernicus lay dying, his precious book, which was the result of his life's work, was put into his hands. As he grasped it he murmured, "Lord, now lettest thou thy servant depart in peace."

MAGIC GLASSES

Copernicus was not able to prove his belief, because he had no means of studying the heavens except with his own eyes. It was not until the next century that his theory was proved to be true by an Italian scientist, Galileo. Galileo gave much of his time to the study of astronomy and became convinced that Copernicus was right about the earth and the sun. But how could he prove it?

Just at that time an interesting thing happened which was to be a great help to Galileo in his work. In a little town in Holland there lived a spectacle-maker by the name of Hans Lippershey. One day, so the story goes, while he was working in his shop, his children were playing outside with some of the glasses he used in making spectacles. They happened to hold up two pieces of glass, one in front of the other, to look at a weathercock on a high church steeple, and they made a wonderful discovery. The magic glasses made the weathercock seem quite near, but upside down! Their excited cries brought their father from his shop.

The spectacle-maker took a look himself. Sure enough, with the glasses held about a foot apart he could see the weathercock quite plainly. He began experimenting and finally fastened two pieces of glass in a tube for convenience in holding.

This spyglass, as it was called, attracted a good deal of attention. Someone wrote about it to Galileo. Galileo at once realized what a wonderful help an instrument of that kind would be to him in studying the heavens. He eagerly set to work to make a spyglass for himself. For a long, long time he worked, grinding pieces of glass, curving them first one way and then another. Then he took a piece of old organ pipe and fitted into it two pieces of glass which he had ground so that one of them curved out and the other curved in.

Galileo had made the first real telescope in the world. On the first clear night he pointed his magic glasses to the sky. What exciting things he discovered! To his delight he found that many places which had before seemed like dark empty spaces were really filled with brightly gleaming stars. Night after night he climbed a high tower and pointed

his telescope this way and that, discovering more and more marvels of the heavens.

One night the astronomer saw a star of great size and brilliant light. It was the planet Jupiter. Much to his surprise he saw four bright little stars near it, two on one side and two on the other. The next clear night he looked for the four little stars and made another astonishing discovery. They were now all on the same side of the planet. Galileo was quite puzzled by this and watched and watched for many nights. Finally he came to the conclusion that these stars were circling around the planet. He observed other planets and found stars circling around them also.

At last, after many years of observing and thinking, Galileo decided that Copernicus was right in believing that the earth and other planets revolve around the sun just as the smaller stars revolve around the planets.

The news of Galileo's discoveries spread far and wide. People crowded into his house to look at the stars through his wonderful instrument. They thought that it must have some magic power. Many learned men of the day refused to look through the telescope. They did not want to change their ideas about the stars. They would not accept the theories that Galileo was trying to prove.

"How I wish we could have one hearty laugh together!" wrote Galileo to a friend at that time. "Here the principal professor of philosophy, whom I have repeatedly and urgently requested to look at the planets through my glass, has persistently refused to do so. Why are you not here? What shouts of laughter we should have at this folly!"

To devout Christian men of that time such beliefs as Galileo's seemed wicked. The Bible was thought to teach that the earth was the center of God's creation. Galileo was summoned to Rome to explain his views. Then he was ordered to "abandon and cease to teach his false, impious, and heretical opinions."

Nevertheless Galileo

continued to study. In 1632 he wrote a book in which he stated his views and his reasons for rejecting the old theories about the earth.

For many years the scientist was punished for having what were thought to be wicked beliefs and for spreading such ideas. Galileo believed in the Bible, but, he said, "I am not bound to believe that God, who endowed us with senses and understanding, does not permit us to use them."

At last the judges of the Inquisition summoned Galileo to appear before them. By that time he was an old man seventy years of age. Completely broken by years of suffering, the aged scientist said: "I am in your hands. I will say whatever you wish."

So Galileo was made to swear that he would never again in words or in writing spread his wicked ideas. In time, however, all scientists came to believe that the theories of Copernicus and Galileo were right.

THE STRUGGLE TO ADVANCE KNOWLEDGE

The early scientists were champions in man's struggle to be free in thought and action. Knowledge cannot advance when men are forbidden to think and when research and experimenting are considered dangerous. The basis of the scientist's work is the right to question ideas which have been generally accepted and to find out things that nobody has known before. Through the ages, men of science who were ahead of their time have suffered persecution and death in their struggle for the right to think for themselves and to form their own opinions about nature and the world.

Roger Bacon, Copernicus, and Galileo all made great contributions to man's advancement. They were pioneers in the world of science, leading the people of their day into real knowledge based on observation and experiment. Scientific thinkers who came later owe much to these men.

The Renaissance was indeed a period rich in the development of the mind and spirit of man. There was growth in freedom of religion, in science, in the spread of knowledge and education among the people. Powerful influences were at work freeing the minds of men and laying the foundations of modern times.

TALKING TOGETHER

1. Using the map on page 330, locate the centers of learning. Discuss the ways ideas in science and the arts were spread.

2. How did the invention of printing help in the struggle for freedom? In discussing this question, reread the section telling why government officials feared the printing press.

3. The Renaissance brought leisure and prosperity to merchants and nobles. How did they help to develop the new interest in art and literature?

4. Think of what you have read in this book about the works of Raphael, Michelangelo, and Leonardo da Vinci. Artists of the Renaissance period often chose the subjects for their paintings and sculpture from the Bible. Name some examples.

5. Talk about some superstitions of today which probably came from the Middle Ages. How would science help to destroy beliefs in superstition?

INTERESTING THINGS TO TRY

1. If you have a printing set in school, experiment with setting type by hand.

2. It would be interesting to visit the printing room in a newspaper plant and compare the present-day methods of printing with those used in Gutenberg's day.

3. Read again the description of paper making during the Renaissance and experiment with a simple process for making paper from rags or paper pulp. The paper you make might be decorated with block-print designs and used for Christmas cards.

4. If you have a microscope in your school, look at some small objects through it. Your group may enjoy seeing how things are magnified.

5. You might arrange on your bulletin board an exhibit of pictures by great artists of the Renaissance. Include pictures of some of the beautiful buildings erected at that time.

Words on Wings, by Lillian J. Bragdon. This book gives the story of communication through signs, speech, and writing.

The Story of Old Europe and New America, by Eugene C. Barker, Mabel Rockwood Grimm, and Matilda Hughes. You find more about the "new learning" in this book.

Leaders in Other Lands, by Jeanette Eaton. You will like "The Story of Johann Gutenberg" as told by Miss Eaton.

Martin Luther, by Harry Emerson Fosdick. For the story of Luther's early life read the chapters "The Poor Boy Who Changed the World" and "Martin Gets an Education."

Great Moments in Freedom, by Marion F. Lansing. The chapters "An Old Man's Dream," the story of Copernicus, and "Junker George," the trial of Martin Luther, make interesting reading.

Wings for Words, by Douglas C. McMurtrie and Don Farran. This is another story of Gutenberg and his invention.

Famous Old Masters of Painting, by Roland J. McKinney. Here you will find the lives of Michelangelo, Leonardo da Vinci, and other artists. There are also illustrations of their paintings.

Can You Make a Summary?

An easy and clear way to make a summary is by means of an outline. Select the most important thoughts for the main divisions and mark each one with a Roman numeral. Under the main divisions place the topics covering the less important thoughts. Each of these topics may be marked by a number. See that thoughts which belong together are grouped together.

Make a summary of this unit for a report on one of these topics:

I. Science
   1. Roger Bacon
   2. Nicolaus Copernicus
   3. Galileo

II. Art
   1. Painting
   2. Sculpture
   3. Literature

How Well Do You Remember?

Here is an opportunity for you to show how well you remember the persons you read about in "The Great Awakening." On a separate sheet of paper write the numbers 1 to 10. After each number write the name that will correctly answer the question having the same number. *Be sure that you do not write in this book.*

1. Who translated the Bible into English?
2. Who translated the Bible into the language of the Bohemians and later was burned at the stake?
3. Who was summoned to appear before the Diet at Worms?
4. Who wrote some of the finest plays in English literature?
5. Who carved the well-known statue of Moses?
6. Who was a great artist with interests in science and invention?
7. Who is best known for his many paintings of the Madonna?
8. Who printed the first book from movable metal type?
9. Who first presented the theory that the earth moves around the sun?
10. Who made the first real telescope?

Raphael Sanzio	Nicolaus Copernicus
Michelangelo	Martin Luther
Johann Gutenberg	John Huss
Galileo	William Shakespeare
John Wycliffe	Leonardo da Vinci

X

EUROPE LOOKS EAST

THE FAR EAST. *Riches of Eastern lands drew European traders to distant regions from which they brought back useful ideas, materials, and customs.*

EUROPE LOOKS EAST

THE WORLD GROWS LARGER

During those stirring centuries toward the close of the Middle Ages, when many changes were coming into the lives of the people of Europe, events were happening which greatly enlarged their ideas about the earth on which they lived. To most Europeans of the Middle Ages the world was not much larger than it had been to the Greeks and the Romans. The only lands of which they knew anything were Europe, a small part of Asia, and the northern part of Africa.

The superstitious minds of the time peopled distant parts of the world with all sorts of wonders. Unknown lands were thought to be inhabited by monstrous folk, some with no joints in their legs, some headless, and some with the heads of different kinds of animals. Geographers of the time made maps of the world, but as they knew little about the real world they filled in from their imaginations the places they did not know about. In blank spaces they drew little pictures of the strange beasts and people they thought inhabited far-off places.

At the time of the Crusades the people of Europe came to know something about Palestine and the near-by lands, but the rest of Asia was still a region of mystery to them.

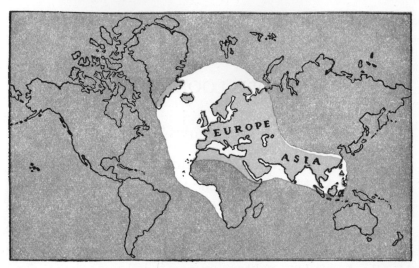

THE WORLD IN THE MIDDLE AGES

Between the Far East and Europe lay high mountains, barren plains, and vast stretches of sandy deserts.

From quite early times there had been trade between the Far East and Europe. Wealthy Romans dressed in Chinese silk, and all through the Middle Ages merchants of Venice and other trading centers brought to the nobles of Europe many luxuries from the East. The people knew that silk and other lovely things came from Cathay, as they called China. They knew that spices, precious stones, and other luxuries came from a region which they vaguely called "the Indies." But almost no Europeans had visited those far-off places, and little was known about them.

For centuries Mohammedan merchants had brought goods from the East over the mountains and the deserts to Constantinople or to Mediterranean ports by long caravans of camels. There the merchants of ports such as Venice and Genoa bought them and carried them home across the Mediterranean Sea to be distributed all over Europe. The Mohammedan merchants wanted to keep the rich trade with the East for themselves, and so they kept secret the places from which they brought their goods.

In the thirteenth century missionaries from Europe traveled through unknown parts of Asia. Adventurous merchants also began making their way to the East. These travelers came to lands of great wealth and culture. They found civilizations more highly advanced than their own. They brought back to Europe strange tales of the magnificence of the East and the thousand and one wonders they had seen. These reports were eagerly received by the people of Europe.

In that distant East were some of the oldest civilizations in the world. In those early days when the Egyptians were building the pyramids, when wise men in Babylon were studying the stars, when Homer in Greece was singing his lays about Troy, and long before Rome was founded, the people of the Far East had built up flourishing civilizations.

ANCIENT INDIA

In the south-central part of Asia is a vast triangle of land called India. To the north of it are the snow-capped Himalaya Mountains. In the snowy peaks of these mountains rise two of the longest rivers of the world. The Indus flows west and the Ganges flows east.

In very early times these two warm, fertile river valleys were settled by tribes of dark-skinned people. Later, the Aryans, a fair-skinned people, made their way from central Asia through the passes in the Himalayas, and came to the valleys of the Indus and the Ganges. They conquered the dark-skinned natives and took possession of the land. They settled in villages and began to cultivate the soil. In the course of time the Hindus, as these people came to be called, built up a great civilization.

The Hindus worshiped Brahma, the creator. They worshiped the gods of nature also, but Brahma was above all other gods. Their early religious writings are called the Vedas. They are the hymns and psalms sung by the priests before the altars, long before they were written down.

The priests, who were thought to have gained their knowledge from heaven to reveal to the people, became the highest class in Hindu society. They were called Brahmans. The next class were the warriors, who defended the

people. Below them were the merchants and farmers, who produced the things which the people needed. Lowest of all were the slaves, who did all the hardest work in the fields and the villages.

This way of dividing society into classes is called the caste system. Nowhere else in the world were classes so fixed as they were in India. People who were born in one class could never become members of another class, no matter what they did. The people of one class did not mingle with those of another class or have anything to do with them.

India was too large to be one nation. It was made up of many states, each state ruled by a Hindu prince. The ruler of a state was called a raja. When a prince conquered a number of states and ruled over them, he was called a maharaja. Many of these rulers were men of great wealth.

In India were to be found gold, silver, and many precious stones—beautiful rubies, glowing blue sapphires, bright green

emeralds, gleaming diamonds. From Ceylon, an island southeast of India, came enormous quantities of pearls. Skilled craftsmen made beautiful jewelry of gold and silver, set with these precious stones. The princes of India had the most beautiful jewels in the world. Their garments were embroidered in gold and ornamented with rare stones.

The people of the higher classes in India lived lives of luxury, while the mass of the people suffered want and often hunger. Their lives were very hard. They lived in little one-room mud huts. Their clothing was an undergarment of cotton which reached halfway down to the ankles, and an upper garment, partly thrown over the shoulder and partly draped in folds around the head. Their principal food was rice, which they raised in their fields.

About the middle of the sixth century before Christ, there lived a young prince in northern India. He had a wife and a young son whom he dearly loved. He had wealth and power and it seemed as if everything that anyone could wish for was his. But the young prince was greatly troubled by the suffering he saw about him. He had a great longing to help his people. One night he left his palace and all the luxury he had known. He changed his fine clothes for simple garments and went to live in a lonely place, where he could think over the things which troubled him.

In his years of quiet meditation it seemed to the young prince that he had found the secret of true happiness. "Happy is he who has overcome all selfishness," he came to believe. "Happy is he who has found the truth. The truth is noble and sweet; the truth can deliver you from evil."

[384]

Later in life the prince went out into the world again and traveled about, trying to teach people how to live the good life. He urged them to think of others rather than about themselves. "Glory not in thyself but in thy neighbor," was one of his teachings. "One should seek for others the happiness he desires for him-  self. To him in whom love dwells the whole world is one family."

Surely this is wisdom, thought those who heard the words of the prince. He gained many followers and they called him Buddha, which means "the chosen one through whom wisdom returned to the earth."

Buddha lived for many years, teaching people and help- ing them to live better lives. Before he died he said to his followers: "From good must come good, and from evil must come evil. That is the first law of life. Go ye now and preach the most excellent law."

The followers of Buddha carried his teachings through India and to other lands. They built beautiful temples in his honor. In each temple was a statue of Buddha in deep thought. Before these images the people burned incense.

In the eighth century, when the Mohammedans were

overrunning many countries, some of them came to India and took possession of many parts of the country. One of their rulers built a magnificent building, the Taj Mahal, in memory of his wife. He wanted it to be the most beautiful building in the world. It is of dazzling white marble, inlaid with colored marble and precious stones in lovely patterns. It is surrounded by a garden with lily ponds and avenues of cypress trees.

IN FAR CATHAY

North of the Himalaya Mountains is China, the land which the people of medieval Europe called Cathay. There in very early times grew up a splendid civilization. Hundreds of years before the birth of Christ tribes of black-haired, yellow-skinned people lived in the fertile parts of that country. They called their country the Middle Kingdom, because they thought that the earth was flat and that their land was in the middle of its flat surface. Sometimes they spoke lovingly of their country as the Flowery Land.

In the early days China was ruled by kings. About two hundred years before Christ the whole land was united under an emperor. The emperor found a number of walls built along the northern boundary of China to keep out the fierce people beyond. He combined these walls into one continuous wall built of brick and stone and mud. For

twelve hundred miles the Great Wall stretched over mountains and valleys, and up the steep sides of high cliffs. It was so broad that armies could march on top of it. At many places were fortresses, where sentinels stood guard.

The Chinese loved their homes and their families. When a son married he did not make a home of his own, but brought his bride to his father's house. The Chinese family came to include not only the children and their parents, but their uncles and aunts, their grandfathers and grandmothers, and their great-grandfathers and great-grandmothers.

In very early days the Chinese made a great discovery. They found that they could unwind the thread of the cocoon made by a little worm and could weave it into a lovely fabric. The story is told that an empress of China became interested in watching a worm feeding on a mulberry tree in her garden. For days it fed ravenously on the tender leaves of the tree. It grew until it was about three inches long. Then it stopped eating and began drawing a cobweb-fine thread out of its mouth. Moving its head this way and that, it wound the thread around and around its body, making a cocoon.

The thought came to the empress that perhaps this beautiful shining thread could be spun and woven into cloth. She ordered her spinners and weavers to try, and they produced silk, the most beautiful material ever seen.

After that the Chinese began raising silkworms and making silk. They embroidered bright-colored birds and flowers on this lovely soft fabric, and perhaps a dragon, with a long, spreading tail. The dragon, the Chinese believed, was not evil but good. A dragon was always embroidered on the robe of the emperor.

The Chinese guarded the secret of silk-making so carefully that for thousands of years no other people knew how to make silk. For centuries Mohammedan traders carried silk from Cathay to the ports of western Asia and from there it was taken to Europe.

There were never more skilled craftsmen than those who lived in ancient China. From very fine clay they made exquisite porcelain which they shaped into dishes, bowls, and vases. When other countries came to know this fine ware, they called it china, from the name of the country where it was first made. Other craftsmen made brightly colored enamel ware. Still others made beautiful articles of wood, which were covered with a thick varnish called lacquer.

Many centuries before the people of Europe knew how to make paper the Chinese had learned how to make it from the inner bark of the mulberry tree and from rags. On this they wrote with brushes, making the characters by different groupings of brush strokes. They made square signs, because it is easier to write with a brush that way. They also learned to print by using wooden blocks.

The Chinese respected their scholars and wise men. More highly honored than any other was the great philosopher, Kung-fu-tse. Europeans found it so hard to pronounce his

學而時習之

不亦樂乎

name that they changed it to Confucius, and that is the name by which he came to be generally known. In the fifth century before Christ, Confucius was teaching the Chinese how to live better lives. His most famous rule of conduct was: "Do not to others that which you would not have them do to you." This is similar to the Golden Rule, which Christ gave to his followers.

For many years Confucius studied and taught. He loved the early history of his country and the old ways of doing things. He believed that his people would be happier if they followed the old customs and ceremonies. He gathered together the ancient writings and put them in a form the people could read.

The teachings of Confucius had great influence on the Chinese people. They were proud of their ancestors and their way of living and they tried to live in the same way. Rich people

[390]

built temples to their ancestors. Even in the humblest homes a special place at which offerings were made was set aside in honor of the ancestors of the family.

After the death of Confucius the people realized how wise he had been. Devoted followers wrote down many of his sayings, which became the sacred writings of the Chinese. They built many-storied temples, called pagodas, with a roof curving up at the edges at each story.

The people of China had no desire to leave the Flowery Land. Their vast, rich country gave them everything they needed and many luxuries, and the people were content with what they had. Not much change came to China from the outside world. Thus the ways of living of the Chinese changed very little.

Northwest of China was a high plateau of desert and grasslands. In that wild region lived tribes of Tartars who were called Mongols. They lived in dome-shaped tents made of felt, and when they moved from one place to another with their flocks and herds, they put their tents on huge carts and carried them along. They were splendid horsemen, for they spent most of their time on horseback riding about from one place to another.

For hundreds of years the Great Wall protected the Chinese from their fierce northern neighbors. But early in the thirteenth century all the Mongolian tribes were united by a fierce warrior named Genghis. He was proclaimed the Khan, which meant the "most mighty ruler."

After Genghis had made himself ruler of all the Mongols, he looked about for other lands to conquer. In 1226 he led his armies south until he came to the Great Wall. Although the wall was heavily guarded, Genghis was able to break through it and enter Cathay. He quickly conquered a large part of the country.

This great warrior then turned westward into Europe and his victorious armies swept over Russia, Poland, and Hungary. After these great victories Genghis went back to the East. Shortly after his return he died. At the time of his death the empire of Genghis extended all the way from the China Sea to the Dnieper River in Russia.

MARCO POLO VISITS THE GREAT KHAN

In 1265, Kublai, the grandson of the all-conquering Genghis, became the Grand Khan of the Mongol empire. He extended his empire even beyond that of Genghis. It was said to be the largest ever governed by one man. "The lord of all the earth," he was called by his people.

Of all his lands Kublai loved Cathay the best. In his time China came to the height of her magnificence. There were splendid cities in which were scarlet palaces with roofs of gold. In the seaports dwelt rich merchants who traded with the whole Eastern world. In and out of the harbors sailed fleets of strange-looking ships called junks, the largest vessels of the time. Kublai built a magnificent city at Cambaluc, which is today called Peiping. There the emperor lived in great splendor.

One day in the year 1275 two merchants from Venice, Maffeo and Nicolo Polo, arrived at the palace of Kublai.

With them was an attractive young man, Marco, the son of
Nicolo Polo. The merchants bowed low in homage before
the emperor, who greeted them in a courteous and friendly
manner.

"Who is this young man?" asked the Great Khan, turning
toward Marco.

"Sire, he is my son and your servant," explained Nicolo
Polo.

"Welcome is he, and it pleases me much to see him,"
replied the Khan.

Once before, Maffeo and Nicolo Polo had visited the
Khan, and when they returned to Venice they had mar-
velous tales to tell of their experiences in the little-known

lands of the East. When they decided to go back, young Marco had begged to go with them and was overjoyed when they consented to take him.

So Marco sailed with his father and uncle down the Adriatic Sea and across the Mediterranean, and landed on its eastern shore. There they set out on the three years' journey across Asia. Over mountains and plains, through deserts and valleys, the Venetians made their way, sometimes on camels, sometimes on horseback, sometimes by boat, and sometimes on foot.

At last the travelers reached the land of Kublai Khan. The Khan heard that they were coming and sent courtiers to bring them to his palace.

Never before had Marco seen such a wonderful palace as that of the Khan. The walls were covered with gold and silver and were adorned with figures of huge dragons.

MARCO POLO'S TRAVELS

"It is altogether so vast, so rich, and so beautiful," he said, "that no man on earth could design anything superior to it. The hall of the palace is so large that it could easily dine six thousand people, and it is quite a marvel to see how many rooms there are besides."

The Khan was much interested in his far-spreading lands and was accustomed to send many agents on missions to different parts of his empire. When they returned they told him little about the places they had visited.

"I had rather hearken to the strange things and the manners of the different countries you have seen," the Khan would say when they returned from missions, "than merely to be told of the business you went upon."

At one time Kublai sent Marco to a distant part of his kingdom. Marco took pains to find out all he could about the lands through which he traveled. When he reported to the Khan, he told of the many strange things he had seen. The emperor was delighted and said, "If this young man live, he will assuredly come to be a person of great wealth and ability."

After that the Khan sent Marco on his most important missions. Far and wide the young traveler journeyed into lands where no European had ever been. For seventeen years he served the Great Khan, "continually going and coming, hither and thither, on the missions that were entrusted to him." Wherever he went he carefully put down in a notebook all that he saw and heard. Thus it came about that he had a greater knowledge of the world than any other man living at that time.

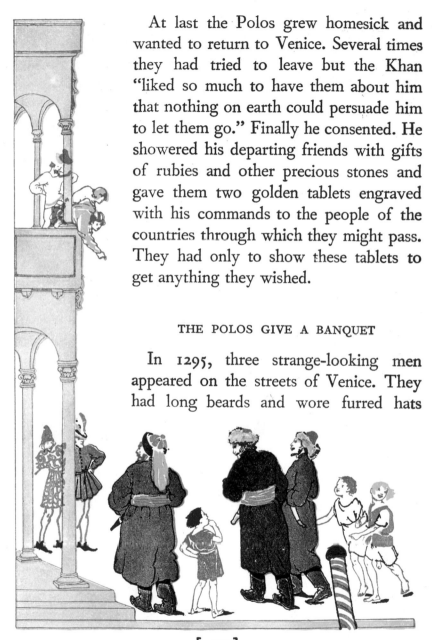

At last the Polos grew homesick and wanted to return to Venice. Several times they had tried to leave but the Khan "liked so much to have them about him that nothing on earth could persuade him to let them go." Finally he consented. He showered his departing friends with gifts of rubies and other precious stones and gave them two golden tablets engraved with his commands to the people of the countries through which they might pass. They had only to show these tablets to get anything they wished.

THE POLOS GIVE A BANQUET

In 1295, three strange-looking men appeared on the streets of Venice. They had long beards and wore furred hats and long padded coats such as were worn by the people of the East. They spoke in a foreign language. The people of Venice stared at the new arrivals curiously. Who were they? No one knew. They said that they were the Polos, but it was hard to believe that these shabby, travel-worn strangers were members of the wealthy Polo family. Marco, who had left Venice as a young boy, was a full-grown man. His father and uncle were quite old.

The three travelers made their way to their old home, the Casa Polo, which was occupied by relatives. They knocked at the door and when it was opened they explained who they were. At first their relatives would not believe them; but at length they agreed to let their kinsfolk in.

An old story tells us how the Polos proved that they were telling the truth about themselves. They prepared a splendid banquet to which they invited all the important people of Venice. It was the strangest banquet the guests

had ever attended. Their hosts appeared in magnificent robes of crimson satin reaching down to the ground. When everyone was seated, they took off these robes and put on others of crimson damask, ordering that those they had taken off should be given to the servants. After the first course the Polos left the room and returned in new robes of crimson velvet, ordering the second suits to be given to the servants. "When the feast was over they did the like with the robes of velvet, after they had put on dresses of the fashion worn by the rest of the company," says the old account.

When all the servants had left the room, the most amazing thing of all happened. Marco went into another room and returned with the old, shabby garments which the travelers had worn when they arrived in Venice. With a

sharp knife he slit open the seams and before the dazzled eyes of the guests poured out a shower of rubies, diamonds, emeralds, pearls, and other priceless jewels. Here was treasure such as they had never before seen in all their lives. The jewels had been stitched up in those dresses in so artful a fashion that nobody could have suspected the fact that the precious stones were concealed within.

Then the guests understood why the Polos had disguised themselves in shabby garments. They had traveled a long distance through dangerous regions where there were many robbers. "Being well aware of the impossibility of carrying with them so great an amount of treasure over a journey of such length and difficulty," they had taken this clever means of bringing their precious jewels safely home to Venice.

"And now," runs the old story of their travels, "the guests recognized that, in spite of all former doubts, these were, in truth, those honored and worthy gentlemen of the Casa Polo that they claimed to be; and so all paid them the greatest honor and reverence."

Such amazing news traveled quickly through Venice, you may be sure, and people flocked to visit "the polite and gracious Marco Polo and ask him questions about Cathay and the Great Khan."

Marco never tired of telling tales about his travels in the far East. People of Venice who perhaps had never journeyed more than a few miles beyond their native city listened spellbound to his stories. Never before had they heard of such things except in fairy tales.

The fabulous tales which Marco told might have been forgotten by the world, but in an unexpected way they came to be written down in a book. For three years Marco remained in Venice. Then a war broke out between Venice and Genoa. During the war Marco was taken prisoner and thrown into a dungeon in Genoa. While he was there he told stories of his journeys to a learned man, Rusticiano, a fellow prisoner. So interested was Rusticiano that he begged permission to write down the stories, for he thought that other people of Europe ought to know about the wonderful lands of Asia.

"We shall set down things seen as seen, and things heard as heard only, so that no jot of falsehood may mar the truth of our book, and that all who shall read it or hear it read, may put full faith in the truth of all its contents," said Rusticiano.

Years afterward, when Marco Polo was an old man, he was asked whether he wished to correct anything in his book. "There is no exaggeration in the book," he declared. "On the contrary, I have not told half the amazing things I saw with my own eyes."

[401]

Many parts of the book described the wealth and splendor of the East. "In the island of Ceylon," wrote Marco, "rubies are found and in no other country in the world but this. They find there also sapphires and topazes and amethysts and many other stones of price. And the king of this island possesses a ruby which is the biggest and finest in the world."

About the island of Cipango, as Japan was called in those days, Marco said:

> I can tell you the quantity of gold they have is endless; for they find it in their own island and the king does not allow it to be exported. Moreover, few merchants visit the country because it is so far from the mainland, and thus it comes to pass that their gold is abundant beyond all measure.
>
> I will tell you a wonderful thing about the palace of the lord of that island. You must know that he hath a great palace which is entirely roofed with fine gold, just as our churches are roofed with lead, in so much that it would scarcely be possible to estimate its value. Moreover, all the pavement of the palace, and floors of its chambers, are entirely of gold, in plates like slabs of stone, a good two fingers thick; and the windows also are of gold, so that altogether the richness of this palace is past all bounds and all belief.

About a prince of India the book said:

> He wears a fine silk-thread string with one hundred and four large pearls and rubies of great price. The king wears on his arms three golden bracelets thickly set with pearls of great value, and gold bands of like kind he wears on his legs. So let me tell you, what this king wears of gold and gems and pearls is more than a city's ransom.

Best of all, Marco learned of many places where the spices and other luxuries of the Orient so much desired by the people of Europe could be obtained. In the islands off Cathay, the sailors told Marco, were many islands from which spices came. "They produce a great variety of spices," said Marco. "For example, in those islands grows pepper as white as snow, as well as the black in great quantities. In fact, the riches of those islands is something wonderful, whether in gold or precious stones, or in all manner of spicery; but they lie so far off from the mainland that it is hard to get to them. When ships do voyage thither, they make vast profits by their venture."

SHIPS IN UNKNOWN SEAS

All over Europe people read Marco Polo's book and longed to get spices directly from the lands where Marco Polo said they grew. How could people get there? Could there possibly be a way of reaching the East by water?

If goods from the East could be loaded on ships and carried directly to Europe without being shifted from camels to boats and back again half a dozen times, the cost of such goods would be much less. Merchants of the country which was fortunate enough to find this water route could then sell their goods for lower prices than could the merchants of Venice. Thus the lucky merchants would secure for themselves the rich Eastern trade.

To reach the East by water seemed an almost impossible task. Ships at that time were equipped with oars and one square sail, which could be used only when the wind was blowing from behind. Such ships were all right for the calm waters of the Mediterranean Sea but were not safe on the rough waters of the ocean. Seamen had no instruments to help them in guiding their ships. Of course, on clear days they could tell directions by the position of the sun, and on clear nights they used the North Star as their guide, just as sailors had done in early days. But in case of fog, or storm, or on nights when there were no stars, they had no idea in which direction they were sailing and they might be hopelessly lost at sea.

By the fifteenth century, men were beginning to build bigger and stronger ships. Oars were given up and ships were built with two or three masts that were equipped with sails. Each sail was made so that one part could be reefed while the rest remained outspread. Sailors learned how to manage their sails so that they caught the wind in whatever direction it blew.

Men of science helped sailors by inventing instruments which made it possible for them to guide their ships over the pathless seas. First came the compass. In quite early times, the Chinese had discovered that if a needle was rubbed with a certain kind of stone and floated on a cork in a basin of water, one end would always point toward the north. Later on someone placed a magnetized needle on a pivot over a card marked with the four principal directions, north, east, south, and west, and with many others in between, and placed it in a box for convenience. This "nautical box," as it was called, was the first compass.

The compass was brought to Europe by Arab traders. At first many sailors refused to use it. They thought there must be some kind of magic in it and were afraid to have anything to do with it. Gradually, however, seafaring men came to recognize its usefulness. They found it reliable and a wonderful help in steering their ships.

Sailors were also aided by new charts and maps. Men who sailed to faraway places began writing out descriptions of the coasts they had seen and directions as to how to get there. These "sailing directions" could be purchased by sea captains. Later, instead of writing out the directions, seamen made drawings of the coasts along which they

sailed. Map makers worked over these, correcting errors and making the maps more and more accurate as new information came in. These charts and maps were trustworthy guides for sailors.

Another instrument was the astrolabe. With it sailors could find out how far north or south of the equator they were by measuring from the position of the sun. When the pitching and rolling of the ship made it difficult to use the astrolabe, still another instrument, the cross-staff, which could be held more steadily in the hands, was used.

With larger, better ships to sail in, with the newly invented aids to navigation, and with charts and maps to guide them, seamen became more confident of finding their way about in strange seas. They now began exploring the unknown waters of the earth.

PRINCE HENRY'S DREAM

The first people to make the search for a water route to the East were the Portuguese. The youngest son of King John of Portugal was Prince Henry. When he was quite young Henry had "a magnificent desire to find a way to where the spices grew." To find a sea route to the East became the dream of his life. So he gave up the gay life at his father's court and went to live on a lonely spot on the southern shore of Portugal. There he built a high tower on a rocky cape overlooking the sea. He invited noted geographers and map makers from other lands to come there. He set up a school to train sea captains in the use of the new nautical instruments and the best ways of managing ships.

The prince's days and nights were filled with greatest toil. "It would be hard to tell how many nights he passed in which his eyes knew no sleep," wrote someone who knew him. His brother brought back from one of his journeys the book of Marco Polo, which the prince studied eagerly.

In those days the continent of Africa was almost entirely unknown to the people of Europe. No one knew how large

it was or whether ships could sail around it. For many years Portuguese sailors had explored the northern coast to trade with the natives. Was there a way around the southern end of Africa by which ships could reach the spice lands of the Indies?

If such a water route could be found, it would be much shorter than the long caravan routes then used by Eastern traders. The Portuguese would now be able to buy spices and jewels for themselves in Eastern markets.

The more Prince Henry studied, the more certain he became that if the west coast of Africa were followed far enough, it would end in a cape. If a ship could round this cape, a sea route to the East and its riches would then be opened. He decided to send seamen to find out whether his belief were true.

Now it was almost impossible to get sailors to venture beyond a certain cape a few hundred miles down the coast of Africa. "Cape Non," they called it, which means "Cape Not." Beyond that cape, they said, the sea was so full of terrible currents that no ship, having passed it, would ever be able to return.

Prince Henry paid little attention to such foolish ideas. He believed that if he could once get his ships past that point, men could find their way around Africa and might reach the land of gold and spices which Marco Polo had seen. Finally the prince persuaded one of his captains to pass the dreaded cape.

Soon another dangerous cape barred the way. Most sailors believed that beyond that point the sun poured down sheets of liquid flame and kept the sea boiling with its fiery heat. Would not sailors who ventured there be boiled alive or scorched brown?

In 1434, the prince called to him a captain named Gil Eanes, in whom he had great faith. His orders to Gil were to pass this cape and not to return "without a good account of the cape and the seas beyond." Instead, Gil came back with terrible stories he had heard.

The prince rebuked him for being afraid. "If there were the slightest authority for such stories," he said, "I would not blame you. But you come to me with tales of seamen who don't know how to use the needle [compass] or sailing chart."

Then the prince urged Gil to make another attempt. "Go out again," he said, "for, by God's help, fame and profit must come from your voyage, if you but persevere."

The next year Gil, "despising all danger," started out again. This time he succeeded in passing the cape and found "the waters as easy to sail in as the waters at home."

After that success it was easier for the prince to persuade other captains to push on down the coast. Seven years passed before one of them reached the next cape, which he named Cape Blanco. Another captain "never lowered his sails" till he arrived at another cape, which he named Cape Verde, meaning the "Green Cape." "The land here," he said, "is full of fine large trees which are continually green. The trees never wither like those in Europe. They grow so near the shore that they seem to drink, as it were, the waters of the sea."

Hence south and still farther south the Portuguese seamen sailed. Every important discovery was carefully noted by Prince Henry on an enormous wall map made by an Italian monk, Fra Mauro. For forty years the prince's ships explored unknown seas, but though his captains sailed and sailed, they did not reach the southern end of the continent of Africa.

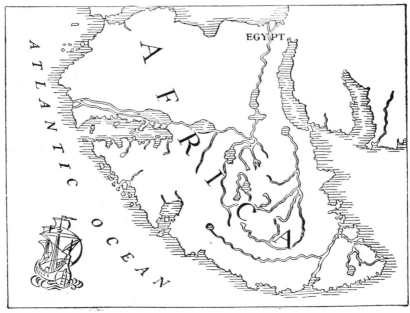

AFRICA ON FRA MAURO'S MAP

Sad to say, Prince Henry did not live to see his dream of finding a sea route to India come true. In the year 1460 he died. But his forty years of patient work were not spent in vain, for later explorers profited by what his seamen had learned.

THE CAPE OF GOOD HOPE

King John of Portugal took up Prince Henry's unfinished task. In 1487 he sent out an expedition in charge of Bartholomew Diaz, well known as a daring seaman. These ships reached a point farther south than any others. They came to a place where terrible storms raged. Mountainous waves at one moment seemed to toss the little ships to the very skies and, at the next, to dash them down to the bed of the ocean. "All cried out for mercy upon their souls, for now they no longer took heed of their lives."

A thick fog came up and hid everything from sight. For two weeks no land was visible. The ships, driven before the wind, drifted southward on the unknown sea. Where were they going? No one knew.

At last the wind ceased. When Diaz next looked at the compass he was amazed to find that they were sailing north. Without knowing it, he had rounded the cape which Prince Henry had believed was at the southern end of Africa. The way to the Indies was now open.

Diaz wanted to go on but his men, worn out by the terrible trip, refused to go farther. Sadly he turned back. As the ships made their way homeward, a tall headland

loomed high above the sea and Diaz realized that this was the cape at the southern point of Africa which they must have passed in the fog. Remembering the terror of passing it, he named it the Cape of Storms.

At last Diaz was back in Portugal once more. Quickly he made his way to the king to tell his good news. When Diaz said that he had named the cape at the tip of Africa the Cape of Storms, the king shook his head.

"The Cape of Storms? Nay! If we call it the Cape of Storms, our sailors will be afraid to pass it. Does it not point the way to India and the riches of the East? Call it then the Cape of Good Hope."

Thus the cape was named, and it still bears that name on modern maps of Africa.

The news of the great achievement of Diaz spread over Europe. When the people of Venice heard about it they were deeply disturbed, for they realized that with the discovery of the way around the southern tip of Africa, the success of the Portuguese in reaching India by sea would be only a matter of time. When that happened, the trade with the East upon which the wealth of Venice depended would be gone and the days of her greatness would come to an end.

"On receiving the news of Diaz's voyage," said a Venetian writer, "the whole city was distressed and astounded, and the wisest take it to be the worst tidings we have ever had. For it is well known that Venice reached the height of her glory and riches through commerce alone, and now by this new route the spice cargoes will be taken straight to Lisbon, where Germans, Flemish, and French will flock to buy them. They will find the goods cheaper in Lisbon than they can be in Venice, for before the freights reach Venice by the old route they must pay enormous dues for passage through Syria and the land of Egypt."

TALKING TOGETHER

1. In discussing reasons why Asia remained so long a place of mystery to the people of Europe, use the map on page 378. Why were they so eager to find a new trade route to the East?

2. Form groups to report on Oriental culture in India and China.

3. Describe some of the new ideas and inventions traders brought back from the East. What changes were brought about in European ways of life as a result of these ideas from the Orient?

4. Explorers made use of several improvements in navigation at this time. How did Prince Henry of Portugal aid men who sailed ships into unknown waters?

5. The people of Venice were disturbed when they heard that Diaz had found a new route to the Indies. How did they think this would affect Venetian trade?

INTERESTING THINGS TO TRY

1. When you are studying Marco Polo, trace on the map, page 395, his route of travel from Venice down the Adriatic Sea, eastward across the Mediterranean, overland to Bagdad, down to the Persian Gulf, and across the country to Peiping.

2. You might like to dramatize the return of the Polos, unrecognized by their friends, and then the banquet scene. Can your class show the wonder and surprise of the guests?

3. To show how the known world has grown, make a map of the world that was known at the time of Marco Polo. Use the map on page 380 of your book as a guide. Then compare your map with a map of the world today.

4. You will be interested in the motion picture "People of Western China." If your teacher can get this for your class, take notes on the parts you find most interesting.

5. After studying the pictures in this unit make a frieze for your classroom on life in India. Include the Taj Mahal in the background.

They Sailed and Sailed, by Frances M. Fox. The stories of "Marco Polo's Surprise Party" and "A Book That Was Written in Prison" are interesting.

He Went with Marco Polo, by Louise Andrews Kent. This gripping story makes Marco seem like a living character.

The Romance of Discovery, by Hendrik W. Van Loon. In this book is a chapter on "Prince Henry of Portugal."

The Past Lives Again, by Edna McGuire. Read "The Three Travelers Return" and "The Story of the Polos' Travels."

Made in China, by Cornelia Spencer. This book tells about silk making, pottery, lacquer work, and other Chinese crafts.

How the Great Religions Began, by Joseph Gaer. Read the accounts of Buddha and Confucius in this book.

The Man Who Changed China: The Story of Sun Yat-sen, by Pearl Buck. This story tells of the struggles and triumphs of a brave leader.

China's Story, by Enid L. Meadowcroft. You will be interested in "Days of Glory and Grandeur."

Adventures and Discoveries of Marco Polo, by Richard J. Walsh. This is based on Marco Polo's own book.

Nehru's Story, by Shakuntala Masani. A bold and courageous man who sacrificed wealth and patiently endured years in prison for love of country.

Made in India: The Story of India's People and of Their Gifts to the World, by Cornelia Spencer. The descriptions of Mogul painting and the Taj Mahal are of great interest.

GETTING READY FOR A PANEL DISCUSSION

In a panel discussion the conversation is begun by a panel, or a small group. People in the audience also take part by raising questions and making comments. For an assembly program arrange a panel discussion of important topics in this unit.

All the members of your class may write on slips of paper the questions they want to hear discussed. Besides points from this book, they may have other ideas from travelers they have met, other books they have read, or films they have seen.

Choose a committee to select the best questions for your panel discussion.

Select a panel of five or six pupils from your class to study and discuss these questions before a school assembly.

Another committee may be chosen to prepare exhibits of pictures and objects to make the program vivid and interesting.

Quiz Yourself

Can You Tell?

1. How did the people in Europe hear of the wealth and civilization of the East?
2. What was the difference in the life of the higher and lower classes in India?
3. What great teacher arose in India and told the people to think of others rather than themselves?
4. Why was the Great Wall in China built?
5. Which of all the lands Kublai governed did he love best?
6. What good results came from Marco Polo's imprisonment?
7. Whose studies of maps and geography greatly helped in the discoveries of the fifteenth century?
8. Why was Cape Verde so named?
9. By whom was the Cape of Good Hope discovered?
10. How did the people of Venice receive the news of the discovery of the Cape of Good Hope?

XI

FINDING A NEW WORLD

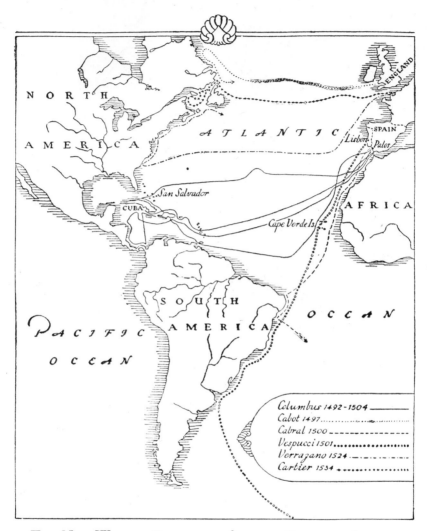

Map labels:

NORTH AMERICA

ATLANTIC

ENGLAND

SPAIN

Lisbon   Palos

San Salvador

CUBA

AFRICA

Cape Verde Is

SOUTH AMERICA

PACIFIC OCEAN

OCEAN

Legend:
Columbus 1492-1504 ———
Cabot 1497 ....
Cabral 1500 - - - - -
Vespucci 1501 •••••••
Verrazano 1524 -·-·-·-
Cartier 1534 •-•-•-•

THE NEW WORLD. *From ports of western Europe, explorers set out to discover a short route to Asia by sailing west and found a new continent.*

FINDING A NEW WORLD

IS THE EARTH ROUND?

For over half a century the Portuguese sent ships farther and farther down the coast of Africa seeking a water route to the East. During that time no mariners, so far as we know, had sailed very far out on the Atlantic Ocean, which lay to the west of Europe. Centuries earlier, those fearless sailors, the Vikings, had explored the north Atlantic in their dragon boats; but the rest of Europe knew little about their explorations.

The sea, so full of strange creatures, stirred the superstitious fears of sailors. They were afraid to venture far out on the Sea of Darkness, as the Atlantic Ocean was called, because of the terrible tales told about it. It was said to be infested with great monsters, which dragged ships down and devoured all on board. It was believed that somewhere beneath its surface was a magnetic mountain which would draw a ship toward it, pull out the nails and all the other iron parts which held it together, and leave nothing but the timbers strewn over the water. Map makers of the time pictured on their maps sea serpents, which they imagined lurking in the unknown sea, and treacherous whirlpools.

It is no wonder that mariners refused to sail far out on such dangerous waters. There was little to be gained by doing so. All the things for which the people of Europe longed came from the East. There was no need to sail west.

For centuries no one knew how far the Atlantic Ocean stretched away to the west of Europe. It was, says an old writer, "a vast and boundless ocean on which ships dared not venture out of sight of land. For even if the sailors knew the direction of the winds, they would not know whither those winds would carry them, and as there was no inhabited country beyond, they would run great risk of being lost in mist and vapor."

One of the questions greatly debated at that time was whether the earth was flat or round. Most people thought that it was flat. One man wrote, "Can anyone be so foolish

The World before the Discovery of America

as to believe that there are some men whose feet are higher than their heads, or that there are places where trees are growing with their tops hanging downward, or rain falling upward?" On the other hand, learned men of the time believed the earth to be round. If that were so, they reasoned that Asia might be reached by a westward voyage across the Sea of Darkness.

According to the maps of the time, the possibility of reaching the East by sailing west seemed simple enough, for on none of them was there any sign of the two huge western continents blocking the way to Asia. No one knew anything about them or about the Pacific Ocean, and no one had any idea that the earth is as large as it really is. To the learned men who thought that the earth was round the western route to Asia seemed shorter than the eastern route the Portuguese were seeking.

One of the most famous geographers of the day was Paolo Toscanelli, who lived in Florence. Toscanelli began thinking about new ways to the lands of the spices. He declared that it was possible to reach the East by sailing west. He drew a map of the world, based on the descriptions of Marco Polo. On the map, the eastern coast of Asia was located opposite the western coast of Europe.

The king of Portugal became interested in Toscanelli's ideas through a gentleman of the royal household who was a friend of the great geographer. The friend wrote to Toscanelli asking whether he would explain his ideas to the king. Toscanelli sent a copy of his map of the world to the king with a letter explaining his views.

Many times I have reasoned concerning the very short route which there is by the sea from here to India—the native land of the spices—and which I hold to be shorter than that which you take by Guinea. For greater clearness I have made a chart such as is used by navigators, on which is traced this route and I send it to Your Majesty and I will show you how you may reach the places most productive of all sorts of spices. You must not be surprised if I call those parts where the spices grow "west," when they usually call them "east"; for if a person should sail continuously westward, he would come to those parts of the earth where those lands be.

Of course Toscanelli, like everyone else in Europe at that time, knew nothing about the two western continents and the Pacific Ocean, so he represented the earth as being much smaller than it is.

WESTWARD TO THE INDIES

During the years when Prince Henry was sending his ships down the coast of Africa, a boy, Christopher Columbus, was growing up in Genoa, Italy, dreaming of becoming a sailor. At that time Genoa was one of the great trading cities of Europe. From his earliest days Columbus haunted the busy wharves of the city, to see the ships coming in laden with their rich cargoes of beautiful things from the East. Their holds were fragrant with sweet-smelling spices. He listened to the sailors telling their adventures, and he picked up many strange tales about distant lands and peoples. His greatest ambition was to be a sailor himself,

and when he was only fourteen years old he went to sea for the first time.

Columbus spent years sailing on the Mediterranean Sea, and later went to Portugal to live—a very attractive place to a seafaring man in those days. There he made maps and charts, and sailed on many voyages with Portuguese seamen. He read all the books he could get and learned all he could about the earth as it was known by the best scholars of his day. He got a copy of Marco Polo's book and studied it carefully. As he read, he wrote in the margins of the book the comments that came to him.

If the earth is round, as learned men stated, and if there is an ocean east of Cathay, as Marco Polo said, it must be the same body of water that washes the western coast of Europe, reasoned Columbus. So why could he not sail west across the Sea of Darkness and reach the riches of the East? But how far would a ship have to sail to reach the East by sailing west? That was the great question in the mind of Columbus.

Columbus wrote to Toscanelli, and the noted geographer replied: "I observe thy great and noble ambition to pass over to where the spices grow." He sent Columbus a map similar to the one he had sent to King John. This led Columbus to believe that Asia lay only about twenty-five hundred miles west of Europe. He was sure that a western route to the riches of the East would be much shorter than the one the Portuguese were seeking around the tip of Africa.

A second time Columbus wrote to Toscanelli, and Toscanelli replied: "I regard as noble and grand your project of sailing from east to west according to the map which I sent you and which would appear still more plainly on a sphere. When the voyage shall be accomplished it will be a voyage to powerful kingdoms and to cities and provinces

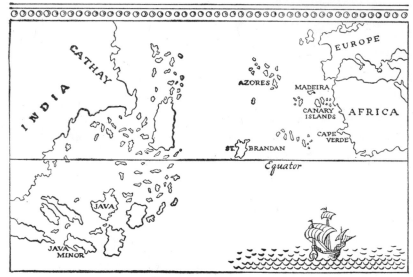

TOSCANELLI'S MAP

most wealthy and noble, abounding in all sorts of things desired by us; I mean, with all kinds of spices, and jewels in great abundance."

By 1484 Columbus had his plan carefully worked out. To get together a fleet of ships and supply them with men and provisions for such a voyage took a great deal of money, and Columbus was a poor man. So he appealed to King John of Portugal for aid. Portuguese ships were steadily making their way down the west coast of Africa, and the king and his advisers were sure that soon the sea route around Africa would be found. They were not interested in the ideas of Columbus.

Then Columbus made application to the court of King Ferdinand and Queen Isabella of Spain for help. At that time the king and queen were trying to drive the Moors out of Spain and had neither the time nor the money for an expedition.

Sad and discouraged, Columbus went on his way. The head of a monastery where he stopped for shelter urged him to try once more. Again he was unsuccessful.

Seven years passed. Columbus had tried in vain to get ships and men for his venture. Finally he decided to seek help from the king of France. He started for the little seaport of Palos. There, perhaps, he might find a ship that would take him to France. Before he got there, Queen Isabella sent for him and promised him help with his undertaking. But again there were disputes and delays, and again Columbus set out for France. Suddenly he heard the clatter of a horse's hoofs. Someone had convinced the queen that she had lost a chance for glory and riches and she had sent a royal messenger, mounted on a swift horse, to persuade Columbus to return.

So in April, 1492, it was decided that Columbus should have the men and ships needed for his voyage. It was very difficult to get sailors for such a wild undertaking. Some men were let out of prison on condition that they would go with Columbus.

CROSSING THE ATLANTIC

Shortly after sunrise on August 3, 1492, three little ships, the *Santa María,* the *Pinta,* and the *Niña,* with about ninety men, were ready to set sail on the great adventure. The sailors bade their families and friends a sorrowful farewell, for most of them thought they would never return. The vessels left the harbor of Palos in Spain and boldly set their course across the mysterious and terrifying Sea of Darkness.

Day after day the little ships sailed westward. As time passed and the sailors saw nothing but the unknown sea stretching about them on all sides, they became more and more frightened. Where were they? Where were they going? How could they get back? They came to a part of the ocean where there were vast masses of seaweed drifting about. They feared that their ships would get tangled in it and they could not get through. Then, for many days, the wind blew only from east to west. "My people were much excited," Columbus tells us, "at the thought that in those seas no wind ever blew in the direction of Spain."

One night the compass began acting strangely. Instead of pointing steadily north, it swerved toward the west. The sailors were panic-stricken. They thought that the sea must be bewitched. "We have no other guide but the compass," they cried, "and now we are coming into seas where the compass will be no guide to us. We shall never be able to find our way back!"

The Admiral explained to them that the compass could not fail to guide them in those seas. The reason it varied once was because a star had moved its place. This explanation calmed the crews and there was for a time no more talk of turning back.

Signs seemed to indicate that land was near. Little land birds flew up into the rigging of the ships and sang.

One evening, about sunset, the lookout on the *Pinta,* which was leading the other ships, suddenly shouted, *"Tierra! Tierra, Señor!"*—that is, "Land! Land, sir!"

Quickly the crew scrambled up the rigging to feast their eyes on the sight. Yes, there it was, straight ahead of them, gleaming in the evening sunlight. Columbus fell on his knees to thank God.

But alas, in the morning the "land" had entirely disappeared. It had been only clouds, lying so low on the horizon that they looked like islands. Again and again the sailors thought they saw land, only to be disappointed.

As September changed into October, the crew grew desperate. Was there never to be an end to this terrible voyage? They begged Columbus to give up his plan and go back to Spain. "But the eternal God gave him the strength and spirit to withstand them all," says the old account of the voyage. "He encouraged them as best he could, giving them good cheer and adding that it was useless to murmur, because he had come in search of the Indies and he must keep on until he had found them."

THE INDIES AT LAST

On October 11, birds which never venture far from land were seen circling around the ships, a green reed floated by, and the sailors of the *Pinta* saw a branch with red berries on it in the water. These were sure signs that land was near. Everybody looked excitedly for the first glimpse of it.

In the evening Columbus made a little speech urging the night watch to keep a sharp lookout. To the man who first sighted land would be given a silk doublet and a purse

of gold which the king and queen had promised. At ten
o'clock that night Columbus thought he saw a moving
light, "like a little wax candle rising and falling," but he
was not sure.

By two o'clock the next morning the moon was high
in the heavens, throwing a bright light over everything
ahead. The watchful eyes of the lookout on the *Pinta*
caught sight of something like a white sandy beach gleaming in the moonlight.

"Land in sight!" he shouted.

"Land! Land!" echoed through the ships.

By sunrise it was clear that the ships were near an island.
The Indies at last! The dream of Columbus had come
true. He believed he had found the western route to the
riches of the East.

Columbus and his men went ashore. "The whole company kneeled on the shore and kissed the ground for joy

returning to God thanks for the great mercy they had experienced during their long voyage through seas hitherto unpassed, and their now happy discovery of unknown land." Columbus unfurled the gorgeous red and gold flag of Spain and set it up.

All of this was watched with amazement and awe by a curious crowd of men, women, and children who had gathered at a distance on the shore. Who were these half-naked, copper-colored people? wondered Columbus. They were not dressed in the splendid clothes he had expected to find the people of the East wearing. But as he was sure that the land he had reached was India, he called them Indians. Actually he had reached a small island north of Cuba, one of a group called the Bahamas.

Everything Columbus saw and heard convinced him that he had arrived at the edge of the Great Khan's kingdom. He thought the little islands he saw were "those innumerable ones that are depicted on the maps of the world in the Far East." Somewhere among those islands must be Cipango. By signs he asked the Indians which way he should go to find Cipango. They made signs to him indicating a rich island to the south.

"I shall set sail for another very large island which I believe to be Cipango according to the indications I have received from the Indians. As I find gold and spices in abundance I shall determine what to do. At all events I am determined to proceed on to the continent, where I shall deliver the letters of Your Highnesses to the Great Khan," wrote Columbus in his journal.

After sailing this way and that, Columbus was puzzled by his failure to come upon the land of the Great Khan. A cruise of ten days among the islands convinced him that he was east of Cathay. He decided to return to Spain and report to King Ferdinand and Queen Isabella what he had found on this first voyage.

Just seven months after he had sailed away, Columbus was back in Spain again. Bells rang out joyously and cannon boomed; cheering, shouting crowds of people lined the streets. Columbus had found Cathay! The king and queen sent nobles to bring to the court "Don Christopher Columbus, our Admiral of the Ocean Sea and Viceroy and Governor of the Islands Discovered in the Indies."

A strange procession made its way through the streets, thronged with cheering people. First came some Indians, decked with feathers and paint and decorated with gold

ornaments. Then followed the weather-beaten sailors, carrying parrots and other strange birds with brilliant blue, yellow, and green plumage. Last came Columbus on horseback, surrounded by nobles dressed in velvet and lace, with caps from which long plumes waved.

As Columbus approached the king and queen, they rose from their throne to do him honor, and most graciously invited him to sit with them and tell them about his voyage. He told his story simply, and when he had finished, the whole court fell upon their knees and gave thanks to God.

Columbus became the idol of Spain. Honors were heaped upon him. He was given a coat of arms and was granted an income from the royal treasury. News of his success spread like wildfire over Europe. Everywhere it was reported that Columbus had "discovered the coast of the Indies and found that way never before known to the East."

Spain was very proud of her Admiral. The people thought that all the wealth of the East would now pour into Spain, making her the most powerful nation in Europe. They were eager to share in this wealth.

A second expedition must be sent out as soon as it could be made ready. This time Columbus was sure he would find and bring back unbounded wealth for the king and queen. "The gate to the gold and pearls is now open," he said, "and precious stones, spices, and a thousand things may surely be expected." He had no trouble getting men to go on this voyage. Hundreds of men wanted to go with him. No one doubted that this time the land of spices would be found.

The second expedition was, of course, no more successful than the first. Still Columbus and the people of Spain did not lose hope.

[433]

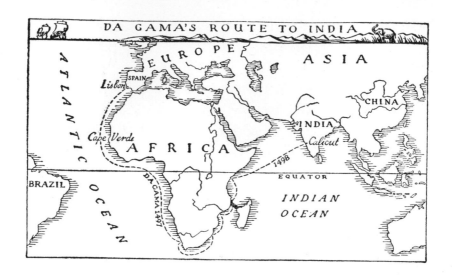

PRINCE HENRY'S DREAM COMES TRUE

The Portuguese were downcast when the news came to them that Columbus had sailed west and found land. Their rival, Spain, was getting ahead of them in finding a way to the riches of the East. It was not very pleasant for the king of Portugal to remember that it was his country to which Columbus had first applied for help and that the glory which had come to Spain might have come to Portugal. If only Portugal could find a sea route to the East around Africa!

A new king, Emanuel, had come to the throne. He decided to send out an expedition at once. Who would undertake such a perilous voyage? Who could be entrusted with such a task? One man after another was suggested. At last the king decided upon Vasco da Gama, a nobleman of high rank, and asked him to head an expedition.

Columbus begged the queen to let him go back once more. In May, 1502, he sailed on his fourth voyage. It was his last. He returned to Spain sick and worn out with his many years of disappointment and disaster. He had been home only a short time when his friend of many years, Queen Isabella, died.

After the death of the queen, the king would do nothing for Columbus, who was poor and friendless. "I receive nothing of the revenue due me," he said in a letter. "I live by borrowing." In another he said sadly, "Such is my fate that twenty years of service through which I have passed with so much toil and danger have profited me nothing, and at this very day I do not possess a roof in Spain that I can call my own."

At last, in 1506, the great discoverer died, broken-hearted at his failure to find the rich lands of the East. To the end of his life he was firmly convinced that he had found the outer fringe of the empire of the Great Khan. He never knew that he had led Europe across the Sea of Darkness to a New World.

DISCOVERIES IN THE WEST

By his daring and courage Columbus had broken through the superstitious fear which for centuries had kept the men of Europe from sailing across the Sea of Darkness. After he had led the way to the west, other venturesome seamen followed, and a great age of exploration and discovery set in. For two hundred years explorers pushed farther and farther into the unknown western world. With each exploration the size of the known world grew.

Explorers from Spain took the lead. They explored the coasts of South America. They toiled through the jungles and over the mountains of Central America from the Atlantic Ocean to the Pacific. They made their way to Mexico and to the mainland of North America. Everywhere they went they claimed the land for Spain "for all time, both now and as long as the earth endures."

They found undreamed-of wealth in the new lands. Fleet after fleet of treasure ships laden with gold, silver, and precious gems returned to Spain, making her the richest nation in Europe.

The great good fortune of Spain stimulated the rulers of other countries of Europe to send out explorers and gain wealth by the discovery of new lands. In 1497, Henry VII, king of England, sent out John Cabot, an Italian seaman in his service, with "the full and free right to sail to all parts, countries, and seas of the east, of the west, of the north, to seek out and discover and find whatsoever isles, countries, regions, or provinces of pagans, in whatsoever part of the world."

Cabot crossed the Atlantic with one small ship and only eighteen men. He reached the continent of North America somewhere in the region of Labrador or Nova Scotia, but, like Columbus, he believed that he had reached Cathay. On Cabot's return from his first voyage a fellow Venetian wrote of him: "The Venetian, our countryman, who went with a ship from Bristol in quest of new islands, is returned and says he discovered land, the territory of the Great Khan. Vast honor is paid to him. He dresses in silk and the English run after him like mad people."

Meanwhile the Portuguese kept pushing on farther and farther east. In 1500, a Portuguese fleet, commanded by Pedro Cabral, was sailing down the coast of Africa, intending to follow Vasco da Gama's route to India. Strong winds and currents carried the ships so far west that they touched the coast of South America. Cabral and his men landed and took possession of the territory for their native Portugal. Later this land came to be known as Brazil, from the Portuguese name for a hard red wood found in the new region.

France was not to be left out in the search for wealth. Francis I, king of France, looked with jealous eyes at the great possessions of Spain and Portugal. He sent a letter to the king of Spain, asking him "by what right he and the king of Portugal undertook to monopolize the earth. Had our father, Adam, made them his sole heirs? If so, it would be more than proper of them to produce the will, and meantime he would feel at liberty to seize all he could get."

In 1524 Francis sent an Italian seaman named Verrazano to explore. Verrazano crossed the Atlantic and sailed all along the eastern coast of North America. Ten years

later a bold French sea captain, Jacques Cartier, entered the Gulf of St. Lawrence and sailed far up the river of the same name. After that, many French explorers made their way up that great inland waterway and also down the Mississippi River to its mouth. All the land which they discovered they claimed for France.

Before the end of the sixteenth century Spain had a vast empire in the New World. It included Mexico, Central America, and all of South America except Brazil. In what is now the United States it extended as far as the northern part of California. The French had an empire in the heart of North America and built up a vast fur trade in that region. Early in the next century English settlers came to the eastern coast of North America, cleared the land, built homes, and laid the foundation for the nation which, in later times, was called the United States.

AMERICA GETS ITS NAME

For many years the explorers who followed Columbus believed that they had reached Asia. In the course of time, however, they realized that this was not true.

Living in Spain at the time Columbus was making his voyages was an Italian named Amerigo Vespucci, or, in Latin, Americus Vespucius. He was much interested in maps and charts, and he was fascinated when he read of Marco Polo's travels in Asiatic countries. As he studied his charts, he dreamed of making voyages to the new lands just being opened up. He is supposed to have joined an  expedition which sailed for the New World in 1497 and to have made four voyages in all. Most of his explorations were along the South American coast.

Vespucci wrote interesting letters to his friends about his travels. In a letter about his voyage in 1501, he spoke of the land he had visited. "It is proper to call it a New World," he said. "Men of old said over and over again that there was no land south of the equator. This last voyage of mine has proved them wrong, since in these southern regions I have found a country more thickly inhabited by people than is Europe, or Asia, or Africa."

A copy of this letter fell into the hands of a map maker named Waldseemüller, who was writing a Latin pamphlet containing maps of the new explorations. In it he said: "Now truly, as these regions have been more widely explored,

[443]

it is clear that a new part of the world has been discovered by Americus Vespucius. This may be learned from his letters which are herewith printed.

"I see no reason why this new part of the world should not be called after Americus. That is, it should be called the land of Americus, or America, from its discoverer, a man of much wisdom."

Thus the name America was first suggested and it was not long before the land later known as South America was called America on maps.

For a long time the people of Europe did not realize that the land to the north of that which Vespucci saw was also a new continent. They still thought of the northern continent as a part of Asia. On maps made in the early part of the sixteenth century North America was called Asia, and the East Indies were shown near by. Not until 1541 was the name America given to both the western continents.

A WORLD MAP DRAWN IN 1507

The people of Europe had discovered a New World. That New World was to benefit by all that the people of the Old World had learned since the time when the first steps toward civilization were taken. For thousands of years the people of earlier ages had been learning new ways of living and finding ways of making man's life on the earth better and happier.

Many nations and people contributed to this great forward march of man through the ages. For a while one nation took the lead, then for some reason it was unable to advance farther. But always a new nation arose to take up the work of world progress. Greece carried civilization far beyond the point reached by earlier nations. The Romans learned much from the Greeks and made their own contributions. They spread the ancient learning throughout the Mediterranean world. In later times tribes north of the Roman Empire learned civilized ways of living, and civilization spread northward and westward over Europe.

For centuries the people of Europe were interested in the East and were shut off from the West by the Sea of Darkness. In the fifteenth century they looked out over the Atlantic Ocean and wondered whether ships could sail over its unknown waters and come back laden with the riches of the East. At length came a great mariner who dared to venture across that dreaded sea. He did not find the riches of the East; he found something far more important, a New World. In later times people from many countries came to settle and make their homes in the land which he had discovered.

During all the early ages the people were governed by despots, who had little thought for the happiness of their people. Most of the people were slaves, forced to do all kinds of work by those in authority over them. Slaves, working under the lash of the whip, moved the huge blocks of stone to build the pyramids of Egypt. Slaves, chained to their seats, rowed the great triremes which made their way to every part of the ancient world. The tombs, the temples, and all the great structures of ancient times were built by slaves.

In feudal days the mass of the people were powerless in the hands of a few nobles who owned the land. Then, in the time of the great awakening of the people which began in the latter part of the Middle Ages, men began saying that every man, no matter how humble his station, had the right to freedom and opportunity.

Recall the words of John Ball, speaking to the peasants of England about the nobles of his day: "By what right are they, whom we call lords, greater folk than we? And what reason do they give why they should be more masters than ourselves? They have leisure and fine castles, while we must brave the wind and the rain in our work in the fields. And yet it is by our toil that these men have the wherewithal to support their pomp."

Thus spoke John Ball, the poor priest, in 1381, and the people of his day and of later days struggled for better conditions in life, for greater freedom and justice, for the right to worship God in their own way, for the right to think and to act as they thought best.

The people who came to the New World were the heirs of all the past. They brought with them many of the customs and ways of doing things they had known in their Old World homes. To that new land they carried the precious heritage of freedom and justice which their ancestors had struggled for centuries to achieve. And in that new land was to be written a wonderful new chapter in the story of man's effort to make the world a better and happier place to live in. Out of the society which the people of Europe created in the New World developed the United States and the other American nations—nations of free people.

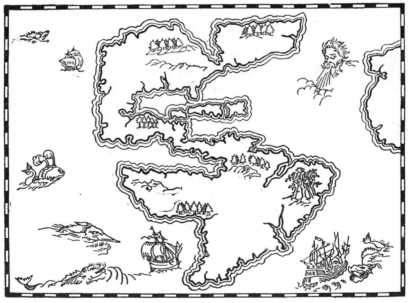

THE NEW WORLD ON A MAP OF 1540

[447]

TALKING TOGETHER

1. Discuss the reasons people once had strange ideas about the shape of the earth. How did these false notions keep ship captains from sailing the Atlantic?

2. Portugal refused aid to Columbus. Why was Portugal not interested in seeking a route to the Indies by sailing west?

3. Select members of your group to report on the explorers who followed Columbus to the New World. Others may report on the eastward voyage of Vasco da Gama.

4. Fate was unkind to Columbus. Even the country he discovered was named for another man. America has honored Columbus by naming places for him. Can you mention some of these?

5. The New World owes many ideas of freedom and justice to the past. Read again the section in your book telling about our heritage from the Old World.

INTERESTING THINGS TO TRY

1. In the days when men sailed the Sea of Darkness, sailors sometimes sealed brief statements of their voyage in bottles or casks, and cast them into the water with the hope that they would be picked up by other seamen. Imagine you were one of Columbus's crew. Write a message of this sort.

2. Study the pictures in this unit. Make a mural showing events in the story of Columbus, from his unsuccessful efforts to gain aid at the court of Portugal to his triumphant return to Spain after crossing the Atlantic.

3. If you have an opportunity in your classroom to see the movie "The Story of Christopher Columbus," list the discouragements which he overcame.

4. Ask a member of your group to find and read to the class Joaquin Miller's poem "Columbus."

5. Add to your time line the dates of the explorations and events in this unit.

[448]

The Story of Old Europe and New America, by Eugene C. Barker, Mabel Rockwood Grimm, and Matilda Hughes. The chapters on "Finding a New Way to the Far East" and "How Christopher Columbus Found America" will tell you more about exploration in Columbus's time.

Heroes of Civilization, by Joseph Cottler and Haym Jaffe. The chapter "India at Last" is a story about Vasco da Gama.

Christopher Columbus, Discoverer, by Alberta Powell Graham. You will enjoy following the adventures of the bold discoverer who sailed on and on.

America Begins, by Alice Dalgliesh. Find and read "The Dragon Ships," "Tales Told by a Traveler," and "The Story of Christopher Columbus."

These United States, by Gertrude Hartman. Read "The Great Days of Spain" to learn more about the Spanish explorers.

The First Book of the West Indies, by Langston Hughes. The beautiful land which Columbus discovered is made very real in this book. From the stories and illustrations you can imagine the excitement and delight of these early discoverers as they landed.

Ship Boy with Columbus, by Enid L. Meadowcroft. This story tells the adventures of Pedro, who sailed with Columbus on his first voyage to the New World.

CAN YOU FIND THE STORY BEHIND MAPS AND GLOBES?

Maps tell you about the change in man's idea of the size of the world. Look at the map of the New World on page 418. Then look at Toscanelli's map on page 424. How did each explorer broaden people's idea of the world?

Secure a map showing the airplane routes of the world. As air transportation develops, how are world travel routes changed?

It is interesting to trace the voyages of the early explorers on a globe.

[449]

List of Dates

THE list gives 53 dates selected for their importance in Old World history. They may be of aid to pupils in making time lines.

B.C.		Unit	Page
3400	Upper and Lower Egypt were united under Menes.	II	46
3000	The Pharaohs began to build the Pyramids.	II	71
2000	Hammurabi put Babylonian laws in writing.	III	90
1500	Egyptian power reached its greatest height.	II	77
1230	Moses led the Hebrew people out of Egypt.	III	102
753	Early people began the settlement of Rome.	V	165
722	Assyria conquered the northern Hebrew kingdom.	III	104
612	The Chaldeans destroyed the city of Nineveh.	III	95
586	Nebuchadnezzar of Babylon captured Jerusalem.	III	104
539	Cyrus and the Persians conquered Babylonia.	III	113
490	Athenians overcame the Persians at Marathon.	IV	144
480	Greeks defeated the Persians at Salamis.	IV	149
461	The Golden Age of Pericles began in Athens.	IV	150
399	Socrates was brought to trial for his teachings.	IV	154
336	Alexander began the conquest of a vast empire.	IV	158
275	Rome controlled the entire Italian peninsula.	V	179
146	Carthage was destroyed by the Romans.	V	182
58	Roman legions under Caesar began to conquer Gaul	V	189
44	Caesar was killed by Romans who feared his power.	V	192
31	Roman Republic became an empire under Augustus.	V	193

A.D.			
375	Huns from Asia invaded the land of the Goths.	VI	208
400	Germanic invaders began to enter Roman lands.	V	201
410	Goths under Alaric took possession of Rome.	VI	209
449	Angles and Saxons began to invade Britain.	VI	222
476	Roman Empire was broken up by invading tribes.	V	201

		Unit	Page
481	Clovis united the Franks under one ruler.	VI	216
622	Mohammed fled from enemies in Mecca.	VI	211
711	Arabs from Africa established kingdom in Spain.	VI	211
732	Moslem invaders were driven back by the Franks.	VI	216
800	Charlemagne was crowned ruler of a vast empire.	VI	218
871	Alfred the Great became ruler of Saxon England.	VI	224
1000	Leif Ericsson explored Vinland in North America.	VI	231
1066	William the Conqueror invaded England.	VI	232
1099	Army of the First Crusade captured Jerusalem.	VII	272
1154	Henry II, who introduced jury trial, began rule.	VIII	297
1215	Magna Charta was signed by King John of England.	VIII	301
1265	Common people were represented in Parliament.	VIII	307
1275	Marco Polo reached the palace of Kublai Khan.	X	393
1340	Gunpowder was brought to Europe from the East.	VII	288
1381	Peasants revolted against serfdom in England.	VIII	318
1434	Prince Henry's mariners began to seek a route east.	X	409
1453	Turks took possession of Constantinople.	IX	359
1456	The first book was printed from movable type.	IX	353
1487	Diaz discovered the Cape of Good Hope in Africa.	X	411
1492	Columbus set out to find a route to the Indies.	XI	426
1497	Vespucci joined an expedition to the New World.	XI	443
1497	John Cabot reached coast of North America.	XI	440
1497	Da Gama began voyage to India around Africa.	XI	435
1500	Portuguese mariners discovered and named Brazil.	XI	441
1517	Martin Luther preached his beliefs in Germany.	IX	334
1524	Verrazano explored the coast of North America.	XI	441
1543	Copernicus laid foundation of modern astronomy.	IX	368
1632	Galileo wrote an early book on astronomy.	IX	372

List of Maps

Unit   **Page**

I. WESTERN EUROPE   2
Traces of prehistoric people have been found in many places.

II. EGYPT AND THE NILE VALLEY   44
Egyptians founded a great nation in this fertile valley.

EGYPTIAN TRADE ROUTES   53
The early Egyptian traders traveled over land and sea.

III. THE FERTILE CRESCENT   82
Different tribes formed early nations in this fertile area.

PHOENICIAN TRADE ROUTES   110
Phoenician traders sailed their ships to many far-off lands.

IV. ANCIENT GREECE   120
The Greek city-states made great gains in government.

GREEK COLONIES   142
Greek civilization spread along the Mediterranean coast.

V. ANCIENT ITALY   164
Rome became the center of a great nation.

THE ROMAN EMPIRE   188
Rome's great empire included most of the civilized world.

VI. TRIBES OF WESTERN EUROPE   206
Wandering tribes settled down and formed new nations.

MOSLEM LANDS   212
The Moslems spread into Persia, North Africa, and Spain.

VOYAGES OF THE VIKINGS   227
The Vikings made long voyages in their small ships.

VII. A MEDIEVAL MANOR   246
Each castle-community was ruled by a lord.

ROUTES OF THE FIRST CRUSADE   273
Crusaders from Europe made their way to Jerusalem.

Unit		Page
	TRADE ROUTES FROM THE EAST	287
	The riches of the East were carried over these routes.	
VIII.	OLD LONDON	294
	London Town grew up along the Thames River.	
IX.	WESTERN EUROPE	330
	New ideas spread from these cities in Europe.	
X.	THE FAR EAST	378
	Traders and explorers found great civilizations in the East.	
	THE WORLD IN THE MIDDLE AGES	380
	Only a small part of the world was known at that time.	
	MARCO POLO'S TRAVELS	395
	These travels covered a period of about twenty-four years.	
	AFRICA ON FRA MAURO'S MAP	410
	This is part of a world map made in Prince Henry's time.	
	PORTUGUESE VOYAGES	412
	Portuguese mariners named the capes on the west coast.	
XI.	THE NEW WORLD	418
	Many explorers sailed westward seeking new trade routes.	
	THE WORLD BEFORE THE DISCOVERY OF AMERICA	420
	People at that time thought that this was the whole world.	
	TOSCANELLI'S MAP	424
	Columbus studied this map before sailing.	
	DA GAMA'S ROUTE TO INDIA	434
	Da Gama reached India by sailing around Africa.	
	A WORLD MAP DRAWN IN 1507	444
	This is the first map bearing the name "America."	
	THE NEW WORLD ON A MAP OF 1540	447
	Map makers now knew something of its true shape.	

ā as in dāte ⎮ ē as in bē ⎮ ō as in hōpe
ă as in ăm ⎮ ĕ as in mĕt ⎮ ŏ as in hŏt
â as in fâre ⎮ ę̄ as in hęre ⎮ ô as in lôrd
à as in àsk ⎮ ē as in makēr ⎮ ū as in ūse
a̍ as in a̍bout ⎮ ī as in bīte ⎮ ŭ as in ŭp
ä as in fär ⎮ ĭ as in bĭt ⎮ û as in bûrn

th as in thin ⎮ o͞o as in fo͞od
th as in then ⎮ o͝o as in fo͝ot
tū as in pictū̦re ⎮ ou as in out

A

Abraham (ā′bra̍ hăm), 99, 102, 281

Acropolis (a̍ krŏp′ō lĭs), 123, 132, 151–152

Aegean (ē jē′a̍n) Sea, 121; map, 120

Africa, 182, 212; Portuguese explorations, 407–413, 425, 434–435; maps, 410, 412, 420, 434. *See also* Carthage; Egypt; Punt

Age of Metals, 14. *See also* Bronze Age; Iron Age

Agriculture: in prehistoric times, 29–32, 34; in Egypt, 46–50; in Greece, 126–127; of Romans, 184; under feudal system, 258–260

Alaric (ăl′a̍ rĭk), 209–210

Alchemists (ăl′kĕ mĭsts), 364

Alcuin (ăl′kwĭn), 218, 219

Aldine (ôl′dīn) press, 356

Alexander the Great, 158

Alfred the Great, 224–226, 354

Alhambra (ăl hăm′bra̍), 214–215

Alphabet, 110–111

Alps, Hannibal's march over, 181

America: Viking voyages to, 231; discovery by Christopher Columbus, 422–433; European exploration of, 439–442; naming of, 443–444; maps, 418, 444. *See also* North America; South America

Amphitheaters, Roman, 184

Amusements: in prehistoric times, 17; in Greece, 133–136; in Rome, 184–185; of Norsemen, 228–229; in medieval castle, 249, 252–257; at fairs, 282

Ancestor worship, 390–391

Angles, 207, 221–222, 239, 295; map, 206

Anglo-Saxons, 221–226, 300; language, 233–234

Animals: in prehistoric times, 4–6, 7, 22–24; in Egypt, 61; in Middle Ages, 254–255

Answerers (àn′sēr ērz), 62

Apollo (a̍ pŏl′ō), 130, 132

Apprentice (a̍ prĕn′tĭs), 278

Aqueducts (ăk′wē dŭkts), Roman, 175

Arabia (a̍ rā′bĭ a̍), 211, 285; maps, 82, 212, 395

Arabic (ăr′a̍ bĭk) numerals, 358

Arabs, 211–214, 270, 405. *See also* Mohammedans; Moors

Arch, triumphal, 179

Archaeologists (är kē ŏl′ō jĭsts), 3, 18

Architecture (är'kĭ tĕk tūr): Egyptian. 71–76; Babylonian, 87–89; Assyrian, 94–95, 97–98; Persian, 114; Greek, 125, 151; Roman, 176, 193–194; Moorish, 213, 214–215; medieval, 247–249, 263, 275–277; Renaissance, 340–342

Arena (*a* rē'n*a*), 135

Arithmetic, 36, 86, 128, 177

Armor, 247–248

Art: in prehistoric times, 18–19; Egyptian, 75–76; Greek, 151–152; Italian Renaissance, 340–346

Arthur, King, 249

Aryans (âr'ĭ *a*nz), 382

Asia, 379, 444; maps, 380, 420

Assemblies: German, 208; Anglo-Saxon, 222–223

Assisi (äs sē'zē), Saint Francis of, 267–269

Assyria (*a* sĭr'ĭ *a*), 94–96, 104, 115; map, 83

Astrolabe (ăs'trō lāb), 406

Astrology (*a*s trŏl'ō jĭ), 89

Astronomy (*a*s trŏn'ō mĭ), 89

Athena (*a* thē'n*a*), festival of, 131–132; statue of, 151, 152; temple to, *see* Parthenon

Athens: map, 120; location, 123; life in, 124; crafts, 124–125; education, 128, 129; oath of citizenship, 129; gods, 130–132; democracy in, 141; Persian wars, 143–144, 147–149; Golden Age, 150–153; war with Sparta, 153; conquest by Macedonia, 158

Atlantic Ocean, medieval ideas of, 419–420

Atrium (ā'trĭ ŭm), 174

Augustine (ô'gŭs tēn), 239–240

Augustus (ô gŭs'tŭs), Emperor, 191, 196

B

Babylon (băb'ĭ lŏn), 84, 85, 97–98, 104, 112–113; map, 82

Babylonia (băb ĭ lō'nĭ *a*): map, 82; geography, 84; life of people, 84–86; weights and measures, 86; religion, 87–89; legal system, 90–91; books, 91–92; education, 93; conquest by Assyria, 95; conquest by Chaldea, 95; under Nebuchadnezzar, 97–98; conquest by Persia, 104, 112–113, 115

Bacchus (băk'ŭs), 175

Bacon, Roger, 365–367

Ball, John, 316–317, 318–319; quoted, 446

Banks, Egyptian, 85

Barons, English, struggle with kings, 298–308

Barter, 35, 36

Baths, Roman, 194

Battering ram, 178, 247

B.C., meaning of, 196

Bellows, early, 15

Belshazzar (bĕl shăz'zēr), 112–113

Benedict (bĕn'ĕ dĭkt), Saint, 262–265

Bernardone, Francesco (bär när dō'nā frän chäs'kō). *See* Francis, Saint

Bethlehem (bĕth'lē ĕm), 196; map, 82

Bible, 105–106, 332, 343, 344, 348, 350–353, 358–359

Bill of Rights, 339–340

Bireme (bī'rēm), 108

Black Death, 314–315

Blanco, Cape, 409; map, 412

dāte, ăm, fâre, *a*sk, *a*bout, fär, bē, mĕt, hẽre, makẽr, bīte, bĭt, hōpe, hŏt, lôrd, ūse, ŭp, bûrn, thin, then, pictụre, fōōd, fŏŏt, out

Block printing, 348–349
Boar's head, 252
Boats: in prehistoric times, 27–29;
Egyptian, 53–54; Babylonian, 85;
Phoenician, 107–109; Viking, 227–
230; Chinese, 393; in later Middle
Ages, 403–404; of Columbus, 426
Bohemia (bō hē'mĭ ȧ), 333; map, 330
Book of the Dead, 63
Books: Egyptian, 55; Babylonian, 91–
92; manuscript, 265–266; block,
348–349; early printed, 350–353.
See also Hornbook; Ink; Papermak-
ing
Bow and arrow, early, 8
Boys, education of: in Babylonia, 93;
in Greece, 126, 127–129; in Rome,
177; in Charlemagne's palace school,
218–220; for knighthood, 249–251;
in monasteries, 264, 354
Brahma (brä'mȧ), 382
Brahmans (brä'mȧnz), 382
Brazil, 441, 442; map, 434
Breadmaking, in prehistoric times, 30
Brickmaking: in Egypt, 51; in Baby-
lonia, 84
Britain, 109, 194, 221–222; maps, 188,
227. *See also* England
Britons, 221–222; map, 206
Bronze, 14, 109
Bronze Age, 14
Brutus (brōō'tŭs), 192
Buddha (bŏŏd'ȧ), 384–385
Buildings. *See* Architecture
Burgundians, 207; map, 206
Buttresses, 275–276; flying, 275

C

Cabot (kăb'ŭt), John, 440–441
Cabral, Pedro (kȧ bräl', pā'thrōō), 441
Caesar, Julius (sē'zēr, jōōl'yŭs), 189–
192, 193, 216

Calendar: Egyptian, 58, 191; Roman,
190–191
Calicut (kăl'ĭ kŭt), 436, 437; map,
434
Caliphs (kā'lĭfs), 212
Cambaluc (kăm'bȧ lōōk). *See* Peiping
Cambyses (kăm bī'sēz), 114
Canaan (kā'nȧn), land of, 99, 100, 102,
103. *See also* Palestine
Canute (kȧ nūt'), King, 226
Caravans (kăr'ȧ vănz), 381
Carthage, 180–182; maps, 110, 164
Cartier, Jacques (kȧr tyā', zhäk), 442
Caste system, 382–383
Castle, medieval, life in, 247–261
Catapult (kăt'ȧ pŭlt), 178
Cathay (kă thā'), 403, 423, 431; map,
424. *See also* China
Cathedrals, 275–277
Catholic Church, 336, 337, 338, 339.
See also Church, Christian; Cru-
sades; Francis, Saint; Monks
Cave dwellers, 16–19
Caxton, William, 356
Central America, 440, 442
Ceres (sē'rēz), 175
Ceylon (sē lŏn'), 384, 402; map, 378
Chaldeans (kăl dē'ȧnz), 95, 97
Chariot races: Greek, 135–136; Ro-
man, 184
Charlemagne (shär'lē mān), 217–220,
354
Charles V, emperor of Germany, 334–
336
Charles Martel, 216
Charter, 284, 289. *See also* Magna
Charta
Cheops (kē'ŏps), 71
Children of Israel. *See* Hebrews
China: papermaking in, 214, 347, 389;
early European trade with, 380,
389; early civilization, 386; Great

[456]

Wall of, 387, 392; family life, 387; silk-making, 388–389; crafts, 389; religion, 389–391; Mongol rule in, 391–393; visit of Polos, 393–397; and compass, 404; maps, 378, 395, 434

Christ. *See* Jesus Christ

Christians, persecution of, 199

Christmas, celebration of, in Middle Ages, 252

Church, Christian: origin, 106, 196; spread of, 198, 238–241, 381; organization of, 241. *See also* Catholic Church; Church of England; Crusades; Inquisition; Lutheran Church; Protestant Church; Reformation

Church of England, 338–339

Cicero (sĭs'ĕ rō), 359

Cincinnatus (sĭn sĭ nā'tŭs), 169–171

Cipango (sĭ păng'gō), 402, 431; map, 378

Circus, Roman, 184–185

City-states, Greek, 121–123, 141

Civilization, contributions to: by primitive man, 38–39; by Egypt, 77; by Hebrews, 105–106; by Phoenicia, 110; by Greece, 159, 445; by Rome, 195, 445; by German tribes, 210; by Moorish Spain, 213, 214; by medieval England, 324–325; by Renaissance, 372–373

Clay, use of: in prehistoric times, 12, 19; in Egypt, 51; in Babylonia, 84, 91–93; in Greece, 124; in China, 389

Clergy, in early church, 241

Clermont, council at, 270; map, 273

Clock, shadow, 57

Cloisters (klois'tĕrz), 263

Clothing: in prehistoric times, 16, 24; Egyptian, 69–70; Roman, 174; German tribes, 207

Clotilda (klō tĭl'dà), 238–239

Clovis (klō'vĭs), 216, 238–239

Colonies, Greek, 142; map, 142

Colosseum (kŏl ŏ sē'ŭm), 193

Columbus, Christopher, 422–433, 438–439

Common law, origin of, 298

Compass, 365, 404–405

Confucius (kŏn fū'shĭ ŭs), 389–391

Constantinople (kŏn stăn tĭ nō'p'l), 270, 286, 359, 380–381; maps, 273, 287, 395

Consuls, Roman, 172

Copernicus, Nicolaus (kō pûr'nĭ kŭs, nĭk ō lā'ŭs), 367–368, 370, 372, 373

Copper, discovery of, 13–14

Cordova (kôr'dō và), 214; map, 206

Cornelia, mother of Gracchi, 186–187

Counting-frames, Roman, 177

Craftsmen: in Egypt, 51–52; in Babylonia, 84–85; in Greece, 124–125; in India, 384; in China, 388–389; in Middle Ages, *see* Guilds

Crito (krī'tō), 155–156

Cross-staff, 406

Crusades, 270–273, 284, 285, 379; map, 273

Cyrus (sī'rŭs), king of Persia, 104, 111–113

D

Dancing, in prehistoric times, 17

Danes, 224–225

Daniel, 112–113

Danube River, 194, 200, 207, 209; maps, 188, 206

dāte, ăm, fâre, ȧsk, ȧbout, fär, bē, mĕt, hēre, makēr, bīte, bĭt, hōpe, hŏt, lôrd, ūse, ŭp, bûrn, thin, then, pictūre, fōōd, fŏŏt, out

Dardanelles (där dȧ nĕlz'). *See* Hellespont

Darius (dȧ rī'ŭs), king of Persia, 114–115, 143, 145

Dark Ages, 210

David, King, 103; statue, 343

Delphi (dĕl'fī), oracle at, 132, 147

Delta, Nile, 45

Demeter (dē mē'tēr), 130, 131, 175

Democracy (dē mŏk'rȧ sĭ): in Greece, 141–142, 150–151; in England, 325

Demosthenes (dē mŏs'thĕ nēz), 157–158, 359

Denmark, 224, 227

Diaz, Bartholomew (dē'ȧs, bär thŏl'ō mū), 411–413

Diet of Worms (vōrms, wûrmz), 334–336; map, 330

Dionysus (dī ō nī'sŭs), 131, 175

Discus-throwing, 134

Division of labor, 34

Dnieper (nē'pēr) River, 392

"Do-nothing kings," 216

Drama: in prehistoric times, 17; Greek, 152; of guilds, 280–281; Elizabethan, 361–362. *See also* Mummers

Drawbridge, 247

Dress. *See* Clothing

Drum, first, 17

E

Eanes, Gil (yȧ'nēsh, zhĭl), 409

East: trade with, 285–287, 380–381; map, 287; search for water route to, 403–413, 419. *See also* Columbus, Christopher; Gama, Vasco da; Polo, Marco

East Indies, 444; map, 378

Education: in Babylonia, 93; in Greece, 126, 127–129; Rome, 177; Moorish Spain, 214; in France under

Charlemagne, 218–220, for knighthood, 249–251; in monasteries, 264, 354; in universities, 357–360; in the Renaissance, 358–360

Edward I, king of England, 308–309

Edward VI, king of England, 339

Egypt: maps, 44, 53, 82, 188; geography of, 45; government of, 46; agriculture, 46–48; irrigation, 49–50; crafts, 51–52; trade, 53, 66–67; trade routes, map, 53; writing, 54–57; telling time, 57; calendar, 58; religion, 59–65; daily life in, 68–70; pyramids, 71–74; temples, 75–77; Hebrews in, 100–102; conquest by Persia, 115; conquest by Rome, 194

Elizabeth, queen of England, 339

Emanuel (ē măn'ū ĕl), king of Portugal, 434, 437–438

England: maps, 110, 330, 418; growth of Britain into, 221–223; under Alfred the Great, 224–226; Norman Conquest, 231–234; development of representative government in, 297–325; contribution to medieval civilization, 325; in Renaissance, 361–362, 365, 367; and New World, 440–442. *See also* Britain

Eric (ĕr'ĭk) the Red, 230

Ericsson (ĕr'ĭk s'n), Leif, 231

Etruscans (ē trŭs'kȧnz), 168

Euphrates (ū frā'tēz) River, 84, 85, 99, 111, 113, 114; maps, 53, 82, 188

Explorers: Phoenician, 108–110; Greek, 142; Viking, 230–231; Portuguese, 407–413, 434–438; Spanish, 422–433, 438–440, 442–444; English, 440–441; French, 441–442

F

Fairs, medieval, 281–282

Falcon, 254–255

Family life: of prehistoric people, 16, 17, 34, 37; in Greece, 125, 127, 129; in Rome, 174; of German tribes, 207; in feudal castle, 249, 252–253; in China, 387–388

Farming. *See* Agriculture

Fasces (făs'ēz), 172

Ferdinand, king of Spain, 215, 425, 431, 432, 439

Fertile Crescent (fûr'tĭl krĕs'ĕnt), 83, 99; map, 82

Feudalism (fū'dȧl ĭzm): rise of, 234–235; life of people under, 247–261

Fire, discovery of, 8–11

Fishermen, Phoenician, 107

Flax growing, in Egypt, 52

Flint, prehistoric tools of, 7

Florence, 340–342, 346, 421; map, 331

Flute, 129

Flying buttress, 275

Folk-moot, 223

Food: in prehistoric times, 5–6, 11, 22, 29–32; in Egypt, 69, 70; in Greece, 124, 126–127; in Rome, 175, 184, 185; of nobles in Middle Ages, 252–253, 254, 258, 261, 285; of serfs, 258, 261, 313; of monks, 263. *See also* Spices

Fool. *See* Jester

Forum, Roman, 176, 177

France: maps, 110, 212, 330; beginning of, 216, 220; under Charlemagne, 217–220; Viking invasion of, 231; and exploration of New World, 441. *See also* Gaul

Francis I, king of France, 441

Francis, Saint, 267–269

Franks, 207, 216–220, 231, 238–239; map, 206

Freedom of press, struggle for, 355–356

Freedom of religion, struggle for, 332–340

Freya (frā'ä), 237

Friars, 268

Furniture: Egyptian, 69, 70; Greek, 125; Roman, 174; in medieval castle, 249, 285

Fust, Johann (foōst, yō'hän), 352–353

G

Galileo (gä lē lâ'ō), 368–373

Gama, Vasco da (gä'mȧ, văs'kō dȧ), 434–438

Games: Olympic, 133–136; in Middle Ages, 249, 253. *See also* Tournaments

Ganges (găn'jēz) River, 381, 382; map, 378

Gargoyles (gär'goilz), 277

Gaul, 181, 189, 216; map, 188

Genghis Khan (jĕng'gĭs kän), 392

Genoa (jĕn'ō ȧ), 286, 381, 401, 422; map, 287

German tribes: invasion of Roman Empire by, 201, 209–210; appearance, 207; houses, 207; sack of Rome, 210; conquest of Spain, 211; map, 206. *See also* names of tribes

Germania (jûr mā'nĭ ȧ), 201; map, 188

Ghiberti (gē bĕr'tē), Lorenzo, 341

Gibraltar (jĭ brôl'tēr), Strait of, 109, 212

Giotto (jôt'tō), 342

Girls, education of: in Babylonia, 93; in Greece, 128–129; in Rome, 177

Gladiators (glăd'ĭ ȧ tērz), 184–185

dāte, ăm, fâre, ȧsk, ȧbout, fär, bē, mĕt, hẹre, makēr, bīte, bĭt, hōpe, hŏt, lôrd, ūse, ŭp, bûrn, thin, then, pictụre, foōd, foŏt, out

Gods: Egyptian, 59–61, 63–65; Greek, 130–132; Babylonian, 87–89; Roman, 175–176, 190–191; Norse, 236–237; Hindu, 382

Golden Age of Pericles (pĕr'ĭ klēz), 150–153

Goldsmiths: in Egypt, 52; in Babylonia, 85; in medieval Europe, 278

Good Hope, Cape of, 411–412; map, 412

Goths, 207, 208–210, 211, 212; map, 206

Government: in prehistoric times, 37; of Egypt, 46, 68; of Babylonia, 90, 97, 98; of Hebrews, 103–105; of Persian Empire, 111–115; of Greece, 141–142, 150–151; of Rome, 168, 171–173, 193–194, 200–201; of German tribes, 208; of Moors in Spain, 212, 214; of Franks in France, 216–220; of Anglo-Saxon England, 222–223, 233; under feudalism, 234–235; of towns in Middle Ages, 283–284, 288–289; representative, growth in England, 298–325

Gracchi (grăk'ī), 186–187

Granada (grȧ nä'dȧ), 214; map, 206

Great Awakening. See Renaissance

Great Britain. See England

Great Charter. See Magna Charta

Great Wall of China, 387, 392

Greece: maps, 110, 120, 142; geography, 121; city-states, 121–122, 141; life in Sparta, 122–123; life in Athens, 123–125; education, 127–129; religion, 130–133; Olympic games, 133–136; literature, 137–140, 359; democracy in, 141–142; colonies, 142; Persian wars, 142–149; Golden Age, 150–153; philosophers in, 153–156; conquered by Macedonia, 156–158; contributions to civilization, 159, 445; conquered by Rome, 182

Greenland, 230, 231; map, 227

Gregory, Pope, 239–240

Guildhalls (gĭld'hôlz), 281

Guilds (gĭldz), 278–281

Gunpowder, 288

Gutenberg, Johann (goo'tĕn bĕrg, yō'hän), 349–353

H

Hammurabi (häm oo rä'bē), 90–91

Hanging Gardens of Babylon, 97–98

Hannibal, 180–182

Harold, king of England, 231

Harp, 69, 224, 229

Hastings, battle of, 232

Hatshepsut (hăt shĕp'soot), queen of Egypt, 66–67, 76–77

Hawking, 254–255

Hebrews: life of early, 99–100; captivity in Egypt, 100–102; return to Canaan, 102–103; government, 103; division of kingdom, 104; captivity in Babylon, 104; conquered by Greece and Rome, 105; religion, 105–106; contribution to civilization, 105–106

Helen of Troy, 137

Hellas. See Greece

Hellenes (hĕl'ēnz), 121

Hellespont (hĕl'ĕs pŏnt), 145; map, 142

Henry II, king of England, 297, 298

Henry III, king of England, 301, 304–307

Henry VII, king of England, 440

Henry VIII, king of England, 338–339

Henry, prince of Portugal, 407–411

Heresy (hĕr'ĕ sĭ), trials for: of Huss, 333; of Luther, 334–336; by Inquisition, 337

Hermits, 262

Himalaya (hǐ mä'lá yá) Mountains, 381, 382, 386; map, 395

Hindus (hǐn'dōōz), 382–384

Hippodrome, 135

Holy City. *See* Jerusalem

Holy Land. *See* Palestine

Homer, 137, 359

Homes: in prehistoric times, 16, 31, 32; in Egypt, 68–70; in Greece, 125; in Rome, 174, 183; of German tribes, 207; of medieval nobles, 247, 248–249; chart, 246; of peasants during Middle Ages, 260

Horatius (hō rā'shǔs), 169

Hornbook, 358

Horus (hō'rǔs), 65

House of Commons, 311–312

House of Lords, 312

Hundred-moot, 223

Huns, 208

Hunting, 24, 254

Huss (hǔs), John, 333

I

Iceland, 230; map, 227

Iliad (ĭl'ĭ ád), 237

India: trade with, 285; geography, 381; early settlers, 382; religion, 382; caste system, 383; government, 383; life of people, 384; Da Gama's voyage to, 434–438; maps, 378, 395, 434. *See also* Buddha; Taj Mahal

Indies (ĭn'dĭz), 380, 408. *See also* East

Indus (ĭn'dǔs) River, 381, 382; map, 378

Ink: Egyptian, 55; for copying manuscripts, 265; for early printing, 352

Inquisition (ĭn kwǐ zĭsh'ǔn), 337

Inventions: prehistoric tools and weapons, 6–8, 10; wheel, 25–26; plow, 47; paper, 55, 347–348, 389; ink, 55; shadow clock, 57; sundial, 86; movable metal type, 350–352; telescope, 368–369; silk-making, 388; compass, 404–405; astrolabe, 406; cross-staff, 406

Iron, smelting of, 15

Iron Age, 15

Irrigation, early Egyptian, 49–50

Isaac (ī'zák), 99, 281

Isabella, queen of Spain, 215, 425, 431, 432, 438–439

Isaiah (ī zā'yá), 106

Israel (ĭz'rā ĕl), Children of. *See* Hebrews

Israel, kingdom of, 104

Israel, Lost Tribes of, 104

Italy: maps, 164, 188, 330; geography, 165; under Etruscan kings, 168; Roman conquest of, 179; and Carthaginian wars, 180–182; Renaissance in, 340–346. *See also* Genoa; Roman Empire; Rome; Venice

Ithaca (ĭth'á ká), 139; map, 120

J

Janus (jā'nǔs), 175, 176, 190

Japan. *See* Cipango

Jerusalem (jĕ rōō'sá lĕm), 103, 104, 105, 106, 270, 272–273; maps, 82, 273, 395

Jester, 249

Jesuits (jĕz'ū ĭts), 337

Jesus Christ, 106, 196–198, 345

Jesus, Society of. *See* Jesuits

Jews. *See* Hebrews

John, king of England, 298–303

dāte, ăm, fâre, ásk, ábout, fär, bē, mĕt, hẹre, makēr, bīte, bĭt, hōpe, hŏt, lôrd, ūse, ŭp, bûrn, thin, then, pictŭre, fōōd, fŏŏt, out

[461]

John, king of Portugal, 411, 425
Joseph, 99–100
Journeyman (jûr'nĭ măn), 278
Judah, kingdom of, 104
Junks, Chinese, 393
Juno (jōō'nō), 191
Jupiter (jōō'pĭ tēr) (god), 175
Jupiter (planet), 370
Jury, trial by, 297–298
Jutes (jōōts), 207, 221

K

Karnak (kär'năk), temple of, 75; map, 44
Khufu (kōō'fōō). See Cheops
Kitchen middens, 3; map, 2
Knighthood, 249–251
Koran (kō rän'), 212, 213
Kublai Khan (kōō'blĭ kän), 393–397

L

Labrador (lăb'rá dôr), 440; map, 227
Lacquer (lăk'ẽr), 33, 389
Lake dwellers, prehistoric, 33
"Land between the Rivers." See Mesopotamia
"Land of No Return," 88
Language: Latin, 216, 264, 361; Anglo-Saxon, 233; Norman-French, 233; English, 234
Lares and penates (lā'rēz, pē nā'tēz), 175
"Last Supper," Leonardo's, 345
Law: in prehistoric times, 37; of Hammurabi, 90–91; of Medes and Persians, 111; Roman, 172–173, 195, 295; of Charlemagne, 218; English, 222–223, 225, 233, 297–298, 310–311, 315, 324–325; of German tribes, 295; common, 298
Leatherworkers: in Egypt, 52; in Babylonia, 85

Lebanon (lĕb'á nŭn), Mountains of, 106, 107
Leonardo. See Vinci, Leonardo da
Leonidas (lē ŏn'ĭ dás), 146–147
Libraries: Babylonian, 92; in Constantinople, 359; in monasteries, 359. See also Manuscripts, medieval
Lictors (lĭk'tērz), 172
Linen, early Egyptian, 52
Lippershey, Hans (lĭp'ẽrs hī, häns), 368–369
Lists, 255, 257
Literature: Greek, 137; in Middle Ages, 249; in Renaissance, 356, 359–360; Elizabethan, 361–362
Litters, 183
Little Brothers of the Poor, 268
Lombards, 207; map, 206
London, 300; map, 294
Loom, early, 23
Lord of Misrule, 253
Lotus (lō'tŭs), 75
Loyola, Ignatius (loi ō'lá, ĭg nā'shŭs), 337
Lute, 249, 252
Luther, Martin, 334–336
Lutheran Church, 336
Lyre (līr), 129

M

Macedonia (măs ē dō'nĭ á), 156–158, 182; map, 120
"Madonna of the Chair," Raphael's, 346
Magna Charta (măg'ná kär'tá), 300–303, 304, 305
Mammoth, 4
Manor, medieval, 258; diagram, 246
Manuscripts, medieval, 265–266
Maps, early, 405, 419
Marathon (măr'á thŏn), battle of, 144; map, 120

Marduk (mär'dŏŏk), 87, 89
Markets: Babylonian, 85; medieval, 281
Mars (märz), 175
Mary, queen of England, 339
Mauro (mô'rō), Fra, map by, 410
Mecca, 211, 213
Medes (mēdz), 111; and Persians, law of, 111
Medici, Lorenzo de' (mĕd'ē chē, lō-rĕn'tsō dā), 342
Medina (mā dē'nä), 211
Mediterranean (mĕd ĭ tĕ rā'nē ȧn) Sea, 109, 110, 182; maps, 53, 110, 142, 188, 273
Memphis (mĕm'fĭs), 46, 71; maps, 44, 52
Menelaus (mĕn ē lā'ŭs), 137
Menes (mē'nēz), 46
Merchants: in Babylonia, 85–86; Phoenician, 108–109; in Middle Ages, 274, 281, 283, 286–287; Mohammedan, 380–381; Chinese, 393. See also Trade
Mesopotamia (mĕs ō pō tā'mĭ ȧ), 84, 97
Metals, Age of, 12–14
Metals, use of: in prehistoric times, 12–15; in Egypt, 52
Mexico, 440, 442
Michelangelo (mī kĕl ăn'jĕ lō), 342–344
Middle Ages, 210
Minstrels, 224, 249; Norse, see Skald
Missionaries, Christian, 238, 240, 381
Mississippi River, exploration of, 442
Moat (mōt), 217
Mohammed (mō hăm'ĕd), 211–212
Mohammedans: in North Africa, 212;

in Spain, 213–215, 216, 425; and Eastern trade, 380–381; in India, 386
Monasteries, 262–266, 359
Mongols (mŏng'gŏlz), empire of, 391–392, 393
Monks, 262–266
Montfort, Simon de, 306–308, 309
Moon-god, Babylonian, 89
Moors, 211, 213–216, 425
Moot (mōōt), 222. See also Folkmoot; Hundred-moot
Mosaics (mō zā'ĭks), 183, 213
Moses (mō'zĕz), 101–103; statue, 343
Moslems (mŏz'lĕmz), lands of, map, 212. See also Mohammedans
Mosque (mŏsk), 213
Muezzin (mū ĕz'ĭn), 213
Mummers, 253
Mummies, Egyptian, 61–62
Music: of prehistoric people, 17; Egyptian, 69; Greek, 129; Viking, 229; of medieval minstrels, 249, 252

N

Nebuchadnezzar (nĕb ū kȧd nĕz'ēr), 97–98, 104, 112, 113
Nero, Emperor, 199
"New learning," 359
New Stone Age, 8
New Testament, 106, 336
New World, 438–447; maps, 418, 447
Newspapers, early, 354
Nile River: map, 44; geography, 45; overflowing of, 46–47, 49–50, 58; festival to, 59; hymn to, 60
Ninus (nē'nŭs), 426
Nineveh (nĭn'ĕ vĕ), 94–96, 104; map, 82

dāte, ăm, fâre, ȧsk, ȧbout, fär, bē, mĕt, hẹre, makēr, bīte, bĭt, hōpe, hŏt, lôrd, ūse, ŭp, bûrn, thin, then, pictūre, fōōd, fŏŏt, out

Nobles: in Egypt, 68–69; in Greece, 141; under feudal system, 234–235, 247–257, 288–289; trial of, 295; struggle with kings, 288–289, 298–308; in Rome, *see* Patricians. *See also* Serfs

Non, Cape, 408; map, 412

Norman Conquest, 231–234

Norman-French language, 233–234

Normandy, 231; map, 227

Norsemen, 207, 227–231; maps, 206, 227

North America, 440, 441, 442; maps, 419, 444

Norway, 207, 227

Nova Scotia (nō′và skō′shà), 440

Numerals: Arabic, 358; Roman, 358

O

Obelisk (ŏb′ĕ lĭsk), 75

Octavius (ŏk tā′vĭ ŭs). *See* Augustus

Odin (ō′dĭn), 236–237, 238

Odysseus (ō dĭs′ūs), 137–140

Odyssey (ŏd′ĭ sĭ), 137, 139

Old Stone Age, 8

Old Testament, 105

Olive, 126, 133, 134

Olympia, 133; map, 120

Olympic (ō lĭm′pĭk) games, 133–136

Olympus, Mount, 130; map, 120

Oracle (ŏr′à k′l), Greek, 132

Ordeal (ôr dē′ál): by fire, 295; by water, 295

Orient. *See* East

Ormuzd (ôr′mûzd), 145

Osiris (ō sī′rĭs), 61, 63

Oxford, University of, 357

P

Page, medieval, 249–250

Pagoda (pà gō′dà), 391

Painting: cave, 18–19; Egyptian

temple, 73, 75–76; Italian Renaissance, 340, 343–346

Palaces: Babylonian, 84; of Darius, 114; of Kublai Khan, 395–396; in Japan, 402

Palestine, 99, 104–105, 270; maps, 53, 82, 188. *See also* Canaan, land of

Palos (pä′lōs), 425, 426; map, 418

Pan, 131

Papermaking: in Egypt, 55; by Arabs, 214, 347; in China, 214, 347, 389; in Europe, 347–348

Papyrus (pà pī′rŭs), 55, 346

Parchment, 265, 346, 347

Paris, Matthew, quoted, 301

Paris, University of, 357

Parliament (pär′lĭ mĕnt), English, 304–312

Parnassus (pär năs′ŭs), Mount, 132

Parthenon (pär′thē nŏn), 151–152

Patricians (pà trĭsh′ánz), 172–173

Paul (pôl), Saint, 198

Peasant (pĕz′ánt) Revolt, 318–323

Peasants. *See* Serfs

Pedagogue (pĕd′à gŏg), 126

Peiping (bā pĭng′), 393; map, 395

Penelope (pē nĕl′ō pē), 140

Pericles (pĕr′ĭ klēz), 150–153

Persepolis (pēr sĕp′ō lĭs), 114; map, 82

Persia: maps, 53, 82, 212, 378, 395; under Cyrus, 104, 111–113; geography of, 111; under Darius, 114–115; wars with Greece, 143–149

Pharaohs (fâr′ōz), 46, 68, 70, 71, 75, 99–102

Pheidippides (fī dĭp′ĭ dēz), 144

Phidias (fĭd′ĭ ás), 151, 152

Philip, king of Macedonia, 156–158

Philosophers: Greek, 153–156; Chinese, 389–391

Phoenicia (fē nĭsh′ĭ à): maps, 53, 82, 110; geography, 107; fishermen,

107; purple dye, 107; ships, 107–108; trading voyages, 108–110; alphabet, 110–111

Picts, 221

Pilate, Pontius (pī'lȧt, pŏn'shŭs), 198

Pillars of Hercules (hûr'kū lēz). *See* Strait of Gibraltar

Pinta, 426, 427, 428, 429

Plato (plā'tō), 156

Plays. *See* Drama

Plebeians (plē bē'yȧnz), 172–173

Plow, first, 29

Pluto (plōō'tō), 130

Pnyx (nĭks), 141

Polo (pō'lō), Marco, 394–403, 421

Pope, 241. *See also* individual names

Porcelain (pōr'sĕ lĭn), Chinese, 389

Porsena, Lars (pôr'sĕ nȧ, lärz), 168

Portugal, search for water route to East by, 407–413, 425, 434–438, 441

Poseidon (pō sī'dŏn), 130, 131

Postal system, Persian, 114–115

Pottery: prehistoric, 12, 19; Egyptian, 51; Babylonian, 85; Greek, 124–125; Chinese, 389

Prague (präg), 333; map, 330

Priam (prī'ăm), 137

Priests: in prehistoric times, 21; Babylonian, 89; Greek, 132; in early church, 241

Printing, 348–356, 389

Promised Land. *See* Canaan, land of

Prophets (prŏf'ĕts), Hebrew, 106

Protestant (prŏt'ĕs tȧnt) Church, 336, 338, 339, 359

Psalms (sämz), 103; quoted, 104

Punt (pŭnt), land of, 66–67, 76–77; map, 44

Pylons (pī'lŏnz), 75

Pyramids (pĭr'ȧ mĭdz), 71–74

Pyrenees (pĭr'ē nēz) Mountains, 216

R

Ra (rä), 59

Races: running, 133; chariot, 135–136; 184

Raft, first, 29

Raja (rä'jȧ), 383

Raphael (răf'ā ĕl), 346

Red Sea, 66, 100; maps, 44, 53, 82, 188, 212

Reformation (rĕf ôr mā'shŭn), 336

Religion: in prehistoric times, 20–21; in Egypt, 59–65; in Babylonia, 87–89; of Hebrews, 105–106; Christian, 106, 196–199, 238–241; in Greece, 130–133; in Rome, 175–176; among German tribes, 236–241; in Middle Ages, 262–273, 275–277; in Renaissance, 332–340; freedom of, 338–340; in China, 389–391; in India, 382, 384–385

Remus (rē'mŭs), 165–166

Renaissance (rĕn ĕ säns'): defined, 331; and religion, 332–340; and the Reformation, 336; and art, 340–346; and printing, 346–356; and drama, 361–362; and science, 363–373

Representative government, growth of, in England, 298–325

Republic, Roman, 171–173, 189

Rhine (rīn) River, 194, 200, 207, 216; maps, 188, 206

Rialto (rē äl'tō), 287

Richard II, king of England, 318–323

Roads: prehistoric, 26; Persian, 114; Roman, 195; medieval, 289

dāte, ăm, fâre, ȧsk, ȧbout, fär, bē, mĕt, hẽre, makēr, bīte, bĭt, hōpe, hŏt, lôrd, ūse, ŭp, bûrn, thin, then, pictŭre, fōōd, fŏŏt, out

Robber barons, 283
Roland (rō'lånd), 249
Roman Empire: expansion of, 105, 182, 189–190, 193–194; system of roads, 195; system of laws, 195; invasion by German tribes, 200–201, 209–210, 216; end of, 201, 210; map, 188
Roman numerals, 358
Rome: maps, 164, 206; founding of, 165–168; under Etruscan kings, 168; early heroes, 168–171; as republic, 171–173; homes, 174, 183; dress, 174; water supply, 175; religion, 175–176; architecture, 176, 193–194; education, 177; conquest of Italy, 178–179; and Carthaginian Wars, 180–182; life in, 183–185; sacking of, by Goths under Alaric, 209–210
Romulus (rŏm'ū lŭs), 165–167
Rubicon, (rōō'bĭ kŏn), 190
Runnymede (rŭn'ĭ mēd), 300–301

S

Sailboat, first, 28
St. Lawrence, Gulf and River, 442
Salamis (săl'å mĭs), battle of, 147–149; map, 120
Santa María, 426
Sanzio, Raphael. See Raphael
Saul, King, 103
Saxons, 207, 221–222, 295; map, 206. See also Anglo-Saxons
Schools. See Education
Science: in Babylonia, 89; in Renaissance, 363–373
Scipio (sĭp'ĭ ō), 186
Scots, 221
Scribes, Egyptian, 56–57
Sculpture: in Egypt, 74, 75; in Assyria, 94–95; in Persia, 114; in Greece, 151;

152; in Middle Ages, 276; in Renaissance, 340–343
Sea of Darkness, 419–421, 423, 426, 439, 445
Seals, Babylonian, 92
Senate, Roman, 172, 179, 189, 190
Serfs, 258–261, 312–314, 315–317. See also Peasant Revolt
Shadoof (shä dōōf'), 50
Shadow clock, 57
Shakespeare (shāk'spēr), William, 362
Shepherds: in prehistoric times, 23; Egyptian, 58; among Hebrews, 99; in early Rome, 165
Ships. See Boats
Sidon (sī'dŏn), 107; map, 82
Silk: trade in, 285, 380, 389; manufacture of, 388–389
Sinai (sī'nĭ), Mount, 102, 343; map, 82
"Sistine Madonna," Raphael's, 346
Skald (skôld), 229
Slavery: in Egypt, 54, 62, 70, 446; in Greece, 126, 142; in Rome, 174, 183, 184, 239; in India, 383; early, 446
Socrates (sŏk'rå tēz), 154–156
Solomon (sŏl'ō mŭn), King, 103, 104
South America, 440, 441, 442, 443, 444; maps, 419, 441
Spain: Phoenician voyages to, 108; Moors in, 211–215; and exploration of New World, 422–433, 438–440; empire of, in New World, 442; maps, 110, 188, 206, 212, 330, 418, 434
Sparta: map, 120; location, 122; patriotism, 122–123; education, 127–128; war with Persia, 143, 145–147; war with Athens, 153
Spear, first, 8
Sphinx (sfĭngks), 74
Spices, 285–286, 403, 422, 424, 433, 437, 438; maps, 378, 395

Spinning: in prehistoric times, 23; silk, in China, 388
Spyglass, 369
Squire, medieval, 250–251
Stone Age: Old, 8; New, 8; end of, 14
Stylus (stī′lŭs), 128
Sumerians (sū mḗr′ĭ ȧnz), 84
Sundial, 86
Superstitions, medieval, 363, 379
Surveying, origin of, 50
Susa (sōō′sȧ), 114; map, 82
Sweden, 207, 227

T

Taj Mahal (täj mȧ häl′), 386
Tapestries, 285
Tarquin (tär′kwĭn), 168, 171
Tartars, 391
Taxation: under Caesar, 190; in Roman Empire, 193, 200; in England, 298, 304, 310, 312
Telescope, 365, 369–371
Temples: Egyptian, 74, 75–77; Babylonian, 84, 88; tower, 88; Solomon's, 103; Greek, 151–152; Roman, 176; Buddhist, in India, 385; Chinese, 391. *See also* Cathedrals; Mosques; Taj Mahal
Ten Commandments, 103
Tents, first, 31
Thames (tĕmz) River, 300; map, 294
Theater: Greek, 152; Elizabethan, 361–362. *See also* Drama
Thebes (thēbz): (Egypt), 75; maps, 44, 53, 82; (Greece), map, 120
Themistocles (thē mĭs′tō klēz), 148–149
Thermopylae (thẽr mŏp′ĭ lē), battle of, 145–147

Thor (thôr), 236, 237, 238
Thoth (thōth), 61
Threshing, in Egypt, 48
Tiber River, 165, 168–169, 179; map, 164
Tigris (tī′grĭs) River, 84, 111; maps, 53, 82, 188
Time, methods of telling: in Egypt, 57; in Babylonia, 86
Tin, 14, 109
Toga (tō′gȧ), 174, 177
Tolls, 283
Tombs, Egyptian, 71–74
Tools: prehistoric, 6–8, 14–15, 16, 18, 29, 30; Babylonian, 85
Toscanelli, Paolo (tōs′kä nĕl′lē, pä′ō lō), 421–422, 424; map, 424
Tournaments (tōōr′nȧ mĕnts), 255–257
Tours (tōōr), battle of, 216; map, 206
Tower-temples, 88
Town-moot, 223
Towns, medieval, 274–275, 283–284
Trade: in prehistoric times, 35–37; Egyptian, 53, 67; Babylonian, 85–86; Phoenician, 108–110; Greek, 124, 142; in Moorish Spain, 214; European, with Far East, 285–287, 379–381, 422; in China, 393; Arab, 405. *See also* Fairs; Guilds; Markets
Trade routes: Egyptian, 53, 66; map, 53; Phoenician, 108–109; map, 110; Eastern, 286–287, 380; map, 287
Trade schools, 358
Travel, land: in prehistoric times, 24–26; in Rome, 183–184; in Middle Ages, 264
Travel, water: in prehistoric times, 27–29; in Egypt, 53–54, 69; in

dāte, ăm, fâre, ȧsk, ȧbout, fär, bē, mĕt, hẽre, makēr, bīte, bĭt, hōpe, hŏt, lôrd, ūse, ŭp, bûrn, thin, then, pictŭre, fōōd, fŏŏt, out

Babylonia, 85; by Phoenicians, 107–108. *See also* Boats
Trial: by ordeal, 295; by combat, 295–296; by jury, 297–298
Tribes: in prehistoric times, 37–38; Hebrew, 103–104; German, 201, 207–210, 216, 221–222, 227
Trireme (trī'rēm), 108
Trojan horse, 138
Trojan War, 137–139
Tunic, 174
Turks, 270, 273, 359
Tyler, Wat, 318–322
Type, movable, 352, 353
Tyrants (tī'ránts), Greek, 141
Tyre (tīr), 107; map, 82
Tyrian (tǐr'ǐ án), purple, 107

U

Universities, 214, 357, 360
Ur (ûr), 99; map, 82
Urban (ûr'bán) II, Pope, 270–271

V

Valhalla (vǎl hǎl'á), 237
Valkyries (vǎl kǐr'ǐz), 237
Vandals, 207; map, 206
Vassals (vǎs'álz), 234–235, 288
Vedas (vā'dáz), 382
Vellum, 265
Venice (věn'ĭs), 286–287, 356, 381, 393, 394, 397, 401, 413; maps, 164, 287, 395
Verde (vûrd), Cape, 410; map, 412, 434
Vergil (vûr'jǐl), 359
Verrazano, Giovanni, (vär rä tsä'nō, jō vän'nē), 441
Vespucci, Amerigo (věs poo'chē, ä mä-rē'gō), 443–444
Vesta, 176
Vestal Virgins, 176

Vikings (vī'kǐngs), 227–231
Villages: in prehistoric times, 32; in Middle Ages, 260
Vinci, Leonardo da (věn'chē, lā ō-när'dō dá), 344–345
Vinland, 231

W

Waldseemüller (vält'zā mūl ēr), Martin, 443–444
Weapons: prehistoric, 6–8, 14–15; Egyptian, 52; Roman, 178; in Middle Ages, 247–248, 288
Weaving: in prehistoric times, 23–24; in Egypt, 52; in Babylonia, 84; among German tribes, 207; silk, in China, 388
Weights and measures, Babylonian, 86
Wheel: invention of, 25–26; potter's, 85
William the Conqueror, 231–233
Wine making, in Greece, 127
"Witches' Sabbath," 363
Witenagemot (wĭt'ě ná gě mōt'), 223
Wittenberg (vĭt'ěn běrg), 334; map, 330
Woden (wō'd'n). *See* Odin
Worms (vōrms, wûrmz), Diet of, 334–336; map, 330
Wrestling. *See* Olympic games
Writing: Egyptian, 54–57; Babylonian, 91–93; Phoenician, 110–111; in Middle Ages, 265–266; Chinese, 389
Wycliffe (wĭk'lĭf), John, 332–333

X, Y, Z

Xerxes (zûrk'sēz), 145–149
Yule log, 252
Zeus (zūs), 130, 133, 175
Zodiac (zō'dǐ ăk), 89